THE JOHNS HOPKINS UNIVERSITY STUDIES IN HISTORICAL AND POLITICAL SCIENCE

Under the Direction of the Departments of History,
Political Economy, and Political Science

SERIES LXXXI   Number 2
(1963)

ELBEUF DURING THE REVOLUTIONARY PERIOD:
HISTORY AND SOCIAL STRUCTURE

ELBEUF DURING THE REVOLU-
TIONARY PERIOD: HISTORY
AND SOCIAL STRUCTURE

By

JEFFRY KAPLOW

BALTIMORE
THE JOHNS HOPKINS PRESS
1964

© 1964 by The Johns Hopkins Press, Baltimore, Md. 21218
Printed in the United States of America
Library of Congress Catalog Card Number: 64–15091

This book has been brought to publication with the assistance of a grant from The Ford Foundation.

TO THE MEMORY OF TED

" I think continually of those who were truly great. . . ."

Stephen Spender

PREFACE AND ACKNOWLEDGMENTS

This study of social structure in the period of the French Revolution was originally undertaken because of an interest in certain new techniques of historical research first employed in France by such scholars as Georges Lefebvre and Ernest Labrousse. These involve the use of fiscal and demographic documents as a means of acquiring greater understanding of the divisions within French society on the eve of the Revolution.

Social structure is, like the weather, something about which much is said, and, until recently, nothing was done. Yet it is clear that we cannot hope to comprehend the very complex nature of revolutionary change without a thorough knowledge of the composition and function of the several classes that make up a national community. To neglect these fundamentals is to run the risk of writing the history of revolutions as merely a series of conflicts between " ins " and " outs," between groups of men fighting one another for power because the struggle itself is amusing and violence and nastiness are part of human nature.

Now it seems to me that any appeal to human nature and its so-called inalienable qualities as a principle of historical explanation is a sign of intellectual bankruptcy. Beyond the desire to survive that they hold in common, men change from generation to generation and from year to year. Their problems, and therefore their conflicts, are specific to the time in which they live and to the society of which they are a part. If one accepts this statement, the problem then becomes one of finding out just what it was that divided men from one another in a given historical epoch and to ask how these divisions made themselves manifest in the process of change itself.

Revolutions, those moments in historical time when the aspirations of great masses of men come together to destroy the existing order of things, possess the fascination of the unknown. And this is most true of France after 1789, when for the first time in the

9

history of Europe almost all citizens of the nation were, in one way or another, personally involved in carrying out their Revolution. But even though all this took place on a national scale, it would be incorrect to assume that the circumstances surrounding the upheaval were the same in all parts of the country. It is precisely the task of local studies such as this to show the variety of considerations to which men responded and thus to pave the way for a larger synthesis.

In this light, the study of the smallest French village would be justified. If I have chosen Elbeuf for analysis, it is because it seemed to me to offer a rather more specific advantage. Because of its importance as one of the most highly developed textile producing centers of eighteenth-century France, it provides an opportunity to study a budding industrial bourgeoisie, the very class that was to profit so greatly from the Revolution, in action.

From its creation in 1790 until World War II, the Department in which Elbeuf is located was called the Seine-Inférieure. When the Fourth Republic was organized in 1946, the name was changed to Seine-Maritime, because of the unfortunate connotation of the earlier title.

This book was originally planned as a doctoral dissertation for the department of history at Princeton University. Professor R. R. Palmer, my advisor, first suggested Normandy as a field of study and helped me with his suggestions during the early stages of the work.

I would like here to express my deep gratitude to M. Marc Bouloiseau of the Sorbonne. As an historian of the French Revolution who has studied the history of Normandy for nearly thirty years, M. Bouloiseau helped infinitely by directing me to the proper archives and libraries in Paris, Rouen, and Elbeuf. He gave unsparingly of his time and energy throughout the successive stages of this work during the two years I spent in France, 1959–1961. It is no exaggeration to say that without his constant aid and encouragement this study would never have been finished.

Professor Marcel Reinhard of the Sorbonne generously offered advice and criticism of several chapters. My fellow graduate students at Princeton have often helped me by reading portions of the manuscript and suggesting ways in which it might be improved. Finally, I would like to thank the members of the staff of the following institutions for their help in locating and using the materials on which this study is based: The Bibliothèque Nationale, the Bibliothèque Mazarine, the Bibliothèque de la Ville de Rouen, the Archives Nationales, the Archives Départementales de la Seine-Maritime, the Archives Municipales de la Ville d'Elbeuf, the Princeton University Library, and the Widener Library of Harvard University. A special word of thanks is due MM. Leroy and Lafond of the Archives Départementales de la Seine-Maritime, and M. le secrétaire général and his fellow administrators of the city of Elbeuf.

I alone am, of course, responsible for any errors either of fact or interpretation contained herein.

J. K.

Paris
August, 1963

TABLE OF CONTENTS

LIST OF TABLES

15

ELBEUF DURING THE REVOLUTIONARY PERIOD:
HISTORY AND SOCIAL STRUCTURE

CHAPTER 1

ELBEUF: THE TOWN AND THE INDUSTRY

The eighteenth century was one of exceptional growth for the city of Elbeuf. Starting out as the smallest of manufacturing towns, it was, during the Revolution, to attain the dignity and status of a *chef-lieu de canton*. Unfortunately, it is difficult to associate definite population figures with the several stages of the town's development. Early population statistics were not calculated by numbers of persons, but by *feux* or households. And when this procedure was put aside, there still remained the problem of confusion between several entities all called Elbeuf—canton, municipality, *arrondissement*—and the thousand natural shocks to which unsystematic counting is heir.[1] It is understood, then, that reliability for the figures given here is claimed only in so far as they represent orders of magnitude.

The first estimates of population have come to us from the late nineteenth-century historian of Elbeuf, Henri St. Denis. He states that in 1707 there were 300 *feux* or between 1,400 and 1,800 inhabitants, depending on whether one adopts the coefficient 4 or 5.[2] In 1748 he finds that this figure had more than quadrupled to 1,600 *feux* or between 6,400 and 8,000 persons.[3] The value of both sets of figures is almost nil, for no one knows on what they are based. Moreover, the use of a coefficient is probably the most inaccurate means of estimating population, family size being itself subject to great variations over relatively short periods of time.

The Abbé Expilly in 1764 counted 919 *feux*, or, at the coefficient

---

[1] Marcel Reinhard, "La Population des Villes, sa Mesure sous la Révolution et l'Empire," *Population*, IX (1954), 279–88.
[2] Henri St. Denis, *Histoire d'Elbeuf* (Elbeuf, 1894–1905), IV, 221.
[3] *Ibid.*, V, 182.

19

of 4.5 that he chose, 4,135.5 inhabitants. But the utility of the calculation is destroyed by the fact that he took the number of *feux* from Doisy's *Royaume de France* (1743) who had himself copied it from Saugrain's *Dictionnaire Universel* of 1726.[4] Saugrain may have come close to the truth for the date at which he wrote, but for the latter period Messance is probably more worthy of trust. He abandoned the use of coefficients. On the basis of a head count of 106 Norman localities, not including Elbeuf, he determined that the proportion of births to population was 1:27.55. The average annual number of births in Elbeuf over the ten-year period 1752–61 was 246.4 which, when multiplied by 27.55, would result in a population of 6,788. But, for some unknown reason, Messance himself multiplied by only 25 and obtained 6,150 as a result.[5] The trouble here is considerably greater than a debate over numbers indicates. It is that the method makes the unwarranted assumption of a constant birth rate extending over a ten-year period.

During the seventeen-eighties, the town's population was estimated by the subdelegate of Pont-de-l'Arche at 4,852, distributed among two parishes, that of St. Etienne with 1,839 and that of St. Jean with 3,013.[6] But once again, the basis of this estimate is not known. It differs from results obtained by applying Messance's method to the birth statistics of the same period, the yield in that case, at one birth per 25 inhabitants, being 5,550 Elbeuvians in 1783 and 5,350 in 1787.[7] In 1787 an investigation ordered by Calonne calculated the population at 5,772 on the basis of 222 births and a coefficient of 26.[8] With all these figures at hand, the best estimate of the population of Elbeuf on the eve of the Revolution is between 4,800 and 5,800. It is impossible to make

---

[4] L'Abbé Expilly, *Dictionnaire Géographique, Historique et Politique des Gaules et de la France* (Amsterdam, 1764–1766), II, 731; Edmond Esmonin, " L'Abbé Expilly et ses Travaux de Statistique," *Revue d'Histoire Moderne et Contemporaine*, IV (1957), 241–80.

[5] Messance, *Recherches sur la Population des Généralités d'Auvergne, de Lyon, de Rouen, etc.* (Paris, 1766), pp. 65, 213–14.

[6] *Archives Départementales de la Seine-Maritime*, C 185.

[7] *Arch Nat.*, D IV *bis* 46. Généralité de Rouen—Etat des Naissances, Sépultures et Professions en Religion, année 1783; Etat des Paroisses Composant la Généralité de Rouen, Classées par Ordre d'Election sous les Bailliages et Autres Juges Royaux, dont Elles Ressortissent, avec l'Indication des Naissances et des Morts Pendant l'Année 1787.

[8] *Arch. Nat.*, H[1] 1444 (86).

any meaningful statement about the growth of the city in the half century preceding the Revolution—except that it did, in the opinion of demographers, government officials, and compilers of dictionaries, grow.

There is a difference between the figures available for 1791 (6,570 persons) and the year II (5,862).[9] This is explained by the area chosen for measurement. In the first year certain rural apanages of Elbeuf were included in the municipality, whereas this was not the case in the year II. Another population estimate for the year II states that there were 5,862 persons in the city (the two documents for the year II correspond) and 803 rural inhabitants, making a total of 6,665 as against 6,570 in 1791.[10] The possibility of a small natural increase explains the difference of 95 between the two numbers. Moreover, it is no doubt the variations in territory of the communes that explain the great discrepancies in the population figures of the communes surrounding Elbeuf in the same years. When the estimates for all the communes are added up, the variations between the totals (21,796 in 1791 and 22,396 in the year II) are not greater than might be expected in a two-year period, which fact leads us to believe that the changes in the individual communes are largely due to redistribution of citizens among the lot.

On 16 Vendémiaire V (October 7, 1796), the estimate of population reported by the municipality, evidently not including the rural population, was 5,683, of whom 1,147 were married men or widowers, 1,741 married women or widows, 1,176 unmarried men or boys, 1,433 unmarried women or girls, and 166 soldiers, 16 of whom had recently been killed.[11] There were two estimates for the year VIII, the one 5,521 and the other 5,600.[12] In 1808, there were also two estimates given, both by the Prefect of the Seine-Inférieure, Savoye-Rollin. The first puts the total at 6,777, of whom 3,459 are men and 3,318 women, the second at 6,325 or 2,979 men and 3,346 women. It should be noted that while both estimates are for January 1, 1808, the first and highest was made in July of the same year, and the second bears the date April 12, 1810. Is it possible that this large discrepancy, particularly apparent on the male side of the register, was due to increased

[9] *Arch. Nat.*, D IV *bis* 52.
[10] *Arch. Dép.*, L 2371.
[11] *Arch. Nat.*, F²⁰ 125.
[12] *Arch. Nat.*, F²⁰ 399.

army recruitment, retroactively calculated by the Prefect?[13]   Be
that as it may, these figures suffice to give us a picture of Elbeuf's
demographic growth that was to reach, by one estimate, 7,515
persons at the end of the Empire in 1814. A nominative census
carried out by the municipality in November-December, 1814,
showed 7,343 inhabitants, including those in the rural hamlets
attached to the city.[14] In other words, Elbeuf had gained between
773 and 945 inhabitants or 10.76 to 14.38 per cent in the twenty-
three year period, 1791–1814.

How can this progression be explained? Much of it was no
doubt natural, that is, due to the excess of births over deaths. For
instance, in 1783 the excess was 92, in 1787, 58, and in 1792, 86.
In 1808, there were 120 male and 93 female births as against
80 male and 85 female deaths, an excess of 48.[15] Is this enough to
account for the demographic rise just noted? The answer to this
question must be affirmative, although it is also possible that
immigration from the surrounding countryside may have played a
small role in the process.[16] In either case, there is good reason to
consider the growth of population in Elbeuf during the whole of
the eighteenth and the nineteenth century as a corollary of the
phenomenon of industrialization.

Elbeuf in the eighteenth century was in the process of becoming
the largest wool-producing center in Normandy. To be sure, the
factories of the city experienced their ups and downs, their share
of business cycles, but the general picture that emerges is one of
intense growth. Although the weaving of woolen cloth had been
known in Elbeuf since the fifteenth century, it was only with the
decline of Rouen woolen manufactures in the face of competition
from cotton cloth that the city rose to pre-eminence in this field.[17]
Contemporary testimony to the fact is not lacking. Almost every
traveler and compiler of a directory of French commerce was
struck by what he saw in Elbeuf. In 1718 Piganiol de la Force
noted that " la manufacture d'Elbeuf est la plus considérable de
toutes." Because he was under the impression that this manufacture dated only from 1667, he was even more impressed by

---

[13] *Arch. Nat.*, F[20] 256.
[14] *Arch. Nat.*, F[1b] II Seine-Inférieure 13; *Arch. Mun.*, F[1].
[15] *Arch. Nat.*, F[20] 256.
[16] See Chapter 3, Section III.
[17] Pierre Dardel, *Histoire de Bolbec des Origines à la Révolution* (Rouen, 1947),
II, 57.

the existence of 300 looms producing 9,000–10,000 pieces of woolen cloth annually worth more than 2,000,000 livres and providing a living for 8,000 persons in Elbeuf and the surrounding area.[18] In fact, 1667 did not mark the establishment of the Elbeuf woolen industry but was only the date of the creation of a unified rule for it. Savary de Bruslons confirmed these remarks in 1723,[19] and Saugrain used Piganiol's very words in 1726.[20] *L'Etat de la France* published in 1737 and based on material compiled earlier in the century furnishes us with some interesting comparisons. After noting the existence in Elbeuf of an additional 70 looms occupied in the production of bergamot cloth, it gives us figures for the production of woolen cloth in other Norman cities. Rouen, at this time at least 12–15 times the size of Elbeuf, employed 3,500 workers on 183 looms, in addition to operating 60 looms of camlet, 200 of *petite tapisserie* called Porte de Paris and 60 of bergamot which, moreover, was generally thought to be inferior to that of Elbeuf. Darnetal had 102 looms and 3,000 workers, while Louviers gave work to 1,900 workers on 60 looms. It should be noted that much of the woolen cloth produced in these cities is spoken of as being of "Elbeuf style," indicative of Elbeuf's already established leadership in the field.[21]

The first impetus to the growth of Elbeuf as a large-scale producer of woolen cloth came early in the seventeenth century from one Nicolas Lemonnier, a Protestant manufacturer. He learned the method of manufacturing fine woolens "Holland style" from his family in the Netherlands and proceeded to introduce this process in Elbeuf. Together with the six associates LeCointe, he occupied the leading place in Elbeuf industry at that time, employing Protestant master craftsmen on long-term contracts. By 1667, the year of the establishment of the Manufacture Royale, that is, of the regulation of the industry, for all the manufacturers automatically became members of the Manufacture Royale, Elbeuf was producing 2,000 pieces of highly esteemed cloth annually. By 1685, Elbeuf was already in possession of 300 looms and gave work to 3,000 workers.

Contrary to what one might expect in a city where Protestants

---

[18] St. Denis, *Histoire*, IV, 354.
[19] *Ibid.*, IV, 418–19.
[20] C. M. Saugrain, *Dictionnaire Universel* (Paris, 1726), I, 1095.
[21] St. Denis, *Histoire*, IV, 34–35; Expilly, *Dictionnaire*, V, 228.

played so important an industrial role, the revocation of the Edict
of Nantes in 1685 seems to have had little effect. Although one-
fifth of the population was in the proscribed category, there is
no evidence of large scale emigration from Elbeuf.[22] And the
industry continued to grow. At the end of the century, there were
thirty-seven master manufacturers in Elbeuf.[23]

The important place assumed by the manufacture was further
recognized in 1731 by the removal of the bureau of inspection
of woolen cloth from Rouen to Elbeuf, which freed the industry
from both a transport charge and a sales tax charged in the Rouen
market.[24] This act, together with the permission granted to Elbeuf
in 1758 to produce any kind and quality of cloth, removed the last
legal obstacles in the path of industrial expansion. The manufacture
continued to fluorish so that in 1762 we read that: " Les manufactures de drap qui sont à Elbeuf au nombre de quatre-vingt,
en font une ruche où personne n'est dans l'inaction; de sorte
qu'Elbeuf qui n'est cependant qu'un bourg, est bien plus vivant
que Verneuil, capitale du Perche et même qu'Evreux, qui est un
évêché. On y file aussi le coton en grande quantité pour les manufacturiers de Rouen." [25]

In order better to understand the social structure of Elbeuf, we
must be familiar with the processes of its first industry. What

[22] It appears that the Protestants of Elbeuf even failed to maintain contact with
the clandestine organizations of the region. In 1744 the Protestant Minister
Preneuf, although he found 1,077 families and 4,441 individuals in his " parish "
of Upper Normandy, reported no members in Elbeuf. In September, 1788, the
municipality reported eighteen Protestants but thought that the number would
increase as a result of the Edict of Tolerance of 1787. Where would they come
from? It is likely that the municipal officers were referring to persons who had
been obliged to become Catholics and who would now resume their true identity.
Such a conformity would have been in keeping with Léonard's description of
bourgeois Protestants, their legalistic temper, their reluctance to join the Eglise
du Désert, their preference for small " cultes de société." See *Arch. Mun.*, BB[8];
Francis Waddington, *Le Protestantisme en Normandie depuis la Révocation de
l'Edit de Nantes jusqu'à la Fin du Dix-Huitième Siècle* (1685–1797), (Paris,
1862), p. 72; Emile G. Léonard, " La Bourgeoisie Protestante et sa Position
Politique et Religieuse du XVIIIe Siècle à la Restauration," Commission de Recherche, *Assemblée Générale 1939* (Besançon, 1942), I, 171–85, and " Les Protestants Français aux XVIIIe Siècle," *Annales d'Histoire Sociale*, II (1940), 5–20.
[23] Charles Brisson, " Origines et Développement de l'Industrie Drapière à Elbeuf
et à Louviers," *Etudes Normandes*, livraison 5, numéro 13 (1952), pp. 215–16.
[24] *Ibid.*, p. 218.
[25] Abbé P. Bernier (ed.), " Voyage de Antoine-Nicolas Duchesne au Havre et
en Haute Normandie, 1762," in Société de l'Histoire de Normandie, *Mélanges*,
IV, 263.

went into the production of a piece of woolen cloth? Fortunately, I am in possession of a document that enables me to answer this question. It is a report on the town's manufacture of woolen cloth dated 1779 and written by Le Page, who was studying to become an inspector of manufactures at the factory of Benoist Delarue, under the supervision of the then inspector, Du Boisroger.[26]

The types of wool that could be used in Elbeuf were limited in number by government regulations. All were first and second quality Spanish wools. The first operation that had to be performed was the removal of grease from the raw wool. This was done by putting the raw material into a vat containing a solution of four-fifths water and one-fifth urine and heating it just to the point where one could no longer hold one's hand in it without being burned. The wool was then left to soak for half an hour, after having been stirred round a bit. After this time had elapsed, it was allowed to drip dry on a piece of wood atop the vat. It was then thrown into a basket resting in a continuous flow of cold water. Two men were employed to move the wool around from time to time with sticks, until all the fat floated free. For more difficult wool, that which was dry, thick, or old and consequently had its fibers held together by dried fat, the proportion of urine in the solution had to be increased. The process was known to be at an end when the wool began to come apart on the sticks used to take it out of the vat, and the tufts stretched out. The wool was then white.

The presence in Elbeuf of a fast flowing stream called the Puchot greatly facilitated this operation. As a manufacturer was to write some years later, this stream " ayant sa source et son embouchure dans la ville même, conserve dans le court trajet le degré de fraîcheur que nos pères considéraient comme indispensable pour le lavage et le dégraissage des laines." On the other hand, an old prejudice held that the Seine should not be used for this purpose, because the water was too warm, having been heated by the sun during its long course from the interior toward the sea. Not until 1820–22 was this prejudice overcome, and then only because of necessity, the Puchot no longer being sufficient for the needs of a rapidly growing industry.[27]

[26] *Arch. Nat.*, F^{12} 560.
[27] P. Delarue, " Histoire Appliquée à l'Industrie Normande," *Revue de Rouen* (Août, 1835), pp. 3n, 4.

The next operation was that of dying, begun while the wool was still wet. This done, the material was stretched out on thin rods in a cool place such as an attic and allowed to dry. Then it was placed on a wattle, usually made of rope rather than wood, since the former was more resilient and there was less chance of tearing the wool while it was being threshed. The threshing or beating of wool served to stretch it, to open the tufts, and to purge it of any foreign bodies it might contain. Just a little wool was put on the wattle at a time, perhaps 3 or 4 pounds. After the beating, it was plucked by hand to remove all parts that could not be subjected to further processing, such as the galls, tars, and dead wools. In wool that had been dyed a solid color, all the parts that had not taken exactly the desired tint were painstakingly removed.

There remained now for the wool to be carded before it could be spun. For the purpose of carding, each pound was soaked in 4 ounces of olive oil, the thicker the better. This made the wool supple and gave it the capacity to stretch while being worked on without tearing. In order to obtain wool suitable for spinning, it had to be carded several times, twice for solid colors, three times for colors of mixed composition. The whole process required a good deal of skill and even more attention, for the wool was constantly in danger of knotting and breaking into short lengths, causing separations in the card and making it difficult, if not impossible, to spin. Elbeuf had an advantage in the performance of this operation due to the presence in the region, around Lery, of the teasel plant, whose panicles, armed with long, curved teeth, when used in carding wool rendered the nap of the finished cloth fine and smooth in quality. The importance of this plant in the woolen industry is proved by the interest shown in its culture by the Société d'Agriculture of Rouen and by complaints of the manufacturers against its export in 1816. At that date, it appears that Belgian manufacturers were buying up the entire Norman crop, thus forcing the price up sevenfold from 40 to 50 francs the bale to 300–350. If exports were not forbidden, said the Elbeuvians, they would be forced to use less teasel and thus reduce the quality of their products. The result would be a loss of reputation and clients.[28]

[28] A. J. Bourde, " L'Agriculture à l'Anglaise en Normandie au XVIIIᵉ Siècle," *Annales de Normandie*, VIII (1958), 224–25; *Arch. Nat.*, F¹² 1559.

Spinning came next, and there a problem arose. The wool was both carded and spun by craftsmen living in the countryside around Elbeuf. They were supposed to bring in a certain amount of skeins of spun wool per pound of raw material, each measuring five-fourths of an *aune* (1.185 meters), the size in which most of Elbeuf cloth was woven and called a *perot*. They did indeed bring in the required number of skeins, but, if we can trust the authority of Le Page (and he was in a good position to know), the workers often cheated on the composition of the skeins. They were often 0.5 of a quarter *aune* shorter than required and contained less than the requisite number of threads. It appears that the manufacturers rarely bothered to check on the spinners, so that the latter got away with impunity.

When the spun wool had been returned to the manufacturer, he gave it out to be woven, most often to rural weavers. These weavers usually owned their own looms,[29] and they were in direct contact with the manufacturer. That is to say, they did not deal with a middleman, as was often true in the region immediately around Rouen.[30] They worked in pairs, because it was necessary for one to operate the machine while the other threw the shuttle when it reached the end of the loom.[31]

After the weaving was done, the cloth was gone over to remove irregularities, and the grease left in as a result of the preparatory processes was taken out, before fulling, by a bath of fuller's earth. This substance, also known as smectite, is a clay found in abundance in Normandy. When mixed into water and beaten, it sudses like soap, but has detergent qualities much superior to those of ordinary soap for removing fatty particles. When this bath was over, fulling could begin. Its purpose, accomplished by pressing the cloth between two rolling cylinders, is to make the cloth firmer and give it a more closely woven texture. Here again, the availability of water was of great importance, both for the bath and as providing power for the fulling mills. Expilly noted the advantage so provided when he wrote: "Un petit ruisseau qui vient d'un coteau voisin d'Elbeuf fait aller les moulins à foulon, qui

[29] E. V. Tarlé, *L'Industrie dans les Campagnes en France à la Fin de l'Ancien Régime* (Paris, 1910), pp. 50–51.

[30] F. Evrard, "Les Ouvriers du Textile dans la Région Rouennaise (1789–1802)," *Annales Historiques de la Révolution Française*, No. 108 (1947), p. 339.

[31] *Arch. Nat.*, F[12] 560.

sont en grand nombre dans ce bourg; ce qui est fort avantageux à ses manufactures." [32] Years later, in 1812, the municipality wrote that poor maintenance of the Puchot was reducing its usefulness. The sources that fed it " font la richesse d'Elbeuf; sans elle point de fabriques," it said. It was absolutely necessary to keep it clean and flowing strongly at its proper width of 7–8 feet, whereas it had narrowed to 5 feet in some places.[33] It should be noted that this problem did not date only from 1812 but was a matter of concern throughout the Revolution. There were simply not enough fulling mills in Elbeuf; they had to be supplemented by others at Pont St. Pierre, Brionne, and Romilly 4 to 6 leagues from the city. The distance created problems, for there was a lack of roads between Elbeuf and the other towns. The municipality and the manufacturers several times solicited a remedy to this situation. In the year IX, for example, the latter wrote that the extant roads were so bad that two days were needed to make the trip instead of one, and the carriages often " restent embourbées dans les trous nombreux qu'elles rencontrent et d'où elles ne sortent qu' avec des avaries également préjudiciables aux voitures et aux propriétaires des draps." The loss caused was enormous, for each of the cloths manufactured in Elbeuf had to be fulled twice, in other words, had to make this difficult trip two times.[34]

After fulling, the wool was scoured and set out to dry. Only then was it brought back to the manufacturer who had it picked over for impurities once again, trimmed, washed, sheared and, if necessary to add luster, pressed, the number of times these operations were repeated depending on the quality of goods desired.

The numerous and complicated operations required in the processing of woolen cloth gave rise to a need for a large amount of manpower, much more than in the cotton industry, for instance. Who were the workers? Where did they come from and how were they organized? To what extent were they wage laborers or independent artisans? Under whose control were they? All of these are questions which must now be answered.

[32] Expilly, *Dictionnaire*, II, 731.
[33] *Arch. Mun.*, Déliberations de la Municipalité (hereafter Délib.), Vol. VIII (April 13, 1812).
[34] *Arch. Dép.*, Series M—Statistique de l'an VI; *Arch. Mun.*, Délib., Vol. A (22 Ventôse IX); St. Denis, *Histoire*, VIII, 30–32, 118.

In 1788, the industry employed 15,300 persons, of whom only one-third were domiciled in Elbeuf.[35] The rest were in the surrounding countryside, peasants owning or farming small plots of land who looked to the industry for a supplement to their income. But this arrangement was undergoing change in the last years of the old regime. Peasants' industrial income was growing to a point where it would cease to be supplementary and become their principal means of making a living. Why should this be so?

First of all, there was the enclosure movement resulting in the suppression of common rights, a movement that had made considerable advances in Normandy as compared with the rest of France.[36] Royal policy favored this trend by granting land and tax concessions to persons who would clear and enclose common lands. Moreover, the Coutume of Normandy as interpreted by the Parlement of Rouen sharply limited the right of *vaine pâture* under certain conditions that were simple for the proprietors to fulfill. In only one way were the peasants of the Elbeuf region, at least those of the communes bordering on the Forest of Elbeuf, sheltered against too brutal a suppression of their common rights. The Forest belonged to the Prince de Lambesc. The royal administration could not, therefore, grant concessions to entrepreneurs as had been done in royal forests.[37] It was only during the Revolution, when the Forest was nationalized, that the peasants saw their rights infringed and finally destroyed.

The evolution of the land as described here was all to the advantage of the urban bourgeoisie. As much cannot be said for the peasants. Although they were not forced off the land at this stage, they had to look more and more to artisan-type work within Elbeuf industry in order to make ends meet. That the movement was extensive in the communes neighboring on Elbeuf is proved by the following remark made by Jean-Christophe Quesney, comptroller of the *vingtièmes* for the Election of Pont-de-l'Arche, about Caudebec-lès-Elbeuf in 1780: "L'occupation des habitants est pour une faible partie la culture des terres, le surplus des ouvriers travaille pour la manufacture d'Elbeuf." [38]

---

[35] *Arch. Mun.*, BB[8]. Even one-third seems too high a figure in light of what we have said about population.

[36] Bourde, "L'Agriculture," p. 217.

[37] Jules Sion, *Les Paysans de la Normandie Orientale* (Paris, 1909), pp. 210–22.

[38] Henri St. Denis, *Notice Historique sur la Ville de Caudebec-lès-Elbeuf* (Elbeuf,

Are we justified in explaining the move toward industry as a matter of necessity on the part of the peasant? To do so is to assume that we are dealing with small, indeed marginal, producers, whose financial equilibrium might be disturbed by even the smallest loss of agricultural prerogative. The assumption cannot be proved with figures as to size and number of peasants' holdings, the study of which, were the relevant statistics available, falls outside the scope of this work. But this is known: that eighteenth-century peasants were neither occupationally nor geographically mobile, that they did not change their way of making a living simply because industry might afford better wages than the land. Indeed, there are cases in which peasants would not change even in the face of the negative sanction of impending starvation.[39] Would they then seek release from agricultural pursuits in the absence of that sanction?

The possibility cannot be denied that industrial wages may have been attractive. They may thus have reinforced the trend toward the absorption of peasants into rural industry. In the absence of estimates of farm income, comparisons are impossible. It seems to me, however, that higher wages alone are not sufficient to explain the extent of the change seen in Elbeuf.

Government policy did not always favor rural industry, but this was less and less true as we move toward the Revolution. In 1749 the Parlement of Rouen had forbidden master manufacturers to put out work in the countryside from the opening of the harvest season until September 15, at the risk of a 500 livre fine for the master and a 100 livre fine for the worker who accepted the work.[40] This was clearly an attempt to keep industry from absorbing manpower to the detriment of the harvest. Does this indicate that peasants were more eager to work in cottage industry than in the fields because of higher wages? Perhaps, but this is not necessarily so. It is just as likely that the manufacturers obliged the peasant spinners and weavers to work on a year round basis, so as to keep the goods coming in at a regular rate. Unlike a craft guild, which would have been overjoyed at this edict, the Elbeuf manufacturers protested vigorously. They had nothing to fear

1888), p. 414; see also Charles Leroy, " Les Paysans Normands au XVIIIe Siècle," Association Normande, *Annuaire*, LXXI (1904), 138–45.

[39] Arthur Redford, *Labour Migration in England, 1800–1850* (Manchester, 1926), p. 82.

[40] St. Denis, *Histoire*, V, 159.

from rural competition, because they controlled it. A blow to rural industry was a blow struck at them. Certainly, the order in no way significantly hampered the growth of rural industry, and when the Order in Council of November 7, 1762, gave country workers the right to perform all manufacturing operations of the textile industry, it did nothing more than give legal recognition to an already established fact. In 1765 the same provisions were renewed for an indefinite period of time, and in 1779 even greater liberty was accorded by the repeal of the rules that obliged each town to manufacture only certain kinds of cloth. Such rules as did remain were unenforceable and were not respected, especially in the countryside.[41] Sion suggests that the Edict of 1762 was prompted by fear of proletarianization and urbanization of the peasantry, which might lead to the development of class consciousness. This possibility was obviated by the authorization to work outside the cities. Moreover, the agricultural income of the peasant allowed him to settle for a lower wage for his industrial work, so long as his income from the latter source was no more than a supplement to his fortune.[42]

All the members of the peasant family worked—man, woman, and child. The men were occupied in weaving, shearing, carding, dying, etc., while women did most of the spinning, wool picking, and burling, and the children assisted their parents—by throwing the shuttle on the loom, for instance. A normal working day was 15 hours long. If pay varied somewhat according to the operation performed, there were even greater differences in wages according to age and sex. A weaver got about 20 sols per day in the last years of the old regime, a spinning woman got 10 sols, and her companions who worked as winders and warpers were paid 12 sols. The best paid women workers were the burlers at 15 sols per day. A child might receive as much as 7 sols a day, but a lower wage was not unknown. The average wage of a family of three all working in textiles was 1 livre, 15 sols to 2 livres per day in 1788.[43]

All the work of the industry was under the direction of the manufacturer who was proprietor of the raw material at all stages

[41] Tarlé, *L'Industrie*, pp. 5, 66–68.
[42] Sion, *Paysans*, p. 179.
[43] *Arch. Mun.*, BB⁸; E. Le Parquier, *Ouvriers et Patrons dans la Seconde Moitié du XVIII⁰ Siècle* (Rouen, 1933), pp. 46–47, 51–53.

of the manufacturing process. It was he who bought it, ordered its preparation, spinning, weaving, dying, finishing, and finally sold the end product. If only a few of these operations were performed in the factory owned by the manufacturer, there was enough to distinguish him from a simple merchant capitalist operating on an uncomplicated putting out system. The factory operations were limited to the initial preparation of the wool for spinning and the finishing of the wool for sale. The rest was done elsewhere. Dying required rather large installations and was run on a factory basis, but by a sub-contractor who sold his services to the manufacturer. Transport was assured by another contractor, as was fulling. In other words, the industry was not yet an integrated one in which a single corporation raised the lambs, grew the dyestuffs, made the cards, dyed, transported, and fulled the wool; it is much too early for that. To what extent did the manufacturer, nonetheless, control the industry? The answer is: totally, for, in the final analysis, all the entrepreneurs and all the workers depended on him.[44]

Let us look at the example of the spinners, carders, and weavers. In the case of the first two, the manufacturer often dealt only indirectly with the workers, giving out his commissions to " maîtres fileurs qui ont des ouvriers jusqu'à 10 et 12 lieues [d'Elbeuf]. . . . Ces maîtres fileurs traitent avec les manufacturiers et se chargent des détails du filage et rendent aux manufacturiers l'ouvrage dans le temps marqué." [45] Thus, the spinner was already a kind of industrial wage earner, albeit still closely attached to the land. He was, unlike the weaver, no longer an artisan dealing on an equal basis with a customer. The great development of spinning machinery was soon to hasten his total transformation into a proletarian. The situation was different for the weaver who, throughout the eighteenth century, dealt directly with the manufacturer on an artisan-like basis. He generally owned his own tools and, because of the slow introduction of weaving machinery, was proletarianized much less rapidly than the spinners.

We see, then, that according to the function studied, there had been varying degrees of progress made toward the kind of industrial capitalist organization that was to reach its height in

[44] Charles Ballot, *L'Introduction du Machinisme dans l'Industrie Française* (Paris and Lille, 1923), pp. 165–66.

[45] Sion, *Paysans*, p. 176.

the nineteenth century. To the extent that the workers were still closely associated to the land, that they owned their tools, that they were artisans working on orders given them by a manufacturer, they were not yet proletarians, and class structures and lines between wage earners and petit bourgeois artisans were still very fluid. But to the extent that the workers were dependent on a manufacturer's orders for their livelihood, a start toward the capitalist organization of the industry as a whole had already been made, even though factory organization was still in its infancy.[46] Moreover, unlike many nascent industries of the period, the woolen manufacture of Elbeuf was not subject to the control of merchant capital originating outside the city. The manufacturers had themselves started as craftsmen and provided their own capital. Because it was through control of markets that outsiders, particularly Rouen merchants, might have taken control of the industry, the manufacturers had started to employ traveling salesmen between 1720 and 1740. Until this time, Elbeuf trade had been in the hands of " marchands et commissionnaires de Rouen qui venaient y acheter les draps et les répandaient ensuite dans le commerce." But the manufacturers succeeded in escaping and remaining clear of Rouen's orbit, selling the largest part of their products through the Paris market.[47]

From 1667, when a definite legal structure was given the industry, relations between wage earners and employers had been regulated by royal *ordonnance*. According to the ruling of 1664, three years of apprenticeship and a masterpiece were required of all candidates for mastership, except sons of masters. Each master could have one apprentice per year. The guild was to elect " guards " who had power to enforce the regulations by means of weekly inspections. The guards had jurisdiction over questions internal to the guild, but appeal might be had to the *bailli* on payment of 20 livres in costs to the guild. No weaver could leave his master's employ without finishing the piece of cloth on which he was working, and he had to give sufficient notice. The master who next hired the weaver was responsible for any debts the latter

[46] Alexandre Choulguine, " L'Organisation Capitaliste de l'Industrie Existait-Elle en France à la Veille de la Révolution," *Revue d'Histoire Economique et Sociale*, X (1922), 195.

[47] Tarlé, *L'Industrie*, p. 47; Brisson, " Origines," p. 218; Prosper Delarue, Notice sur la Ville et sur les Fabriques d'Elbeuf en Brumaire, an XIII. *Bibliothèque de Rouen*, Ms. g. 1 (709), p. 5.

had contracted with his former employer. On the other hand, a master had only to give 24 hours notice in order to dismiss his workers. A worker who left his work " pour aller en débauche " was to be fined 20 sols and put in prison for three days. Anyone, no matter where domiciled, might be employed in the industry. Masters were to refrain from hiring workers away from one another on penalty of a 300 livre fine and of being refused the right to work for a period of six months. A worker who spoiled a piece of cloth while working on it was made to pay for it. In addition, the manufacturers were protected against competition by a provision that gave them the sole right to buy wool in the market until noon of each market day. Finally, no cloth or tools might be seized by police authority, except in the case of arrears of house rent.[48]

These regulations did not remain static. Over the years, changes were made. In 1749 the government instituted the famed *billet de congé*. In order to quit his job, the worker henceforth would need an authorization from his employer. To procure it, he had to give proper notice and be clear of debt toward his employer. If these conditions were fulfilled, the manufacturer had to grant the authorization. If he did not, appeal could be made to the public prosecutor of the tribunal that had jurisdiction over the industry. Any worker who quit work without a *billet de congé* was liable to a 100 livre fine, a sum that was reduced to 30 livres in 1751. An employer who had hired a worker without the prescribed formalities became liable for his debts to his ex-employer, as under the Edict of 1667.[49]

The obligations imposed by these *ordonnances* were evaded by both employers and workers. In 1753 one Mathieu Osmont, a carder, complained that his three children, employed as spinners by the manufacturer Henry, could not subsist on the wages they received, much lower than those paid by the manufacturers of Rouen. He therefore asked for their *billet de congé* and was refused. He appealed to the *bailli*, saying: " En vain que le suppliant se plaignait au bureau de la manufacture; ils sont tous drapiers et se rendent les maîtres des pauvres et les tiennent sous

[48] *Reglemens et Statuts Concernant les Manufactures de Draps Qui Se Font au Bourg d'Elbeuf en Normandie, 1667.* A copy may be found in the Bibliothèque de Rouen under the call number N. *mm. 632.*
[49] Le Parquier, *Ouvriers,* pp. 32–34.

leurs loix. Il n'y a cependant pas d'esclaves en France; il n'y a aucuns maîtres de manufactures qui puissent refuser de billet de congé aux ouvriers quand ils sont bien fondés. . . ." In his reply, Henry wrote of " les abus très considérables qui résultent de l'esprit d'indépendance qui commence à régner chez la plupart des ouvriers de cette manufacture." [50] In 1766, an Order in Council allowed rural workers to escape the formalities of the *billet de congé.* When the manufacturers protested against this ruling in 1781, Joly de Fleury wrote that it was just that " ouvriers attachés par état et par la nature de leur travail [à la manufacture] . . . ne puissent quitter sans billet de congé, mais il n'en est pas de même des fileurs et cardeurs qui travaillent chez eux et sont souvent éloignés de 3 ou 4 lieues de la manufacture." The only obligation for the last named workers before they could leave their work was to return materials and tools belonging to the manufacturers.[51]

Despite these occasional difficulties, worker-employer relations were peaceful throughout the century. As much might have been expected, given the lack of class consciousness engendered by a still fluid social structure and the lack of factories where " combinations " might take place. In only one instance was there any violence over a labor question. That was in 1731 when there were riots of the unemployed, one-half of the looms in the city being idle. Full powers given to the Intendant de Gasville to deal with this uprising resulted in fourteen death sentences and two commitments to the galleys.[52] In general, however, the good conduct of the workers was known and appreciated. If contemporary opinion saw Rouen workers as " paresseux, fainéants, adonnés à l'ivrognerie, à laquelle ils consacrent, par habitude, deux jours entiers [par semaine]" it saw Elbeuvians as " laborieux, actif, obligeant . . . ils sont sobres, beaucoup moins crapuleux que les ouviers des Fabriques ne le sont ordinairement." [53]

Such disputes as did arise were subject to the jurisdiction of the Haute Justice, the Seigneurial Court of the Duchy of Elbeuf. The Edict of 1667 had given primary jurisdiction to the guards of the

[50] St. Denis, *Histoire,* V, 219–20.

[51] *Arch. Nat.,* F^{12*} 156.

[52] Julien Hayem, " La Répression des Grèves au XVIIIe Siècle," in his *Mémoires et Documents pour Servir à l'Histoire du Commerce et de l'Industrie en France* (Paris, 1911), I, 116–77; Brisson, " Origines," p. 218.

[53] Le Pecq de la Cloture, *Collection d'Observations sur les Maladies et Constitutions Epidémiques* (Rouen, 1778), pp. 204, 269.

guild with appeal to the *bailli* or judge of the Haute Justice. But this was changed in 1669. In that year, the first degree of jurisdiction was attributed directly to the Haute Justice, with appeal to the Parlement. It may be said that the acquisition of this power by the *bailli* was accomplished by default. The Edict provided that the mayor and *échevins* or, in their absence, the special police judges should have this power. Only when neither existed were the Seigneurial Courts given jurisdiction over the manufacturers. This arrangement had at least one advantage for Elbeuf: it kept the city clear of the jurisdiction of manufacturers of Rouen and was thus a guarantee of its independence.[54] Only once, in 1780, was an attempt made to transfer this jurisdiction. An Order in Council of February 14 gave the Intendant the police power formerly in the hands of the Haute Justice. The Prince de Lambesc, seigneur of Elbeuf, protested vigorously and by August had got back his rights, no doubt because of his great influence at Versailles. The government demanded only that a part of the revenues from fines collected for the infringement of manufacturing rules be attributed to the support of the poor. Agreement was easily reached on the basis of one-third for the Prince, one-third for the poor, and one-third for the informer.[55] Aside from one slight change in 1784, when the Intendant was given jurisdiction over cases in which workers were accused of stealing raw materials from their employers, the system remained intact until the Revolution.[56]

What profit could the manufacturer hope to make on a single piece of material, supposing that he followed all the rules of production? (In fact, he did not always follow these rules, but attempted to make a larger profit by mixing domestic wools into his Spanish supplies, or by stretching the wool while it was drying, or by the application of what one observer called " mille petits tours dont il est difficile de s'apercevoir." Unfortunately, we have no way of measuring the extra profit gained in this way, illegal operators being careful not to leave statistical traces behind them.)

[54] David Houard, *Dictionnaire Analytique, Historique, Etymologique, Critique et Interprétatif de la Coutume de Normandie* (Rouen, 1780–82), IV, 206–7; Robert d'Estaintot, *Recherches sur les Hautes Justices Féodales, etc.* (Rouen, 1892), *passim*, especially p. 38 n.
[55] *Arch. Nat.*, F^{12*} 30; F^{12*} 156; F^{12} 204.
[56] *Arch. Nat.*, F^{12} 1365 (Report of Goy, 1787).

The following, then, is a list of costs involved in the manufacture of a single cloth of a normal size of 30 *aunes* (35.55 meters):

	livres	& sols
75 pounds of wool, which leave 68		
after removal of grease	294	16
Brokerage fees		14
Entry duties on wool		12
Threshing		12
Dying	24	
Sorting	3	
Oil at 17-18 sols the pound	12	15
Carding	12	
Cards	3	
Spinning	47	16
Putting onto bobbin	1	7
Warping	11	
Sizing	2	5
Lists	7	16
Heddles, tenters, and teasel	2	5
Carting	3	5
Soap	5	16
Finishing	6	
Washing	7	
Shearing	7	16
Shears		5
Reworking of broken threads into pattern		15
Pressing	1	
Office Expenses, packing, and taxes	4	10
Total	449	10

Each piece of cloth sold for approximately 500 livres, thus leaving a surplus of 51 livres, 10 sols. But a certain amount must be deducted from this gross profit for overhead not otherwise accounted for, such as depreciation of the factory installation and losses of material during processing. The result is that the net profit on a piece of cloth may be set at about 30 livres.[57]

In an average year of the seventeen-eighties, Elbeuf manufactured 18,700 pieces of cloth worth 9,350,000 livres. Of this, 6,405,785 livres were paid out for raw material. Another 2,383,215

[57] This conclusion is confirmed by another estimate for the same period. It cost 358 livres, 16 sols to manufacture a piece of cloth measuring 25¼ aunes. The sale price was 391 livres, 7 sols, 6 pence. Total profit: 32 livres, 9 sols, 6 pence. See Lucien Barbe, "Histoire de l'Industrie du Drap à Louviers," *Bulletin de la Société d'Etudes Diverses de l'Arrondissement de Louviers*, II (1894), 55–56.

was paid out to workers. Total profit for the manufacturers was 561,000 livres.[58]

The profit seems, then, to have been approximately 6 per cent of the sales price, a small enough margin in the eighteenth century when the extent of commercial risk was normally greater than it is today and was consequently compensated for by higher returns on investment than we are used to. But it should be remembered that this figure remains true only if we ignore the tricks used to draw more value from a given amount of raw wool. The evidence that this practice was common is great. Every report of the Inspectors of Manufactures mentions it. One of them, Goy, wrote in 1767 that: " depuis plusieurs années beaucoup de fabriques en ont altéré la qualité, soit en employment des laines trop communes ou en ne donnant pas les apprêts convenables. Plusieurs même ont mis à leurs chaînes beaucoup moins de fils qu'il n'est ordonné, ce qui à occasionné de justes plaintes." [59] His opinion was confirmed by Taillard *fils* in 1773, who notes this cheating on materials but hastens to assure us that the majority of manufacurers, " jaloux de leurs réputations, n'abusent point de la liberté que le ministre a bien voulu leur accorder et se contentent d'un profit honnête, s'appliquant à perfectionner de plus en plus leurs manufactures." We have no way, then, of knowing what proportion of Elbeuf woolens were inferior in quality to that demanded by the regulations, but we do know that attempts were often made to make inferior woolens pass for better quality goods. The number of seizures made by government officials abundantly testifies to this. Given the small profit made on a single cloth, the inspectors were generally of the opinion that a blind application of the rules would result only in the ruin of the manufacture. But they were firm in demanding that fraud be eliminated. A strict application of the rules " risquerait même de perdre une grand partie de cette branche de commerce si intéressante à conserver." [60] It was absolutely necessary, however, to stop the currently practiced abuse of putting yellow and blue lists on mediocre cloth, which made it resemble the fine cloth of Louviers and served

[58] François de la Rochefoucald, (ed. Jean Marchand), *Voyage en France, 1781–1783* (Paris, 1933), I, 21–23.

[59] *Arch. Nat.*, F^{12} 1366.

[60] *Arch. Nat.*, F^{12} 1366 (Goy).

to fool the customer. If this practice were not stopped, the reputation of the woolen industry would be completely destroyed.[61]

We now have an idea of the advantages provided by the woolen
industry to its entrepreneurs. What of the advantages, if any,
for the State? Did the commerce of woolen cloth strengthen or
weaken the balance of trade? From a strictly mercantilist point
of view, the answer must be a negative one, for raw wool and dye
stuffs purchased abroad cost 309 livres per piece of cloth or
5,778,300 livres for 18,700 pieces, whereas only 10,000 of these
cloths were sold abroad, mainly in Italy, Spain, and the Americas,
bringing in a total of 5,000,000 livres. The result was a net loss
of 778,300 against the balance of trade. However, if we look more
closely, not to say more realistically, at the situation, we find that
France not only did not lose on this commerce but actually profited
from it. First, it must be realized that France did not have enough
raw wool, even of poor quality, to clothe its population. Second,
the foreign purchases produced a total value of 9,350,000 livres
of cloth. The inevitable conclusion, then, is that an expenditure
of 778,300 livres outside the realm was counterbalanced by gross
revenue of 4,350,000, the sum of the industry's production after
deduction of foreign sales. And this is in addition to the employment provided some thousands of workers and eighty manufacturers. It might be also added that, even from a mercantilist point
of view, the national, but not the local, balance of trade in woolens
was positive, if we take into account the numerous lesser quality
woolen goods made with domestic wools that were sold abroad.[62]

Now we must look more closely at the economic position of
Elbeuf in relation to the business cycle. It was already remarked
that there were thirty-seven manufacturers in the town at the
beginning of the eighteenth century. In 1750 there were eighty-
six,[63] and in 1787 there were seventy-six distributed among sixty-
two enterprises.[64] An attempt will be made to analyze the fluctuations of the industry between the last two dates, but leaving aside
for the moment the situation of the manufacture in the last years
before the Revolution, a subject that will be dealt with later. The
tables found on the following pages will serve to orient a discus-

[61] *Arch. Nat.*, F¹² 1365 (Report of 1787).
[62] La Rochefoucauld, *Voyage*, I, 23–25.
[63] *Arch. Nat.*, F¹² 1366 (Report by Goy, 1767).
[64] *Arch. Nat.*, F¹² 1365.

sion of business cycles, although it is evident that these series are
not complete. Still, they are more than enough to serve our

TABLE 1–1

PRODUCTION OF ORDINARY CLOTH   (in livres & sols)

Date [a]	Number of pieces	Price per aune	Value
1750 [2]	9,079	15	3,126,155
1751 [1]	7,637	15	2,634,765
1751 [2]	8,395	15.5	2,944,546
1752 [2]	6,287	15.5	2,208,215
1753 [1]	6,459	15.10	2,302,533
1753 [2]	6,707	15.10	2,391,045
1754 [1]	6,379	15.10	2,274,113
1754 [2]	6,742	15.10	2,403,523
1756 [1]	6,912	15.10	2,464,128
1756 [2]	7,600	15.10	2,709,400
1757 [1]	6,744	15	2,326,680
1757 [2]	7,631	15.10	2,720,451
1758 [1]	6,862	14.10	2,288,477
1758 [2]	7,473	14.10	2,492,245
1759 [1]	6,964	14	2,242,408
1759 [2]	6,436	14	2,072,392
1760 [1]	6,177	13.10	1,309,258
1760 [2]	5,888	14	2,143,232
1762 [1]	6,341	14.10	2,390,557
1762 [2]	6,493	14	2,363,452
1763 [1]	6,506	14.10	2,452,782
1763 [2]	8,194	14	2,982,616
1764 [1]	8,294	14.10	2,826,838
1765 [2]	7,903	15.10	3,182,909
1766 [1]	7,000	15.10	3,038,000
1766 [2]	7,647	14.15	3,156,145
1767 [1]	6,589	15.10	2,859,626
1767 [2]	7,060	15.10	3,064,040
1768 [1]	6,897	15.5	2,945,019
1768 [2]	6,949	15.5	2,965,519
1770 [1]	5,776	14.10	2,077,552
1770 [2]	6,176	14.10	2,328,352
1771 [1]	6,500	14.10	2,450,500
1771 [2]	6,025	14.10	2,271,425

Sources: *Arch. Nat.*, F[12] 1363, F[12] 1364.
[a] The dates on Tables 1–1 to 1–3 represent the semester and year.

purposes. It should also be noted that these are production figures
and therefore reflect commercial trends only indirectly. It is not

known how many of these cloths were sold, or how many remained in the manufacturers' warehouses. Of course, production was bound sooner or later to slow down as markets were closed off,

TABLE 1–2

PRODUCTION OF FINE CLOTH   (in livres & sols)

Date	Number of pieces	Price per *aune*	Value
1750 [2]	40	18	15,560
1751 [1]	15	18	6,210
1751 [2]	20	18.5	8,395
1752 [2]	15	18.10	6,382
1753 [1]	50	18.10	24,975
1753 [2]	18	18.10	7,733
1754 [1]	100	19.10	44,850
1754 [2]	125	21	66,375
1755 [2]	190	21	91,770
1756 [1]	350	20	161,000
1756 [2]	200	21	96,600
1757 [1]	300	19.10	134,550
1757 [2]	150	21	72,450
1758 [1]	300	18.10	127,650
1758 [2]	90	18.10	38,295
1759 [1]	100	17.15	40,825
1759 [2]	10	17.15	4,082
1760 [1]	20	17.15	8,165
1760 [2]	12	17.5	5,382
1763 [1]	6	18.10	2,886
1763 [2]	14	18.10	6,734
1764 [1]	5	18.10	2,405
1765 [1]	4	19	1,976
1766 [1]	29	19	15,428
1766 [2]	15	18.15	2,696
1767 [2]	59	20.10	33,866
1768 [1]	72	19	38,304
1768 [2]	119	20	66,640
1770 [1]	50	17	22,100
1771 [2]	35	17	15,470

Sources: *Arch. Nat.*, F[12] 1363, F[12] 1364.

but the period of time taken by production to align itself with commercial possibilities was more or less long.

At the beginning of the twenty-year period under examination, Elbeuf had reached a high point in its woolen production until that time, producing some 16,500 pieces of cloth per year. That was in 1751. By 1753 this total had fallen by almost 3,000 pieces to 13,600. There was a rise again in 1756 to 15,400 and this

TABLE 1–3

COMPARISON OF TOTAL WOOLEN PRODUCTION OF ELBEUF
AND THE GENERALITY OF ROUEN

	Elbeuf		Generality of Rouen	
Date	Number of pieces	Value (in livres)	Number of pieces	Value (in livres)
1751 [1]	7,973	2,749,666	20,346	5,116,947
1751 [2]	8,719	3,057,044	21,806	5,569,659
1752 [2]	7,454	2,264,297	19,662	4,933,092
1753 [1]	6,710	2,395,482	18,638	4,677,537
1753 [2]	6,889	2,454,862	19,368	4,832,677
1754 [1]	6,569	2,308,478	18,439	4,972,907
1754 [2]	7,032	2,522,760	17,205	4,402,529
1755 [2]	6,985	2,513,620	18,329	4,941,572
1756 [1]	7,353	2,660,822	20,563	5,325,018
1756 [2]	8,037	2,898,452	18,600	5,112,941
1757 [1]	7,126	2,523,988	17,531	4,515,949
1757 [2]	8,135	2,921,264	19,006	5,258,149
1758 [1]	7,243	2,444,330	17,568	4,918,306
1758 [2]	7,804	2,614,806	18,605	4,854,409
1759 [1]	7,211	2,332,018	17,711	4,468,298
1759 [2]	6,585	2,127,076	16,464	4,123,728
1760 [1]	6,263	1,339,987	14,321	2,812,317
1760 [2]	6,574	2,193,111	15,754	4,099,367
1761 [1]	6,308	2,214,354	13,768	3,839,891
1761 [2]	6,027	2,391,716	16,016	4,389,314
1762 [1]	6,453	2,432,896	15,272	4,370,531
1762 [2]	6,707	2,436,358	16,739	4,605,935
1763 [1]	6,644	2,501,708	15,949	4,536,829
1763 [2]	8,319	3,035,882	17,871	5,202,674
1764 [1]	8,378	2,855,195	17,688	5,051,008
1765 [1]	7,958	3,204,824	16,951	5,571,724
1766 [1]	7,060	3,063,935	16,032	5,415,611
1766 [2]	7,734	3,184,836	17,793	5,711,234
1767 [1]	6,630	2,878,746	15,742	5,240,681
1767 [2]	7,159	3,113,830	16,966	5,757,979
1768 [1]	6,987	2,990,227	16,379	5,694,794
1768 [2]	7,090	3,041,003	16,156	5,678,542
1770 [1]	6,000	2,179,524	14,136	4,421,877
1770 [2]	6,381	2,422,375	14,837	4,730,995
1771 [1]	6,818	2,584,689	14,138	4,420,079
1771 [2]	6,359	2,416,457	13,882	4,371,909

Sources: *Arch. Nat.*, F[12] 1363, F[12] 1364.

figure held true in 1758 as well. Down again in 1759 to 13,700, production fell still lower in 1760 to 12,700 and remained stable in that region through 1761 and 1762. There was a marked improvement in 1763, when the 15,000 mark was topped once again. The half-yearly figures which are available for 1764 and 1765 together with the complete totals for 1766 permit us to assume that this level was maintained during those years. The years

TABLE 1–4

BALES OF WOOL USED IN ELBEUF INDUSTRY, 1740–63

Date	Amount
1740	3,802
1741	3,672
1742	3,903
1743	3,727
1744	4,753
1745	4,477
1746	4,521
1747	4,897
1748	5,137
1749	5,830
1750	6,127
1751	4,842
1752	3,190
1753	4,258
1754	4,393
1755	4,381
1756	5,080
1757	5,307
1758	4,008
1759	4,539
1760	3,370
1761	3,968
1762	4,461
1763	4,997

Source: Messance, *Recherches* (Paris, 1766), pp. 305–6.

1767 and 1768 were years of decline, but in neither did the figure reach the nadir of 1760, standing instead at a little under 14,000. The low point of this secular trend at approximately 12,300 was reached in 1770, and 1771 just managed to top 13,100.[65]

Now, although the evolution of the world market was, as we shall see, in large part the force responsible for the vicissitudes of the Elbeuf manufacture, production did not always follow the

[65] See Table 1–3.

price index. In other words, a period of high prices did not necessarily push production up, nor did low prices inevitably depress this activity. Numerous are the examples of exactly the reverse phenemenon. A single one taken from the index of fine cloths will suffice. Thus production fell by 50 per cent, from 300 to 150 pieces, between the first and second semesters of 1757, while the price per *aune* increased from 19 livres 10 sols to 21 livres.

If prices did not necessarily determine the course of wool production, what did? There are a variety of factors which need to be discussed under this heading, and, fortunately, this can be done because of the excellent reports written every six months by Du Boisroger, the Inspector of Manufactures at Elbeuf, which have come down to us almost in their entirety.[66]

The beginning of the lean years in 1752 would seem to have caught the inspector unawares. He had difficulty in explaining the reasons for this decline. Although he noted that the high price of Spanish wool, due in turn to the disease and death of the lambs, was partially responsible, he tended to attribute the sad taste of the industry to less material factors. Thus, for two semesters running, he rang the changes on the theme that " la confiance qui fait l'âme du commerce est entièrement perdue." It was only at the end of 1753 that he ventured to provide a more precise explanation to the effect that, while internal consumption and sales to Italy were holding their own, the Spanish market, both in the Mother Country and in its West Indian possessions, had undergone a disastrous eclipse. That this should have had so great an influence on Elbeuf is readily understandable, when we know that one-quarter of the wool production of the generality (8,000–9,000 pieces annually) was disposed of on this market.

The recovery of 1756 bolstered Du Boisroger's spirit, but he was, and rightly so, slow to be convinced of the coming of the millennium. He continued to complain of the high prices of raw materials, blaming Spanish wool growers for their speculations. But he also wrote that frequent bankruptcies were a factor in sending prices upward. Worst of all, he thought that the apparent augmentation in production could be explained by bad bookkeeping of the previous years. But, if production was not up, at least the increase in sales was cause for optimism.

[66] *Arch. Nat.*, F[12] 560; F[12] 1364.

On the surface, this optimism was well founded. Production held its own through 1758. A closer look at the situation, however, shows that all was not well with the manufacture. In 1757 we hear for the first time of the effects of the Seven Years War on commerce. The naval war made navigation difficult and especially so in New World waters. When we remember the important role of the Spanish West Indies in Elbeuf's trade, we need seek no further to understand the depression of this year. The lack of confidence occasioned by bad business was the least of the manufacturers' worries. The lack of species, whether caused by falling sales or by the hoarding of money that is often practiced in periods of business decline, created ideal conditions for a flowering of bankruptcies. These did not tarry in making their appearance. This intermingling of cause and effect, like parasites feeding on one another, served to make the crisis still deeper. Warehouses remained full as markets were closed off. When an opportunity to sell some of the surplus presented itself, the manufacturers, anxious to have cash with which to meet their obligations, hastened to take advantage of it, even if it meant selling the cloth " au-dessous de la valeur intrinsèque." In 1758 Du Boisroger analyzed the situation as follows:

> Le défaut de confiance du marchand de laine . . . attere le crédit de leurs débiteurs, les uns se sont vus forcés de termoyer, vis-à-vis de leurs créanciers, et d'autres de faillir, en sorte que cette place est devenue dans un discrédit duquel elle aura peut-être bien de la peine à se relever: les maisons les plus solides se tiennent sur leurs gardes, pour ne pas se trouver à découvert, elles diminuent peu à peu leur commerce, afin de laisser écouler insensiblement les draps en magasin.
>
> [A comparison of the years 1757 and 1758 shows that] il est entré dans la première année 5,307 balles [de laine] et la dernière 4,008 balles, ce qui fait une différence de 1,299 balles de diminution. Si une balle de laine produit, suivant le calcul ordinaire qu'on en fait, 3 pièces et demie de drap, c'est de moins de fabriqué d'une année à l'autre 4,546 pièces. On en suppose une même quantité d'invendu et en magasin. Or, on ne peut s'attendre à rien moins de flatteur, mais au contraire à envisager beaucoup de misère qui jette une grande consternation de toute part, qui influe vivement sur les misérables ouvriers, tant de la ville que celui [sic] de la campagne, dont une partie n'a que demiouvrage, une autre un quart et une autre point du tout, et sans cependant pour ainsi dire, d'autres ressources que celles de la providence.

Is it any wonder then that in this time of misery Du Boisroger should complain of the harm caused native industry by clothing members of the French regiments in the service of the Empire in foreign cloth?

The above analysis retains its validity for 1759, 1760, and 1761. If anything, things got worse. Bankruptcies became still more frequent, and all hope of re-establishing trade in Elbeuf woolens was given up for the duration of the war. Du Boisroger wrote: " La rareté de l'espèce jointe aux révolutions qu'on a nommées souvent les guerres qui ôtent la confidence qui fait la base du commerce, refroidissent beaucoup nos fabriquants qui ne se livrent qu'en tremblant relativement aux banqueroutes qu'ils ont essuiées."

The year 1761 saw the dawn of a new hope for the commerce of Elbeuf, a hope which, when it had had time to make its influence felt, was to be in great measure responsible for the recovery of the town's industry. This was the Bourbon Pacte de Famille of August of that year.[67] Already in his report for the second half of 1761, drawn up early in the following year, the Inspector of Manufactures saw a slight augmentation in sales, which had, he felt, to be attributed to the advantages that must

nécessairement résulter du concordat entre la France et l'Espagne au sujet du commerce relativement aux circonstances de la rupture entre l'Espagne et l'Angleterre. Et les préjugés en sont d'autant plus favorables que cette manufacture paraît vouloir sortir de la léthargie pour reprendre la vigueur qu'elle avait dans les dernières guerres de ces deux royaumes, ce qui s'annonce non seulement par le débouché qu'elle a présentement de ses draps, mais particulièrement par la fourniture des matières premières que font journellement les fabricants.

Having once secured the Spanish market, the problem became one of how to keep it; here, Du Boisroger was adamant. In his view, this market could be still further enlarged if the manufacturers paid more attention to the quality of the goods they shipped to it. He blamed those manufacturers whose only concern was a quick profit for injuring the reputation of their product, and he recommended that the inspectors be authorized to countersign the export certificates of goods destined for Spain. In addition, he expressed concern over the lack of spun wool available to the weavers of Elbeuf. Later, in 1764, he was to state his conviction that the fault lay with the overly close supervision which Elbeuf manufacturers sought to exercise over the spinners who, as a

[67] Pierre Muret, La Prépondérance Anglaise (Paris, 1949), pp. 557–60.

reaction, preferred to do other types of spinning " pour jouir de leur liberté."

The four-year period beginning in 1763 marked the height of Elbeuf's prosperity. In 1763 more raw wool was imported than in any year save five of the preceding thirty-five. And 1764 was even better from this point of view, topping every previous year except 1749 and 1750. It was with justification that Du Boisroger could attribute the fall of the Rouen woolen industry to " l'éléva-tion de celle d'Elbeuf qui a envahi à elle seule presque tout le commerce et toutes les manufactures de la province, particulière-ment celle-ci [Rouen] ainsi que celle d'Orival."

But how to protect this advantage, once gained? To a man whose mentality was clearly that of an administrative functionary, there could be only one answer: close regulation of the manu-facture by the agency of which he was a representative. The industry was much too important in the national economy to be left to the discretion of the manufacturers.[68] In the case discussed, this view proved to be correct.

The end of the war put an end to the difficulties of transport and thus increased the number of markets for Elbeuf woolens. A new demand was born for goods that had not been available in wartime. But at the same time the price of raw materials was going up faster than the price of cloth. The results were two-fold. A certain number of manufacturers reduced the quality of their cloth and rushed in to profit from increased demand, while others, not wishing to produce goods of inferior quality, were forced to cut production in order to avoid losses. The less scrupu-lous thus made quick fortunes, while the others had difficulty in making ends meet. But what is worse is that the profiteers them-selves were soon hoist with their own petard. Their excessive shipments to Cadix soon made of their cloth a drug on the market and reduced the reputation of the manufacture to a new low. The result was that a new decline set in, beginning in 1767 and aggravated toward the end of 1768 by a fall in domestic con-sumption. This recession lasted through 1770; only in 1771 did the trend seem to turn slightly upward once again, as can be seen

---

[68] The preoccupation with regulations, their enforcement, and efficacity was constant among the Inspectors. To listen to them, one would get the idea that regulation alone was responsible for the prosperity of the manufacture, which would surely perish if left to itself. See *Arch. Nat.*, F¹² 749ᵇ; F¹² 751.

by the number of bales of wool shipped to Elbeuf during these years. In 1768 there were 4,583.5; in 1769, 4,407.5; in 1770, 4,435 and in 1771, 4,544.75. But the number of pieces of cloth manufactured during these years does not correspond to the number of bales of wool received, if the coefficient of 3.5 pieces to the bale is adopted. This may have meant that some of the wool went unused for lack of good market conditions. Or, on the other hand, some cloth may have been manufactured and sold clandestinely, without undergoing the required official registration.

In their pursuit of profit, Elbeuf manufacturers sometimes stooped to fraud. Frequent efforts were made to mislead the client as to the quality of cloth offered for sale. Theoretically, certain well-defined lists had to be put on each piece of cloth according to its quality, and part of the task of the inspection was to verify the exactness of the relationship between the cloth and its list. But this formality was not demanded of certain types of cloth of inferior quality known as " draps libres," that is, not subject to government control. Certain manufacturers took advantage of this freedom to pass off their freely manufactured goods as regulated cloth of better quality. Although the Intendant of Commerce responsible for the Elbeuf manufacture was aware of this practice and constantly spoke of the need to put an end to it, he seems to have had little success in the matter.[69]

Another and perhaps more important kind of fraud was practiced by the established manufacturers of Elbeuf. Because they worked under government regulation and were known in the market as members of the Royal Manufacture, any contravention committed by them automatically endangered the reputation of the industry as a whole, much more so than did the action of an interloper. Unfortunately, their respected position in the field also protected them from any severe sanctions. When they did decorate a piece of cloth to look better than it actually was, extenuating circumstances were usually found to save them from punishment. There are two such cases which serve as examples, one in 1778 and the other ten years later. In the earlier instance, Alexandre Lefebvre was found to have marked an ordinary piece of cloth with the lists reserved for fine cloths. But as he was a " bon fabricant " and suffering from the effects of a recent bank-

[69] *Arch. Nat.*, F^{12*} 156 .

ruptcy, the Director General of Finances ordered that the goods which had been seized should be returned to him. No disciplinary action was taken. Again, in 1788, one Louis Delaunay was found to be putting lists reserved for the fine cloth of Louviers on his produce. At first, the seigneurial judge who had jurisdiction over the manufacture ordered that a part of the cloth be confiscated and that a notice to that effect be posted in the principal parishes of the *bailliage*. Delaunay was, moreover, to pay the costs of this operation. But the Inspector of Manufactures Goy put forth in his favor the argument that he was a hard-pressed, small manu-facturer who should not be unduly punished for having once given in to temptation. In the end, the cloth was returned minus the misleading borders, and he was forced to pay the costs (12 livres) engendered by the seizure, but no defamatory notice was posted.[70]

The indulgence shown by the government in these cases served only to make the manufacturers bolder in their requests for special privileges in marking cloth. They even came to demand such privileges as a matter of right. In 1782, Pierre Grandin the elder asked that he be permitted to attach his name in gold letters on each of a lot of 29,300 pieces of cloth, this being the condition demanded by the buyer. This seemingly harmless request was denied on the ground that if granted, it would inevitably lead to other demands of a similar nature and create unutterable con-fusion on the market.[71]

Requests of this sort multiplied rapidly during the commercial decline that followed on the conclusion of the Anglo-French treaty of 1786.[72] In 1789, several of the most eminent manufacturers, including Louis Michel Grandin, Henry Grandin, Alexandre Grandin, Louis Joseph Duruflé, and Moyse Duruflé, after having noted that the English might export to France any kind of cloth they wished, under whatever mark that suited them, demanded the right to do the same. The only way to keep the manufacture from falling into complete decay, they argued, was to allow them to

coiffer nos draps d'une lisière arbitraire au goût et suivant les ordres des commettants qu'il nous importe sans doute de satisfaire. Autrement ils porteront ailleurs leurs commissions. Lorsqu'on a des rivaux à craindre, ce n'est pas le cas de dire, telle fabrique est connue pour faire des draps

---

[70] *Arch. Nat.*, F¹² 1365; F¹²* 157.   [71] *Arch. Nat.*, F¹²* 156.

[72] This last sentence should not be taken to be an argument *post hoc, ergo propter hoc*. For the causes of the pre-revolutionary crisis in Elbeuf, see Chapter 3, Section I.

pour telle et telle lisière et ne veut ni ne peut changer son système parce qu'alors nos voisins plus accommodants et toujours aux aguets pour donner de l'activité à leur industrie profiteront de nos fautes et nous supplanteront partout.

If the regulations were strictly followed, orders would have to be refused, and the result would be " deux grands inconvénients, l'un de préparer à la nation du tort irréparable en la frustrant d'un débouché avantageux, l'autre de procurer à nos voisins rivaux, la facilité de s'emparer de toutes les affaires de ce genre." The date of this letter is February 10, 1789, and the petitioners are certainly up to date in their language, as may be seen from their appeal for the good of the nation. Nor were they alone in this. Only two days earlier, their fellow manufacturers Michel and Pierre Grandin had also written to Necker protesting against excessive government supervision. The only way to escape it, they claimed, was " en vivant noblement, c'est-à-dire à ne rien faire." But this alternative they reject with infinite scorn, claiming that they prefer to work, to give others work, and to pass on their business to their heirs. But all their arguments proved fruitless. Necker's reaction was to instruct Goy to go to Elbeuf " pour faire sentir à tous ces fabricants que ce n'est pas en fatiguant sans cesse le Conseil par des projets de la nature de ceux-ci qu'ils pourront mériter la protection du gouvernement." And Goy's inspection tour satisfied him that the " bons fabricants " were wise enough not to want entire freedom in this matter.[73] For the moment the matter was settled by Letters Patent issued even before the manufacturers had a chance to state their case. The ruling of February 7, 1789, reaffirmed that of December 5, 1782, in fixing specific borders for each kind of cloth manufactured in Elbeuf.[74]

Growing pains are common in any city that, like Elbeuf, undergoes a rapid industrial development. Always subject to the vicissitudes of the business cycle, it is not surprising that the manufacturers should have sought some scapegoat to blame for their troubles. The government that practiced close supervision was a perfect target for their wrath. When the government refused to hear their complaints, they often enough passed over its objections and did what their business sense told them to do. Inevitably, this practice created conflict between the manufacturers and the bureaucrats.

[73] *Arch. Nat.*, F^{12} 1366.   [74] *Arch. Nat.*, F^{12*} 31.

I have tried here to provide a picture of the growth of the woolen industry in Elbeuf: the manner of its organization and control, its processes, the respective roles of the manufacturers and workers. Without an understanding of these three things there is no possibility of studying the urban social structure. Throughout the following chapters I shall have to keep in mind that the industry was increasingly organized and controlled from the top down, that the numerous workers necessary to the execution of multiple industrial processes were less and less independent and continually losing any control they once may have exercised over the industry. In other words, the producer gave way in importance to the manufacturer who controlled investment capital, raw materials, markets and, to a lesser extent, the tools of the trade.

CHAPTER 2

THE SOCIAL STRUCTURE OF ELBEUF, 1770–89

I

While an understanding of the industrial structure of Elbeuf is necessary to the comprehension of its social structure, it does not alone suffice. Because our principal sources for the study of the social structure are the tax rolls, we must first understand the fiscal system of the city.

Like all other cities of the *pays d'élection*, Elbeuf was subject to a *taille*. However, the inhabitants had obtained the right in 1708 to subscribe for this tax by means of a *tarif* on all " bestiaux, denrées et marchandises qui entreront et se consommeront, seront vendus ou fabriqués dans ledit bourg d'Elbeuf et lieux en dépendant." Henceforth, the *taille* was to be paid out of the revenues thus procured, the sum to be fixed by the royal government annually. In order to avoid evasion of this tax, it was specifically stated by the government that the inhabitants who cultivated any land outside the city or took any such land on a farm lease would remain subject to the *taille* in the parish where the land was located. By the same token, no manufacturer or *négociant* living in the city could store goods subject to the *tarif* in a warehouse outside of its limits, under penalty of a fine of 500 livres.[1] The former of these two stipulations involved the repeal of a privilege which had allowed the bourgeois of Norman cities to cultivate their own lands for a period of one year tax free, if they were unable to find a farmer.[2] Apparently Elbeuvians felt that the loss of this prerogative was as nothing to what they gained through

[1] J. Darsel, " Les Privilèges d'Elbeuf en matière de Taille et de Capitation," *Annales de Normandie*, IX (1959), 17–20; St. Denis, *Histoire*, V, 237–38.
[2] Loisel de Boismare, *Dictionnaire du Droit des Tailles* (Caen, 1787), I, 109–13.

the creation of the *tarif*. The *tarif* did not by any means produce enough revenue to pay the city's taxes, but in the eyes of the bourgeois it had a greater advantage. They said that it avoided favoritism; what they meant is that it avoided arbitrary taxation according to external signs of wealth. It was also a non-progressive tax in that everyone, rich or poor, bore proportionately the same burden. The *tarif* had been renewed once in 1728, and when it came time to extend it once again, the city solicited an indefinite prolongation, saying that otherwise its industry " tomberait dans l'anéantissement; la haine, la partialité, l'animosité prendraient le dessus et l'on ne tarderait pas à voir le bourg replongé dans l'état de misère et de désolation où il avait été réduit par ces différentes passions avant l'établissement du tarif." Its request was granted, and the *tarif* remained in effect until 1790.[3]

Contemporary observers shared the opinion of Elbeuvians vis-à-vis the *taille*. In 1769 Moreau de Beaumont wrote:

Il n'est pas douteux que l'imposition et le recouvrement de la taille entraînent dans les villes des inconvénients infiniment plus considérables que dans les campagnes; elle ne peut être établie dans les villes sur aucune base certaine, parce qu'elle porte entièrement sur les facultés; elle arrête, ou anéantit même, les progrès du commerce et de l'industrie; la collecte entretient les divisions dans les familles ou détruit les fortunes dans leur principe; les droits sur les consommations s'acquittent au contraire insensiblement et presque toujours dans la proportion des facultés; l'habitant, à l'abri de toute inquiétude, se livre au travail avec l'assurance d'en recevoir les fruits; les deniers du roi sont assurés et rentrent sans peine et sans frais au moyen du produit des droits, dans lequel il doit se trouver un excédent que l'on peut employer aux déstinations les plus utiles des villes.[4]

It was a happy coincidence that the *tarif* seemed to conform to eighteenth-century precepts of reason and bourgeois interests at one and the same time.

The government's decision to extend the *tarif* may have been prompted by the Elbeuvians' argument that it had advantages for the royal government as well as for themselves. Although the *taille* itself did not increase notably between 1708 and 1776, the

[3] St. Denis, *Histoire*, V, 122, 155; for the authorization to abolish the *tarif*, see *Arch. Dép.*, C 2193.
[4] Moreau de Beaumont, *Mémoires Concernant les Impositions et Droits en Europe* (Paris, 1768–69), II, 56, cited in Marcel Marion, *Les Impôts Directs sous l'Ancien Régime* (Paris, 1910), pp. 22–23.

total of all taxes went up two and one-half times. Thus the city paid only about 21,000 livres in 1708, but 47,251 in 1747 and nearly 53,000 in 1776.[5] The *tarif* facilitated the increase in taxes by providing for the *taille* in a manner more or less unfelt by the population, leaving only the capitation to be collected by means of individual assessment. Moreover, the *tarif* permitted the city to take loans when necessary to subscribe for other taxes or to redeem offices, as it was anticipated that any surplus revenue produced by the *tarif* could be used for debt service. This was done, for instance, in the case of the *don gratuit* in 1759–65.[6]

Despite several augmentations that finally raised the *tarif* by 50 per cent on the eve of the Revolution,[7] it was impossible for it to cover at the same time the local expenses of the city and the taxes due by it to the royal government. The years of economic distress in the seventeen-sixties reduced the number of goods coming into the city, and the revenue of the *tarif* decreased accordingly. In 1783 the municipality wrote that before the Seven Years War, 30,000 to 40,000 *pots*[8] of brandy were consumed annually in Elbeuf, but that the total was now down to 12,000. Similarly for pigs, which were the cheapest food animal, the number consumed had dropped from between 7,000 and 8,000 to 250. The drop in consumption not only made it impossible for the *tarif* to produce a sufficient return but it also largely invalidated the special *octroi* on alcoholic beverages established in 1755 to replace a former tax on wool used in the manufacture. The result was a deficit in the city's accounts of 1,463 livres 10 sols in 1783 and of 8,781 livres for the six previous years.[9]

We find that Elbeuf was caught in a vicious circle. Money had somehow to be procured to pay royal taxes. Recourse was had to loans. In 1783 the city owed a total of 124,500 livres, an enormous sum for the time. Then provision had to be made for debt service, and when the *tarif* did not suffice (and this was more and more the case as we come closer to the Revolution), this meant still more borrowing or the establishment of additional

[5] *Arch. Dép.*, C 202; C 274. The *taille* was never higher than 25,400 livres (1752) and stood at 23,980 livres in 1776.

[6] *Arch. Mun.*, CC.

[7] *Arch. Dép. de l'Eure*, C 42 (September 18, 1788).

[8] One *pot* equals 1.688 liters.

[9] *Arch. Mun.*, CC; *Arch. Dép.*, C 202.

taxes in the form of local levies. In other words, the attempt to escape direct taxation was a failure.

At the same time, the central government was applying more pressure in order to get money to meet its own needs. The city, of course, reacted vigorously, but usually with mediocre results. It blamed the new royal taxes for the economic depression and attempted to escape them. In 1771 a royal declaration added 6 sols per livre to the two already being collected on the *tarif*. The citizens of Elbeuf protested that they could not stand this increase:

> Quel serait le sort de ces malheureux habitants, si, Elbeuf érigé en ville depuis peu, sans qu'ils aient jamais eu l'ambition de la demander, ce titre vain pour eux les rendait susceptible des taxes des autres villes du royaume, et que comme taillables il supportassent encore les charges et taxes mises sur les habitants des campagnes? Le montant des 6 sols pour livre qu'on veut établir sur les droits de tarif joint aux deux sols déjà indûment perçu sur le même objet formeraient une surcharge de plus de onze mille livres, somme exhorbitante dans tous les temps pour les habitants d'Elbeuf mais bien plus encore dans ces temps de calamité où la plupart d'entr'eux ne peuvent qu'à peine subvenir à leurs besoins physiques; loin d'être en état de contribuer à des charges nouvelles, ils devraient être dèchargés d'une partie des anciennes dans un temps surtout où par le peu de consommation le tarif ne peut point fournir au paiement de la taille.[10]

As we have seen in Chapter 1, 1771 was indeed a difficult year, and this protest was not just the idle ranting of people trying to evade taxes. Nonetheless, they failed to obtain satisfaction, although the burden was somewhat lightened as the city paid a lump sum of 12,000 livres in lieu of this tax.

Other taxes in Elbeuf included the *corvée*, the *vingtièmes*, and the *vingtièmes d'industrie*. The latter was abolished in 1777 in all "bourgs, villages et campagnes" in an obvious attempt to encourage rural industry. But Elbeuf, having had the bad luck of being declared a city in 1776, did not profit from this measure.[11]

Aside from the *taille*, the major portion of Elbeuf's taxes was covered by the capitation established in 1695. No one was exempt from it, although a few persons, including the farmer of the duchy's revenues and the inspector of manufactures, were taxed

---

[10] *Arch. Mun.*, CC.

[11] Louis Duchemin, "L'Impôt sur le Revenu en Normandie (Dixième et Vingtième) avant la Révolution," *Recueil des Travaux de la Société Libre d'Agriculture, Sciences, Arts et Belles-Lettres de l'Eure*, 5th series, V (1898), 89.

directly by the intendant, rather than by the municipality or its agent. This was no doubt done to protect these highly placed individuals from abusive taxation, in the event that one of the assessors should wish to settle a score with them.

The capitation was a head tax, not a property or income tax. At first, a fixed amount of capitation was paid by each individual according to his occupation and/or status as listed in a table drawn up by the royal government. In later years, however, fixed assessments were abandoned in favor of a tax calculated by an agent of the municipality on the basis of his estimate of each person's ability to pay. And everyone did pay, no matter how poor. In cities where the *taille* was collected by roll, persons paying less than 40 sols of *taille* were theoretically exempt from the capitation, as it was thought that they were too poor to bear the extra burden.[12] This was not, however, the case in Elbeuf.

On the other hand, the manufacturers, assessed as a community, customarily paid no more than two-fifths of the capitation, although as a group they probably controlled more than two-fifths of the city's total wealth. The capitation decided upon by the royal government was made known to the city; a commission was appointed to make the assessments. Two-fifths of the necessary sum was immediately divided by the number of bales of wool that had entered the city in the previous twelve months. The result was the amount each manufacturer had to pay per bale brought in for his account. An attempt was made in 1786 by the receiver of the city to increase the contribution of the manufacturers. He reasoned that the number of manufacturers had grown so that the same tax burden was being divided among a greater number of individuals. Thus, each individual was benefiting from a reduction in taxes. Second, he said that

dans les temps où cette proportion a été établie le corps de fabrique contribuait aux droits de tarif beaucoup plus qu'il n'y contribue actuellement. Le luxe qui s'est introduit depuis quelques années dans Elbeuf ayant fait perdre aux gens opulents l'usage des matières communes qui sont presque les seuls articles imposés au tarif et auxquels l'opulence a substitué la soierie, la porcelaine, les glaces, le sucre, le café et autres articles non-imposés au tarif.

The municipality unanimously rejected this proposal.[13] On the

---

[12] Georges Lardé, *La Capitation dans les Pays de Taille Personnelle* (Paris, 1906), pp. 270, 346–48.

[13] *Arch. Mun.*, Délib., Vol. I (December 16, 1786).

other hand, a general assembly of the city decided two years later to tax manufacturers 3,000 livres over and above the two-fifths due by them on the capitation of that year.[14]

To what extent can the records of the capitation help us in our study of the social structure of Elbeuf? The capitation was the only direct tax individually assessed on a regular basis. As a result, the tax rolls contain a list of the occupations of all persons gainfully employed. It is hoped that occupation will provide at least a clue to the class position of the taxpayers, according to the definitions we shall establish.

What of the assessments as mathematical quantities? Can they help in defining class structure? Here extreme care must be taken. Is there any guarantee, first of all, that assessments are truly representative of income? Hardly, for the capitation was based not on income, but rather on that vague category known as the " ability to pay." In addition, the capitation was an *impôt de répartition*, that is, one whose product was fixed by the government.[15] A certain total had to be collected even if it meant taxing some individuals beyond their means. Finally, even if all this were not true, the use we might make of tax assessments would still be limited, as income is at best an indication, rather than a definition, of class standing.

II

The difficulties involved in coming to agreement on a definition of the bourgeoisie are numerous and evident. This is about the only conclusion that can be drawn from the lengthy discussions of the topic by a group of eminent French scholars at the Tenth World Historical Congress at Rome in 1955. But there is possibly also a moral to the story, and that is that agreement on anything but minimal definitions is, at this stage, unimportant. As Professor Labrousse said, it is better to dispense with making " doctrinal passports " a prerequisite for the study of the bourgeoisie, a study which is susceptible of throwing much light on modern social history.[16]

[14] *Arch. Mun.*, Délib., Vol. I (December 20, 1788).

[15] Lardé, *Capitation*, p. 197.

[16] Ernest Labrousse, " Voies Nouvelles vers une Histoire de la Bourgeoisie Occidentale aux XVIIIe et XIXe Siècles," *Relazioni del X Congresso Internazionale di Scienze Storiche* (Florence, 1955), IV, 395–96. See also the discussion in *Atti*, pp. 515–30, and *Riassunti*, pp. 331–35.

Each historian must, however, propose his own definition, even if it means throwing caution to the winds and giving rise to polemics on the part of fellow researchers. My own is the following.

In the Marxist schema, the bourgeoisie denotes " the class of modern capitalists, owners of the means of social production and employers of wage labor." Each bourgeois is, then, an investor of capital (accumulated labor) who purchases the labor power of the proletariat in order to increase the value of his initial investment. The proletariat is defined as that class which must depend exclusively upon the sale of its labor power in order to survive. The mode of production created by the interaction of the bourgeoisie and the proletariat we call capitalism.

In order for fully developed capitalism, capitalism as a mode of production, to exist, it is clear that there must be both bourgeois and proletarians. One cannot exist without the other. The question is: Did they both exist in eighteenth-century France? Is the Marxist schema relevant to this period of history?

In this connection it is well to remember Marx's dictum that " the epoch of the bourgeoisie has simplified class antagonisms. Society as a whole is more and more splitting into great hostile camps, into two great classes directly facing each other—bourgeoisie and proletariat." The statement is one of tendency rather than of fact. It applies to the nineteenth-century capitalist society in which Marx lived and wrote. In that sense it is what Max Weber would call an ideal type. It is only a theoretical formulation to be built upon in the study of complex social reality.

With this in mind, we must make two preliminary notes. Failure to acknowledge them would make the application of Marxist categories to eighteenth-century society both impossible and ridiculous. First, neither capitalism nor the division of society into two classes which it implies came into being overnight. Both are the products of a long evolution within feudal society. Neither emerges full grown from some sheltering womb; each becomes a noticeable phenomenon long before it reaches maturity. Therefore, at any given specific instant of capitalist development, bourgeoisie and proletariat are more or less fully formed. At the same time other classes continue to exist that have their roots in another form of society.

It has already been indicated in Chapter 1 that the bourgeoisie of eighteenth-century Elbeuf was not yet as fully developed as it was to become a century later. For instance, it had not yet succeeded in organizing the entire textile industry on a capitalistic basis, and it did not yet have the monopoly of the means of production. Workers in the textile industry were not yet fully proletarian, in that many of them still owned the tools of their trade and sometimes, though less frequently, the raw materials. Moreover, many workers were still peasants, even land-owning peasants. To avoid any confusion, I shall refer to these workers simply as wage earners.

Other classes in the population must, I think, be divided into two categories. First, the nobles and the lower bourgeoisie, both of whom may be identified as older classes having grown up in pre-capitalist society. Second, those persons who may legitimately be considered as part of the capitalist order but who are neither bourgeois nor proletarian according to the above definitions. Specifically I have in mind persons in the service occupations. In his study of Orléans society, Lefebvre refers to them as the middle bourgeoisie. And he also considers certain retail merchants, small manufacturers, and commission agents as belonging in the same class.[17]

Is such an approach justifiable? Clearly, the very concept of a middle-class standing between bourgeois and proletarians is a catch-all, a way out of a sociological model which, in describing the nineteenth century and predicting the future, does not trouble to describe in detail developments up to that point. That there should be levels within the bourgeoisie is normal and predictable. So it is possible to speak of a middle class of persons making their living in the productive, as distinguished from the service, sphere of the economy and who conform to the role requirements of the bourgeois. But it is not quite so easy to justify including professionals in the same category. It may be said that an attorney who specialized in commercial law, a doctor whose origins were bourgeois or whose subjective status was high in the eyes of the community, a bookseller who catered to bourgeois or who was a member of the same lodge or academy as the leading manufacturers had a greater affinity to the upper bourgeoisie than to the lower bourgeoisie or the wage earners. If the observation is gener-

[17] Georges Lefebvre, "Urban Society in the Orléanais in the Late Eighteenth Century," *Past and Present*, No. 19 (April, 1961), pp. 52–54.

alized to cover all members of the professions, they can be included in the middle bourgeoisie. At best, it is an empirical approach which later developments—the capital role played by professionals and particularly lawyers in the Revolution—seem to justify.

How may the lower bourgeoisie be defined? If we are to include in this class, as Lefebvre does, " those artisans who, though working for a *négociant* (or a manufacturer), themselves employed workers, as well as those artisans and shopkeepers who, however humble, kept a certain independence because they dealt directly with the consumer," [18] it is because the lower bourgeoisie is recognized as being identifiable with an essentially pre-capitalist era of productive relations. In other words, the lower bourgeois is a handicraftsman who provides both the capital and the labor power needed in production. He owns the means of production and sells the commodity he produces on the open market. That, at least, is the classic schema. By the eighteenth century it had become somewhat more involved. Lower bourgeois producers did sometimes work for *négociants*. Their independence was thus threatened and they had to face the possibility of being reduced to the status of proletarians, as many of them eventually were. On the other hand, some became employers of labor. Those who did so and at the same time ceased to be producers themselves finally became members of the middle and upper bourgeoisie. It is probable, however, that these changes among the lower bourgeois did not noticeably affect their class status in the eighteenth century. Even when they were employers of labor, the relationships that existed between them and their employees were not simply those that exist between bourgeois and proletarians. The lower bourgeois usually remained a producer working alongside his employees, who, in turn, were bound to him not merely by wages but by a whole set of patriarchal relations that carried over from an earlier period. These facts help to explain why lower bourgeois, their employees and industrial wage earners as well, should have acted together to form the political class of *sans-culottes*. Their interests are threatened by developing industrial capitalism and increasing bourgeois social and economic control, albeit often in different ways. They therefore unite to meet the challenge, temporarily at least.

Then there is the nobility, an ambiguous grouping if ever there

[18] *Ibid.*, p. 54.

was one. In so far as " noble " is a legal term and not a social one, a member of the nobility would not necessarily be excluded from the bourgeoisie as herein defined. A noble in this sense could, after all, have been a capitalist owner of the means of production; some, in fact, were.[19] Lefebvre goes so far as to group members of the clergy, nobility, and upper bourgeoisie together in what he designates as the ruling class, not without some justice.[20] But he recognized, as we must, that even if there is no valid economic distinction to be drawn between nobles and upper bourgeois, there is still a certain social distance between them. The very concept of nobility conferred upon its members a psychology and *Weltanschauung* which, bolstered by a certain style of life, habits and traditions that were not quick to die out, made them act differently from, and sometimes in direct opposition to, the bourgeois. On the other hand, it is also possible that " noble " continued to designate a true social class, i. e., large-scale holders of feudal property and most especially land. This was probably true in some parts of France in the revolutionary period. In a study of Elbeuf society, it will be neither necessary nor possible to draw the distinction between the nobility as a still valid social class and the nobility as a legal-psychological group. However it may be, noble individuals were so rare in Elbeuf as to be negligible in a study of urban social structure.

Because I intend to use the above class schema as a framework for the study of the social structure of Elbeuf, it should not be assumed that I intend to ignore other types of stratification. Keeping in mind the noted inadequacy of our fiscal statistics, I shall, nonetheless, make some remarks about differences in income levels. Furthermore, I am perfectly conscious of the role that occupational interests may play in causing intra-class conflict. Table 2–7 shows the relation of taxation to occupation among the lower bourgeois; I shall have occasion to comment on it in the course of this chapter.

There is finally the question of subjective status levels, and I must confess that this will be the most difficult category with which

---

[19] On this point, see Charles A. Forster, " *Honoring Commerce and Industry in 18th Century France: A Case Study of Change in Traditional Social Functions* " (Unpublished Ph. D. dissertation, Harvard University, 1950); H. Lévy-Bruhl, " La Noblesse de France et le Commerce à la Fin de l'Ancien Régime," *Revue d'Histoire Moderne* (1933), pp. 209–35.

[20] Lefebvre, " Orléanais," pp. 47–52.

to deal. There are few documents surviving to tell us what people thought of one another's social position in eighteenth-century Elbeuf. Indeed, the only sources that touch even slightly upon this question are statements made in the course of political debates.

With these definitions established, I can proceed to examine the social structure of Elbeuf.

The first thing that strikes me is that there were, practically speaking, no nobles in the city. To be sure, there were fiscally privileged individuals. In 1787 there were, to be exact, 39 such persons. They had 71 persons as members of their households who were also, on this account, privileged. In addition there were 42 members of the Ursulines Convent with 93 household members. There was also one privileged person at the City Hospital (probably the chief administrator) with 22 employees. The total: 82 privileged persons and 186 dependents.[21] Leaving aside the 14 pensioners of the Convent and the Hospital, we find only 25 privileged persons. Who were they? Thirteen were members of the clergy, 7 were serving in the militia and therefore not taxed during the period of service. There was also a postmaster, a gardener, and the receiver of the city. Why the gardener was privileged is a matter for speculation. Is it possible that he, too, was a member of a privileged household? We cannot be certain. Finally, there was the Chevalier de Beaufort, the concierge of the chateau, and a certain Desilles, chevalier de St. Louis. Thus, of all the privileged only two were noble.[22] At other times between 1770 and 1789, we have found four or five other privileged persons, including Zins, chevalier de St. Louis in the service of the Prince de Lambesc, the *bailli* of Elbeuf, a *controlleur des actes*, a *controlleur des aides*, and one *secrétaire du roi*. So we see that nobles were of no importance in Elbeuf, and the role of the privileged was limited, the more so as the social origins of the thirteen clergymen can all be traced back, without exception, to the local bourgeoisie.

There is only one case in which an Elbeuf bourgeois became noble. In 1782 Michel Grandin, manufacturer and mayor of Elbeuf, petitioned the king for nobility under the terms of the Edicts of 1701 and 1767 concerning ennoblement of wholesale traders.[23] Although he had the support of the Duc de Liancourt

---

[21] *Arch. Dép.*, C 586.
[22] *Arch. Dép.*, L 806.
[23] Foster, *Honoring*, p. 134; Marcel Reinhard, " Elite et Noblesse dans la

and of Madame Louise, daughter of Louis XV, he was refused
on the recommendation of the Intendants of Commerce, who did
not wish to create a precedent by granting the request.[24] Not
content with this rebuff, he and Pierre Grandin the Elder bought
nobility conferring offices as *secrétaires du roi*. They claimed that,
in consequence, they were exempt from the *tarif*. The municipality
answered that according to the ruling of 1708 which set up the
tax no one was exempt and fought and lost the case in the Election
of Pont-de-l'Arche. If the exemption were recognized, it would
be disastrous for the city, as Michel Grandin had four sons who,
together with him, were the owners of five of the most important
factories in the city, and all of them would thereby be exempt. It
was decided to appeal the ruling to the Chambre des Comptes
at Rouen and, in the meantime, to claim a reduction of the *tarif*.
The reduction was not granted, but the municipality did win its
case on December 5, 1788. We do not know, however, what
happened in the case of Pierre Grandin the Elder. As late as
March 26, 1789, he wrote to Necker saying that he had enjoyed
freedom from the *tarif* from 1783 until February 26, 1789, when
the city decided to abolish all such exemptions, save those of the
clergy. Further, he had no objection to the abolition, for he believed in equality of taxation. But he had no intention of paying
back taxes amounting to 488 livres. The city replied by citing
the decision of the Cour des Comptes and added that the petitioner
had a big farm in the parish of Marcouville on which he enjoyed
an exemption. He lived, they said, in Elbeuf only a few months
out of the year and to grant him an exemption in the city would
be to allow him "tirer d'un sac deux moutures." Moreover,
he was a millionaire, while the city had a huge debt and contained "une infinité de malheureux ouvriers qui outre les droits
de tarif paient jusqu'a 20 et 25 livres de capitation." [25] Grandin's
persistence in defending his rights was later to cause some trouble
for his sons, Alexandre Pierre and Pierre Constant Michel. They
both were obliged to resign from the Société Populaire and the
latter from his post of municipal officer in conformity with the
law of 27–28 Germinal II concerning ex-nobles, "parce qu'ils

Seconde Moitié du XVIIIᵉ Siècle," *Revue d'Histoire Moderne et Contemporaine*,
III (1956), 14–15.

[24] *Arch. Nat.*, F¹² 1366.

[25] *Arch. Mun.*, Délib., Vol. I (September 20, 1785); BB⁸.

ont plaidé pour l'exemption des droits du tarif." Their reputation
as good republicans was strong enough, however, for them to
avoid any unpleasant consequences. Pierre Constant Michel Grandin was even allowed to resume his municipal functions, on the
request of the Conseil Général of the city.[26]

We come now to the bourgeoisie, and to a problem. The role
criteria of the definition being fulfilled, how shall the upper from
the middle bourgeoisie be divided? The attempt may be made on
the basis of income as reflected in the tax statistics, although it
must be kept in mind that they do not have an absolute value. But
where is the dividing point to be set?

Vidalenc in his study of Evreux in 1789 put it at 30 livres, but
he does not say why.[27] As a strictly empirical definition, it is perhaps useful. It is known that the last of the one hundred most
highly taxed individuals in Elbeuf in no year paid less than 36
livres in capitation. The tax category in which this number falls
starts at 30 livres, and, for convenience's sake and without doing
violence to the facts, the latter figure can be taken as the point of
departure for the upper bourgeoisie, once the role requirements
have been noted.

This is a matter of convenience, as well as of some speculation.
It is therefore understood that no absolute value is claimed for
the distinction drawn here.

Looking at the upper bourgeoisie from the point of view of
professional activity, we find that it was made up of rentiers,
wholesale merchants, *cultivateurs*, dyers and, above all, woolen
manufacturers.[28] In the smaller of the two parishes, St. Etienne,
this class made up between 7.5 and 8.1 per cent of the population,
while the figure for St. Jean varied between 5.1 and 5.7 per cent.
For Elbeuf as a whole the percentage stood between 6.1 and 6.4 per
cent. The power and influence of this class was, as I shall later
attempt to show, much out of proportion to its size.

The members of the middle bourgeoisie belonged to the same
professions as the upper bourgeoisie. There were also lawyers,

[26] *Arch. Dép.*, L 2350; L 5621; *Arch. Mun.*, Délib., Vol. IV (8 Messidor II).

[27] Jean Vidalenc, "La Bourgeoisie à Evreux en 1789," in Commission de
Recherche et de Publication des Documents Relatifs à la Vie Economique de la
Révolution, *Compte-Rendu de l'Assemblée Générale de 1939* (Besançon, 1942), I,
221–48.

[28] See Tables 2–1 and 2–2.

doctors, notaries, and high civil servants, including the lieutenant of the duchy and the farmer of the tithe. The middle bourgeoisie represented from 2.9 to 5.2 per cent of the population in St. Etienne, 1.6 to 5.1 per cent in St. Jean, and 2.1 to 4.2 per cent in Elbeuf as a whole.

The lower bourgeoisie is a much more heterogeneous grouping than the first two. Essentially it is made up of artisans and shop-

TABLE 2–1

POPULATION BY SOCIAL CLASS, CITY OF ELBEUF, 1770–85

	1770	1775	1780	1785
Men				
Upper bourgeosie	84	85	84	95
Middle bourgeoisie	51	38	42	20
Lower bourgeoisie	340	353	360	387
Wage earners	698	677	654	730
Sick, poor, beggars	22	16	3	5
No profession	7	2	12	8
Total	1,202	1,171	1,155	1,245
Women				
Upper bourgeoisie	7	5	5	2
Middle bourgeoisie	12	9	10	12
Lower bourgeoisie	82	82	74	80
Wage earners	139	128	134	182
Sick, poor, beggars	17	10	3	–
No profession	21	3	3	6
Total	278	237	229	282
Men and Women				
Upper bourgeoisie	91	90	89	97
Middle bourgeoisie	63	47	52	32
Lower bourgeoisie	422	435	434	467
Wage earners	837	805	788	912
Sick, poor, beggars	39	26	6	5
No profession	28	5	15	14
Total	1,480	1,408	1,384	1,527

keepers, as well as of clerks and minor functionaries. For the sake of clarity we have attempted, in so far as possible, to divide this class into several sub-groups according to occupation. These include: the building trades (carpenters and joiners, locksmiths, glaziers, masons, and roofers), the apparel trades (shoemakers, tailors, dressmakers, wigmakers), the food trades (butchers, bakers,

TABLE 2–2

SOCIAL CLASS DISTRIBUTION BY PERCENTAGE OF POPULATION,
CITY OF ELBEUF, 1770–85

	1770	1775	1780	1785
Men				
Upper bourgeoisie	7.0	7.2	7.3	7.6
Middle bourgeoisie	4.2	3.2	3.6	1.6
Lower bourgeoisie	28.3	30.2	31.2	31.2
Wage earners	58.1	57.9	56.7	58.6
Poor, sick, beggars	1.8	1.4	0.2	0.4
No profession	0.6	0.1	1.0	0.6
Total	100.0	100.0	100.0	100.0
Women				
Upper bourgeoisie	2.5	2.1	2.1	.7
Middle bourgeoisie	4.3	3.8	4.3	4.2
Lower bourgeoisie	29.5	34.7	32.4	28.4
Wage earners	50.1	54.0	58.6	64.6
Poor, sick, beggars	6.1	4.2	1.3	—
No profession	7.5	1.2	1.3	2.1
Total	100.0	100.0	100.0	100.0
Men and Women				
Upper bourgeoisie	6.1	6.3	6.4	6.3
Middle bourgeoisie	4.2	3.3	3.7	2.1
Lower bourgeoisie	28.6	31.0	31.4	30.6
Wage earners	56.6	57.3	57.0	59.8
Poor, sick, beggars	2.6	1.8	0.4	0.3
No profession	1.9	0.3	1.1	0.9
Total	100.0	100.0	100.0	100.0

TABLE 2–3

COMPOSITION OF THE UPPER BOURGEOISIE BY OCCUPATION, 1770–85

	1770	1775	1780	1785
Men				
Manufacturers	51	53	54	62
Rentiers	8	5	5	12
Dyers	4	3	3	3
Merchants	14	16	17	16
Cultivators	7	8	5	2
Women				
Manufacturers	2	2	2	1
Rentières	3	3	2	1
Merchants	2	—	—	—
Cultivators	—	—	1	—

millers, caterers, bread and salt merchants, tavernkeepers, fish-
mongers, drysalters), the cloth trades (artisans who are dependent
upon merchants but who also employ workers, including carders,
sizers, makers of worsted and *siamoise* printed cloth), and clerks
and minor functionaries (paymasters, beadles, recordkeepers,
jailors, sergeants of the duchy, members of the *maréchausée*). In
addition, there are many members of the lower bourgeoisie not

TABLE 2–4

COMPOSITION OF THE MIDDLE BOURGEOISIE BY OCCUPATION, 1770–85

	1770	1775	1780	1785
Men				
Manufacturers	8	3	3	1
Rentiers	8	9	11	6
Merchants	18	11	9	7
Cultivators	5	2	6	1
Officials	4	4	8	1
Lawyers	4	5	2	–
Doctors	3	3	2	–
Notaries	1	1	1	–
Dyers	–	–	–	4
Women				
Manufacturers	1	–	–	–
Rentières	7	7	7	9
Merchants	4	2	3	3

so easily classified in occupational groups. We may list a representative selection here: goldsmiths, barbers, tool grinders, school-
teachers, saddle makers, tanners, carters, small rentiers, and agri-
culturists.[29]

The lower bourgeoisie made up from 19.6 to 24.2 per cent of
the population in St. Etienne, 32.8 to 37.4 per cent in St. Jean,
and 28.5 to 31.3 per cent in the two parishes taken together.

Finally, there are the wage earners, the largest class in Elbeuf.
In every year and in each parish they made up a majority of the
population. In St. Etienne they formed 63.1 to 69 per cent of
the population, 50 to 53.9 per cent in St. Jean, and 56.5 to 59.7
per cent in the city as a whole.

The class of wage earners was made up almost entirely of textile

[29] A more complete list will be found in Tables 2–3, 2–4, 2–5, 2–6.

TABLE 2–5

Composition of the Lower Bourgeoisie by Occupation, 1770–85

	1770	1775	1780	1785
Men				
Rentiers	20	17	39	16
Building trades	56	39	55	54
Apparel trades	56	56	51	65
Food trades	52	51	56	61
Cloth trades	12	10	12	20
Cultivators	13	25	19	22
Upholsterers	4	2	3	3
Carters	11	13	8	10
Tool grinders	9	7	7	7
Clerks	8	10	6	10
Gardeners	15	15	19	18
Retail merchants	43	52	52	52
Horse dealers	7	1	3	3
Farriers	5	4	6	5
Painters	1	1	1	–
Dance teachers	1	–	–	1
Chandlers	6	7	8	5
Leatherworkers	4	8	7	10
Schoolmasters	6	7	5	5
Boilermakers	5	4	3	6
Barbers	–	2	2	1
Watchmakers	–	1	1	3
News vendors	2	1	2	1
Jewelers: goldsmiths	1	2	2	3
Engineers	–	–	1	–
Papermakers	1	–	–	–
Contractors	–	–	–	–
Stain removers	1	1	2	2
Tobacco graters	2	1	1	1
Arms manufacturers	–	2	1	1
Stonecutters	–	1	–	–
Musicians	–	2	–	–
Chemists	–	–	1	–
Women				
Rentières	26	31	24	33
Apparel trades	22	17	11	10
Food trades	7	6	10	8
Schoolmistresses	5	6	7	5
Retail merchants	17	19	19	21
Carters	1	–	–	–
Gardeners	2	–	–	–
Cloth trades	1	2	2	1
Dance teachers	1	–	–	–
Cultivators	1	–	–	1
Lead smelters	1	1	–	–
Nurses	–	–	1	–
Civil servants	–	–	–	1
Total number of men	343	343	363	387
Total number of women	84	83	74	80
Total number both men and women	427	426	437	467

workers but also included some porters, gatekeepers, transit workers, and agricultural day laborers. The latter never represented more than 6.8 per cent of all wage earners in St. Etienne, 5.5 per cen in St. Jean, and 5.3 per cent in all of Elbeuf—and this despite Elbeuf's position as one of the prinicipal grain markets of the region.[30] The large percentage of wage earners, and particularly of wage earners employed in the textile industry, was quite extraordinary in eighteenth-century France. Given the pre-industrial capitalist nature of economic organization at this time, one would be perfectly justified to expect a larger percentage of small, inde-

TABLE 2-6

COMPOSITION OF THE CLASS OF WAGE EARNERS BY OCCUPATION, 1770-85

	1770	1775	1780	1785
Men				
Textile workers	570	561	582	610
Dyers	37	35	14	35
Foremen	23	25	—	11
Agricultural laborers	24	25	30	45
Gatekeepers	25	25	24	22
Transit workers	7	6	3	5
Launderers	—	—	1	1
Sewer cleaners	—	—	—	1
Women				
Textile workers	127	119	124	169
Agricultural laborers	4	3	1	4
Laundresses	6	4	8	9
Porters	1	1	—	—
Employers in grain market	1	1	1	—

pendent artisans and shopkeepers who would, by definition, fall into the category of the lower bourgeoisie. That it is otherwise only highlights the predominance of the textile industry in the town's economy.[31] This is not to say that many of the wage earners

[30] See Table 2-6.

[31] For the sake of comparison, we may note that Lefebvre finds the wage earners of Orléans making up approximately 57 per cent of the urban population on the eve of the Revolution. (Lefebvre, *Orléanais*, p. 58.) This figure is obtained by adopting a coefficient of 3 to determine the size of a typical wage-earner's family. Orléans was very active in the textile industry and the *bonneterie* (cap and hosiery manufacture). Paris, on the other hand, was probably less industrialized—at least that is what we are led to believe by available statistics regarding its wage-earning population. These statistics, gathered by F. Braesch ("Essai de Statistique de la Population Ouvrière de Paris vers 1791," *Révolution Française*, LXIII [1912], 288), have only a relative value. Soboul (*Les Sans-Culottes Parisiens en l'an II* [Paris,

TABLE 2-7

INCOME LEVELS OF ELBEUF'S LOWER BOURGEOISIE BY OCCUPATION AS REFLECTED IN TAX PAYMENTS, 1770–85

	1770	1775	1780	1785
Men				
Building trades	56) 11 = 15 + 1 = 20 ++	49) 8 = 15 +	55) 12 = 15 + 5 = 30 ++	54) 10 = 15 + 1 = 20 ++ 2 = 30 ++
Apparel trades	56) 11 = 15 + 3 = 20 ++	56) 6 = 30 ++ 14 = 15 ++ 2 = 20 ++	51) 5 = 15 ++ 2 = 20 ++ 1 = 30 ++	65) 15 = 15 + 2 = 20 ++ 2 = 30 ++
Food trades	52) 10 = 15 + 10 = 20 ++ 7 = 30 ++	51) 10 = 15 ++ 4 = 20 ++ 15 = 30 ++	56) 16 = 15 + 3 = 20 ++ 11 = 30 ++	61) 22 = 15 + 6 = 30 ++ 1 = 50 ++
Cloth trades	12) 3 = 15 + 1 = 20 ++ 6 = 30 ++	10) 1 = 20 ++ 7 = 30 ++ 1 = 50 ++	12) 5 = 15 ++ 7 = 30 ++ −	19) 2 = 15 + 2 = 20 ++ 8 = 30 ++
Merchants	43) 2 = 15 + 3 = 30 ++ −	52) 3 = 15 ++ 2 = 20 ++ 4 = 30 ++	52) 11 = 15 + 7 = 30 ++	52) 14 = 15 + 5 = 30 ++ −
Leatherworkers	4) 2 = 30 +	8) 2 = 20 ++ 2 = 30 ++	7) 2 = 20 + 3 = 30 ++	10) 1 = 15 + 3 = 30 ++ 3 = 20 ++
Carters	11) 1 = 15 +	13) 3 = 15 ++ 1 = 30 ++	8) 2 = 20 ++ 1 = 30 ++	10)
Chandlers	6) 2 = 30 +	7) 4 = 30 ++ −	8) 2 = 15 ++ 2 = 20 ++ 4 = 30 ++	5) 4 = 15 ++ 2 = 50 ++ −
Tool grinders	9) 3 = 15 ++ 4 = 30 ++	7) 3 = 30 ++ 1 = 100 ++	7) 2 = 15 ++ 3 = 30 ++	7) 4 = 15 ++ 1 = 50 +++ 1 = 100 ++
Horse dealers	7) 1 = 15 + 5 = 30 ++ 1 = 30 ++	1) 1 = 30 + −	3) 3 = 30 + −	3) 2 = 20 ++ 1 = 30 ++ −
Papermakers Contractors	1) 1 = 30 +		1) 1 = 15 ++	1) 1 = 50 +
Upholsterers	4) −	2) 1 = 15 +	3) 1 = 15 ++	3) −

TABLE 2–7 (Continued)

INCOME LEVELS OF ELBEUF'S LOWER BOURGEOISIE BY OCCUPATION AS REFLECTED IN TAX PAYMENTS, 1770–85

	1770	1775	1780	1785
Farriers	5) —	4) 1 = 15 +	6) 1 = 15 +	5) 1 = 15 +
Boilermakers	5) 4 = 15 +	4) 3 = 15 +; 1 = 30 +	3) 2 = 30 +	6) 2 = 15 +; 2 = 30 +
Stain removers	1) 1 = 30 +	1) 1 = 30 +	2) 1 = 30 +	2) 1 = 30 +
Painters	1) 1 = 20 +	1) 1 = 30 +	1) 1 = 30 +	—
Gardeners	15) 3 = 15 +	15) 2 = 15 +; 2 = 30 +	19) 3 = 30 +	18) 2 = 30 +
Arms makers	—	2) —	1) 1 = 20 +	1) 1 = 20 +
Goldsmiths	1) 1 = 15 +	1) 1 = 20 +	2) 1 = 30 +	3) 1 = 30 +
Minor functionaries	8) —	10) 2 = 20 +	6) 1 = 20 +	10) 2 = 30 +
Women				
Food trades	7) 1 = 15 +	6) 1 = 15 +; 1 = 75 +	10) 1 = 15 +; 2 = 20 +	8) 1 = 15 +; 2 = 30 +
Cloth trades	1) 1 = 15 +; —	2) 1 = 15 +; 1 = 20 +	2) 1 = 30 +	1) 1 = 30 +
Apparel trades	22) 2 = 15 +	17) 2 = 15 +	11) 1 = 30 +	10) 1 = 30 +
Merchants	17) 2 = 20 +	19) —	19) —	21) 1 = 30 +
Totals	344) 56 = 15 +; 18 = 20 +; 32 = 30 +	338) 49 = 15 +; 15 = 20 +; 48 = 30 +; 1 = 50 +; 1 = 75 +; 1 =100 +	345) 57 = 15 +; 14 = 20 +; 57 = 30 +	375) 76 = 15 +; 11 = 20 +; 40 = 30 +; 5 = 50 +; 1 =100 +

Note: The figure in parentheses represent the total membership of the occupational group within the lower bourgeoisie. The figures that follow show the number of persons who paid more than 15 livres in capitation in each year. The tax categories used are the same as those in Appendix One.

The figure 15 + indicates that the tax payment was between 15 and 19 livres. The next category, 20 + designates 20–29 livres, etc.

Source: Arch. Min., Series CC-Capitation Rolls, 1770–85.

who are classified as industrial workers did not have a subordinate agricultural occupation. It is probable that many of them did, at least to the extent of cultivating a small patch.

An estimate of the influence of Elbeuf industry speaks of 20,000 persons earning their livings from, or being dependent on, it. It is certain that this figure represents not only heads of families, but also their dependents. If this is the case, we may assume that perhaps 5,000 of them were workers—heads of families, while the other 15,000 were workers and/or dependents, but not tax-payers. Of these 5,000, between 800 and 900, according to the year, were domiciled in Elbeuf. The proportion is, by modern standards, small enough. It is, however, significant that in the eighteenth century somewhat more than one-sixth of the persons employed in the industry were already urbanites. Was the peculiar nature of the woolen industry responsible? Was there a tendency toward centralization and urbanization at this early date? Although this was to be true in the nineteenth century, it is not certain that technical advances and the introduction of machinery had already made their influence felt at this time. There were already twenty-nine spinning machines, the nature of which cannot be ascertained, in Elbeuf on the eve of the Revolution.[32] The co-existence of machinery and a large percentage of urban workers is, at least, suggestive.

The last group to be mentioned is not, properly speaking, a social class. It was made up of persons listed on the tax rolls as poor, sick or beggars, and those who had no ascertainable occupation. Even taken together, these individuals were so few as to

---

1958], pp. 435 and notes, and Table II, 1091–92) criticizes them greatly and with reason. They were gathered from employers who sought to exchange large for small assignats in order to pay their employees in 1791, and thus they do not represent a precisely defined wage-earning class. Moreover, they are available for only 41 of 48 sections and do not take into account seasonal variations. With all these reservations in mind, I have nonetheless made the following calculations: there was a total population of 554,141 in the 41 sections, of whom 62,739 were workers. Adopting a coefficient of 3, we find 188,217 members of the wage-earning class. On the other hand, if we take a coefficient of 4, as Soboul does, we come out with a figure of 250,956 wage earners and members of their families. In the first case, the percentage of wage earners is 33.9, in the second, 45.2.

If we can accord even an indicative value to these figures, we see that Elbeuf had a proportionately much greater wage-earning population than Paris. But the real conclusion to be drawn from these figures is that research and analysis of eighteenth-century French cities is still in a rather underdeveloped state.

[32] Brisson, " Origines," p. 220.

form only a negligible part of Elbeuf's population, generally
1 to 2 per cent, except in 1770 when the figure went as high as 4.5
per cent.

Up to this point the status of the sexes in the social structure
has not been discussed. The possible result of this omission is
that the reader may believe that women were of no importance
in the economic life of Elbeuf. The contrary could hardly be
more true. It must be said at the outset that all women who paid
taxes were either widows or unmarried. The status of the male
as chief of the household is not yet challenged; while he lives,
the woman's place is distinctly secondary, although not always in
the home. But where no male is present, the myth of female
inferiority gives way to the realities of earning a living and paying
taxes. In fact, women accounted for between 17.4 and 20.3 per
cent of the taxpayers in the parish of St. Etienne, and in St. Jean
the figure runs from 15.6 to 21.6 per cent. For the city as a whole,
the number fluctuates between 16.7 and 18.6 per cent—which
is far from negligible. In addition, there were many women gainfully employed who did not pay taxes because they were not heads
of families.

According to Table 2–2, we find that a considerably smaller
percentage of women taxpayers than of men belonged to the
upper bourgeoisie. However, in the case of the middle and lower
bourgeoisie, women held their own, their participation in each of
these classes not differing greatly from that of men. The same is
true of female wage earners; indeed, in St. Etienne in 1780, in
St. Jean in 1785 and 1789, and in the entire city in 1785, wage
earners made up a considerably greater part of the female tax-
paying population than of the male. In general, more women than
men fall into the category of the sick, the poor, and the beggars.

Thus far servants have not been included in the calculations.
Even long after the Revolution servants were considered inferior
beings, as if personal service meant not only a loss of dignity
but also of capacity for participation in public affairs. They did
not pay taxes, but were assessed, like real property, through their
masters. Their position in public law was highly unfavorable. The
Revolution followed the example of the old regime in refusing
to recognize them as citizens, notably by withholding from them
the right to vote.

Although I cannot agree with Vidalenc when he makes employment of servants a criterion of social class, it is true that the presence of a servant in a household was a sign of wealth, of a certain style of life, and, as such, may help one to get a closer look at the social structure.

The number of servants in Elbeuf ran from 136 to 194 in steady progression from 1770 to 1785. Who employed them? There were 123 employers of 136 servants in 1770, 154 employers of 174 servants in 1775, 146 employers of 173 servants in 1780, and 158 employers of 194 servants in 1785. About a quarter to a third of the employers were members of the lower bourgeoisie, but the upper bourgeoisie accounted for between 54 and 61 per cent of the employers. Moreover, the upper bourgeoisie employed between 56 and 63 per cent of the servants. In other words, the distribution of servants, in so far as it is a sign of wealth, only serves to confirm the predominant position of the upper bourgeoisie, and particularly of the woolen manufacturers, in the social structure of Elbeuf.

This observation brings us to the more general questions of levels of wealth in the social structure. Although wealth is, as already pointed out, at best an indication rather than a determinant of class status, we would not be justified in ignoring such differences of wealth as did exist within classes in Elbeuf. For a study of this question, the records of tax assessments can be examined, bearing in mind that their relationship to actual income levels may have been, at least in some cases, tenuous.

To begin at the top, there was great variation in the individual fortunes of the upper bourgeois. This should be obvious when it is noted that certain manufacturers paid as much as 500 livres in capitation, while others paid as little as 40 livres. A little later a closer look will be taken at the component parts of the great bourgeois fortunes.

A taxation criterion has been used to separate the middle from the upper bourgeoisie, where there is no essential distinction between the two as regards social role, as is true in the majority of cases. The greatest number of middle bourgeois paid between 15 and 30 livres of capitation. The only exceptions to this rule are the members of the service professions, whose tax assessments varied both above and below these characteristic limits. Thus, in 1770 each of four lawyers and one of two doctors paid less than 15 livres in capitation, while the farmer of the tithe in the

Parish of St. Jean paid more than 30 livres. In 1775 all five lawyers and the *procureur-fiscal* paid under 15 livres, while one of the three doctors paid more than 50 livres. The situation was similar in 1780 when two doctors, two lawyers, the *procureur-fiscal*, and a lieutenant of the duchy paid less than 15 livres, and another lieutenant of the duchy, the tax receiver, the notary, and the two farmers of the tithe paid more than 30 livres. In 1785 all middle bourgeois paid between 15 and 30 livres of capitation.

Income levels, together with professional activities, were more varied among the lower bourgeois. Although it remains true that the great majority of lower bourgeois paid less than 15 livres in capitation in every year of our period, a considerable number were assessed at higher levels. Thus, in 1770, 12.7 per cent of the lower bourgeois paid between 15 and 20 livres, 4.2 per cent paid between 20 and 29 livres, and 7.5 per cent paid more than 30 livres. The corresponding figures for 1775 are: 11.2 per cent, 3.4, and 11.2 per cent; in 1780, 13.1, 3.2, and 13.1 per cent; in 1785, 16.2, 2.3, and 8.5 per cent. In other words, approximately one-quarter of the lower bourgeois paid higher taxes, and may therefore be supposed to have had higher incomes, than the typical member of their class. From a closer look at Table 2–7, it appears that certain lower bourgeois occupations were considerably more lucrative than most. Although members of as many as twenty-two occupational groups paid more than 15 livres of capitation, in only a few cases did they represent a considerable percentage of all persons in the group. This is the case of the food, clothing, apparel, and building trades, in approximately that order. It also holds true for the tool grinders, horse dealers, chandlers, leatherworkers, and goldsmiths.

There seems to have been no great differences of income among the members of Elbeuf's largest class, the wage earners. The great majority paid under 15 livres in capitation throughout the period. In 1770 only twelve wage earners paid more than this amount, eleven of them falling in the 15 to 20 livre category, and only one paying more than 30 livres. In 1775 twenty-six wage earners were assessed 15 to 20; two, 20 to 30; and one, more than 30 livres. In 1780 we find twenty-one wage earners at between 15 and 20 livres, and one over 20. The pattern holds good in 1785, with fourteen persons of this class taxed at 15 to 20, and two at more than 20 livres. These numbers constitute an infinitesimal percentage of all wage earners. Even if it is assumed that the higher level of taxation reflects higher incomes, it is not possible to think of these few individuals as an elite or labor aristocracy whose members had a special skill in common. Most of them were ordinary textile workers, along with a couple of foremen and a dyeworker or two. Why they should have had higher incomes is a moot question. Perhaps they held more than one job or had supplementary incomes of which we are not aware.

Before leaving the question of income levels, it should be noted that very few individuals saw their tax assessments change significantly during this period. A total of 122 persons, including 4 women, paid considerably higher taxes at the end of our period than at the beginning, while 51, including 8 women, paid less than they had started out with. Of the first group of 122, at least 94 underwent neither professional nor class change, and one woman changed her profession but not her class. Of the second group of 51, 23 were subject to neither professional nor class change, and an additional 18 changed professions but not classes. The conclusion is clear: that income levels cut across class lines, and a change in income level in no way presupposed a change in class.

If this be so, it becomes impossible to study social mobility by use of the tax assessments alone. The single exception to this rule is that we may attempt to differentiate between the upper and middle bourgeoisie on the basis of tax payments, at least to a certain extent. But an investigation of mobility between more widely separated classes is closed to us. And this is all the more true, as the sources cover only the twenty-year period 1770–89, thus making it impossible to study the social position of families through several generations, even if genealogical materials were readily available, as they are not. It should be noted that evidence to be gleaned from notarial archives may offer a way out of this dilemma. This is not certain, for the limitations of time and difficulties of consultation have precluded making use of them.

When this has been said, there are nonetheless certain indications concerning social mobility that arise from a study of professional change. On this basis, forty men and eight women who had been wage earners became lower bourgeois during this period, while three men migrated from the lower to the upper bourgeoisie, and six from the middle to the upper bourgeoisie. On the other hand, eleven men and four women moved downward on the social ladder from the lower bourgeoisie into the wage-earning class, and four men migrated into the middle from the upper bourgeoisie. Tentatively, this does not seem to indicate a high degree of social mobility in a town that had an average tax-paying population of 1,448.[33] At most, we may be justified in suspecting that mobility between the lower bourgeoisie and the wage-earning class was somewhat greater than between either of these two classes and the others in Elbeuf society.

The point previously made about income levels cutting across class lines is re-enforced by a glance at the tax assessments of persons who were socially mobile. Of the forty-eight persons who migrated from the wage-earning class to the lower bourgeoisie, thirty did not undergo a change in their tax assessments, while seventeen paid more taxes than previously, and one, less. In the case of those who changed from the lower to the upper bourgeoisie, one, a tool grinder who became a manufacturer, continued to pay the same tax, and two paid more than they had before. Middle bourgeois who became upper bourgeois paid higher taxes, by definition. Of the lower bourgeoisie who became wage earners, eleven continued at the same level of taxation, while two paid more and two less than before.

If the indications, then, are that there was a general lack of social mobility in Elbeuf, an absolute statement cannot be made on this matter. What of the role of marriage in promoting mobility? Was it, first of all, possible for an outsider to marry into the upper bourgeoisie? The answer is no. The members of the upper bourgeoisie tended, rather, to marry among themselves. Take, for instance, the Grandin family. Their family tree shows that in the eighteenth century they intermarried with the Bance, Beranger (twice), Delarue, Duruflé, Flavigny, Flavigny-Gosset, Godet (twice), Lefebvre (twice), Quesné (twice), Piétou, Papavoine, and Renard families. All but one were woolen manufacturers. Papavoine was, like Piétou, from Louviers, but he was a tanner.[34]

That the Grandin family was not atypical is shown by other documents examined. In 1789 each person who subscribed to the first *contribution patriotique* was required to declare the name of

---

[33] See Table 2–8.

[34] Andre Delavenne, (comp.), *Recueil Généalogique de la Bourgeoisie Ancienne*, Deuxième Série (Paris, 1955), pp. 212–15.

his beneficiary, should his death occur before reimbursement. Most of the money was assigned to the children of the contributors, but also on occasion to more distant relatives. A study of the loan declarations reveals that the Grandins were related by marriage to the Lamberts (dyers), and the Mailles (manufacturers). Quesnés were married to Rouvin (rentiers) and Duruflés (manufacturers). A Rouvin was also married to a Delarue (manufacturer), a Flavigny to a Godet, and the rentière Leclerc to Glin, a manufacturer.[35] Beginning with the establishment of the *état-civil laique* in 1792,[36] the marriage records kept in each commune always mention the profession of the groom and of the bride or of the bride's father. It is therefore possible to see what percentage of marriages cut across class lines.

The records from the beginning of 1793 to the end of the year II show that there were thirty-six marriages between wage earners, twenty-seven between lower bourgeois and fifteen marriages between middle bourgeois. There were twenty-one marriages between wage earners and lower bourgeois, in all but three of which the bride was the wage earner. Usually, these were marriages between artisans and female textile workers, and sometimes domestic workers. But there are also instances of a lower bourgeois cultivator marrying a field laborer and a wigmaker marrying an ironing woman, cases in which the commercial no doubt preceded the marital relationship.

In the same period, there were fifteen marriages among upper bourgeois. In only two cases were class lines crossed when a manufacturer married a dressmaker daughter of a wigmaker and a dyer married the daughter of a wealthy dealer in old clothes. The normal pattern was for a manufacturer to marry the daughter of a colleague (five examples), or a rentière (two examples), or the daughter of a dyer, a close business associate. A wholesale merchant might marry a rentière or a manufacturer's daughter.

Samples for the following years confirm the above statements:

[35] *Arch. Mun.*, Series II—Contribution Patriotique, 1789.
[36] *Arch. Mun.*, Etat Civil de la Ville d'Elbeuf, Marriage Registers, 1793, **Year II**, 1800, 1805, 1810, 1815.

Marriages by Social Class and between Classes

Year	Wage earners	Lower bourgeoisie	Middle bourgeoisie	Upper bourgeoisie	Lower bourgeoisie and wage earner
1800	6	6	4	2	1
1805	15	11	4	4	5
1810	15	5	3	2	6
1815	31	13	8	3	13

The pattern does not change at all but remains the one already described. There is not a single marriage involving an upper bourgeois in which there is a crossing of class lines. In only two of twenty-five marriages between wage earners and lower bourgeois were the grooms wage earners, textile workers who married artisans in related fields—two seamstresses, in the event.

At best, then, some wage earners might hope to migrate, by marriage or otherwise, into the lower bourgeoisie. But the average textile worker who earned 20 sols a day for 15 hours work [37] could look forward only to earning his daily bread in the same manner all his life through. The question will be asked later whether the Revolution brought more mobility to Elbeuf society. For the moment, let us look at some of the factors that created the situation of limited mobility by studying the way in which one became a woolen manufacturer, since the manufacturers made up the largest and most influential group in the upper bourgeoisie of Elbeuf.

According to the ruling of 1783, a candidate for mastership had to be at least twenty years of age and to have served a four-year apprenticeship. However, the son of a master might be admitted at eighteen after only two years as an apprentice. A period of apprenticeship was not, for all intents and purposes, required of candidates who had reached the age of twenty-five. They might be admitted after only one year's work under the supervision of an already established master. An oral examination and a masterpiece were required,[38] despite the fact that masters had long since ceased to be producers and had become merchant capitalists with overall control of the industry. The only exception to this requirement was in the case of privileged mastership, one created by the government as a venal office. Four such master-

[37] Brisson, " Origines," p. 219.   [38] *Arch. Nat.*, F^{12} 760.

ships were established in Elbeuf in 1767, and at least one of them was bought by Jacques Lefebvre in 1772.[39]

The requirements for mastership seem stringent in an organization that no longer resembled a guild in the proper sense of the word and in the midst of an expanding economy. But they do not tell the whole story, for it was even more difficult to become a master than they may indicate. From 1717 to 1757 no one but sons of masters could enter the manufacture, and the repeal of this stipulation in the last named year did not sit well with the masters.[40] Not anxious to have increased competition, they justified their position by arguing that new masters would make inferior grade cloth and would contribute to a shortage of materials and workers. The labor shortage would make workers restless and disobedient, and they would do their jobs poorly. Experience had already proved that the more they were paid, the less efficiently they worked. In order to protect their hegemony, the manufacturers demanded, and failed to obtain, a ruling that would forbid any but a master's son to become an apprentice. For the Intendant De Crosne, the demand smacked of monopoly. He reasoned that the more masters there were, the more competition would exist to the benefit of the government and the consumer. The shortage and high price of manpower was no reason to concentrate the woolen industry in the hands of a few. The creation of additional enterprises would protect against unemployment consequent on the introduction of machinery. Following this advice, Joly de Fleury, in 1782, categorically refused even to consider the masters' request, saying that it was "contraire au droit naturel que doit avoir tout citoyen d'acquérir les connaissances nécessaires pour embrasser une profession qui lui convient." [41]

If the liberalism of the minister and the intendant counterbalanced the exclusiveness of the masters, the road was still not clear for someone who wanted to make a career in the Elbeuf woolen industry. There remained the matter of the fees that had to be paid both during the apprenticeship and at the time of admission to master's status. The fees were, respectively, 300 and

[39] Charles Ouin-Lacroix, *Histoire des Anciennes Corporations d'Arts et Métiers et des Confreries Religieuses de la Capitale de la Normandie* (Rouen, 1850), pp. 387–88; St. Denis, *Histoire*, V, 455–57.

[40] St. Denis, *Histoire*, IV, 390–92, 502, 572; V, 61, 271–72.

[41] *Arch. Nat.*, F^{12*} 156.

200 livres. They were paid by the new master to the Prince de Lambesc and were known as " droits des eaux," that is, payment for the right to use the water courses of the Duchy.[42] Moreover, until 1767, when L'Averdy forbade the practice, the guild charged a 300 livre fee for the registration of the *brevet d'apprentissage.*[43] We can be sure that the average worker under these conditions had little hope of acceding to mastership.

The intention of the manufacturers was to perpetuate the control of the industry in the hands of a limited number of families. In order to do so, they had to meet the challenge, not of the workers, but of an entirely different group, made up of persons who had a certain amount of money or experience and who, coming from outside the town, wanted to get into the business without going through all the formalities. The struggle against these interlopers met with only intermittent success, although every means was used to conduct it.

When in 1783 one Galleran, a manufacturer of Elbeuf who had started his business only the year before although admitted to mastership in 1774, sought an authorization to take on an apprentice, his request was denied on the ground that he had not been established in the community for ten years. Galleran protested vigorously to de Tolozan, the Intendant of Commerce, saying that this action was all the more indefensible as the apprentice in question had already worked for twenty years as a foreman in the factory of Louis Flavigny at Elbeuf and was, therefore, thoroughly familiar with the trade. Moreover, Joly de Fleury had written only a year earlier that ". . . tout fabricant au moment de sa réception dans la communauté avait le droit de faire des apprentis." Galleran threatened to sue the masters and administrators of the manufacture for civil damages if his claim were not settled in accordance with the above rule.[44]

It is not known how this case was settled, but there are records of continual protests made by Elbeuf masters. In 1784 they wrote:

pour 10 sols que coûte sa réception l'homme le moins versé dans la fabrication, l'homme le plus inapte à s'en approprier les principes: des émouleurs de forces, des enfants de maçon, maçon cy-devant, se font recevoir fabricant à Orival, village voisin d'Elbeuf. Il y existait jadis une manufacture qui ne subsiste plus. On les admet sans chef d'oeuvre, sans information, sans examen, il leur suffit de se présenter pour être reçus.

---

[42] *Arch. Nat.*, F[12] 751.   [43] *Arch. Dép.*, C 129.   [44] *Arch. Dép.*, C 129.

Munis de leur acte de réception, ils fabriquent quelques draps dans un genre libre et par conséquent à l'abri de toute inspection quant aux matières et quant à la fabrication. Ils les présentent au bureau de la manufacture d'Elbeuf même, et à peine ont-ils joui pendant 6 mois du titre de fabricant d'Orival qu'on les voit descendre à Elbeuf se faire présenter aprentifs par d'anciens fabricants que leur mauvaise conduite ou leur inexpérience ont ruinés et prétendre, à la faveur des dispositions du roi du 6 fevrier 1783 n'être tenus qu'à faire un an d'apprentissage. . . . Ces particuliers pendant l'année à laquelle ils prétendent réduire leur apprentissage travaillent et fabriquent pour leur compte personnel sous les noms de leurs maîtres et à la honte du commerce on y voit reparaître des noms condamnés à un éternel oubli.[45]

How much of this was true? No judgment can be made on those manufacturers who sponsored apprentices, but the statement about Orival is exact. The manufacture there had fallen into decay in the seventeen-fifties, and anyone could be admitted to it without difficulty. This does not necessarily mean, however, that all who came from Orival were frauds. However valid the arguments of the Elbeuf manufacturers were from a strictly legal point of view (for example, their correct assertion that the Ordonnance of 1783 was not meant to apply to the woolen industry),[46] their motives remain clear. They wished to protect their interests by suppressing competition.

The masters were only partially successful in their drive toward exclusiveness. Each case was treated in isolation by the government, legal precedent rarely playing any part in the decision. For example, there is the case of Jean-Baptiste Cavé, who had been a foreman in the manufacture of Pierre Maille the younger at the time of his application for mastership in 1783. On December 30, an Order in Council commanded his admission without need of apprenticeship. Early in 1784, however, the masters, joined in a rare show of co-operation by the manufacturers of Louviers, declared their opposition to this decree. They protested that experience as a foreman could not possibly suit a man for mastership, for a foreman did not undergo the same training as an apprentice. Moreover, the foreman might turn his knowledge of his ex-employer's commercial arrangements to profit by stealing clients and workers from him. His admission, like that of other claimants, could only

[45] *Arch. Dép.*, C 129.   [46] *Arch. Nat.*, F[12] 760.

donner lieu à un plus grand prix des matières premières et de la main d'oeuvre. Le prix des étoffes diminuera dans la même proportion, et les fabricants ne parviendront à se rédîmer que sur la qualité des draps qui, passant à l'étranger, le dégoûtera infailliblement de ceux d'Elbeuf—de là, la ruine de la première fabrique du royaume au très grand préjudice de l'état.

While this argument did not prevail so far as to keep Cavé out of the guild, it had enough strength to obtain an order forcing him to execute a masterpiece, a procedure which had not been demanded in the original decree of 1783. It was the beginning of 1786 before he was finally accepted, a lapse of two years from the time he was first ordered admitted, and even then the masters were not satisfied with the result of his examination. They even talked of appealing to the Parlement of Rouen against the judgment of the *bailli* of Elbeuf.[47]

There is, as far as we know, only one case in which the Elbeuf masters were wholly successful in obtaining their goals. It was that of a certain LeBailly who wished to transfer his trade from Orival to Elbeuf after a one year apprenticeship under Nicolas Lefebvre. He was restrained from so doing by a government ruling of February, 1785, which stated that the Declaration of 1783 was not meant to apply to the woolen industry. Moreover, he was forced to do his three-year apprenticeship under a manufacturer still practicing his profession.[48] On the other hand, the aspirant named Le Fort was admitted in 1785 after only one year's training, although the masters argued in vain that he was guilty of all sorts of fraud in claiming that he had previously worked in the industry for two years. They endeavored to prove that he had been nothing more than the financial agent of the silent partners of Amable Alexandre Lefebvre, and that he had worked in Lefebvre's warehouse only in the capacity of a clerk and cashier. Seeing no future in this, he had then set up on his own in Orival, they said. All their complaints did no good whatsoever, and Le Fort was admitted after production of his masterpiece. The conclusion that must be drawn from this consistent inconsistency on the part of the government is that the law was incapable of resolving these intra-class disputes on anything but an arbitrary basis. Because manufacturers made up the greatest part of the upper bourgeoisie, it is also clear that

[47] *Arch. Nat.*, F¹² 206; F¹² 760; *Arch. Dép.*, C 129.
[48] *Arch. Nat.*, F¹² 206; *Arch. Dép.*, C 129.

access to the ranks of the upper bourgeoisie, almost non-existent for members of other citizens in Elbeuf, was equally difficult for outsiders before the Revolution.

Let us look at the list of the 100 most highly taxed individuals in Elbeuf.[49] Several facts immediately become apparent. First, that there seems to be, as we have already noted, great variation in the size of individual fortunes, for, if everyone on the list paid more than 36 livres of capitation, a few persons paid as much as 300, 400, and even 500 livres. Second, that the great majority of these individuals were members of the upper bourgeoisie. The class distribution of these individuals follows:

	1770	1775	1780	1785
Upper bourgeoisie	84	83	81	81
Middle bourgeoisie	2	1	5	3
Lower bourgeoisie	23	22	20	19
No profession listed	1	–	1	1
Total	110	106	107	104

Note that they add up to more than one hundred in each year. This is due to equality of tax payments, especially at the lower end of the scale. There are few members of the middle bourgeoisie on this list, for by definition all bourgeois paying more than 30 livres in capitation are members of the upper bourgeoisie, with the exception of professional men and members of the service occupations. A still closer look shows the dominance of the manufacturers in the upper bourgeoisie. There were fifty-nine manufacturers on this list in 1770, sixty-nine in 1775, fifty-nine in 1780, and sixty-two in 1785. The next most highly represented upper bourgeois group is the mercantile one, and merchants never had more than twelve persons on the list in any given year. Of the lower bourgeois who showed signs of wealth, the majority were retail merchants, artisans in the food, cloth and building trades, tool grinders, and chandlers.

We come now to the question of the circulation of elites. In the years chosen for study between 1770 and 1785, 193 persons passed through 100 available places in Table 2–9b. But it would

[49] See Tables 2–8, 2–9.

TABLE 2-8

POPULATION TOTALS BY TAX CATEGORY

	1	2	3	4	5	6	7	8	9	10	11	12	13	Total
St. Etienne														
1770	272	106	39	24	28	24	10	7	5	2	—	2	7	526
1775	218	132	52	18	25	26	6	5	5	8	5	2	6	508
1780	279	110	45	16	26	22	10	5	3	4	4	3	8	535
1785	305	86	38	16	22	18	14	6	6	3	1	2	9	526
1787	288	84	39	13	20	16	12	4	8	2	2	1	11	500
St. Etienne—Women only														
1770	81	9	4	6	4	2	1	—	—					107
1775	75	10	5	—	4	3	—	—	—					97
1780	75	10	3	2	2	1	—	1	1					93
1785	86	5	3	3	2	—	—	1	1					100
1787	80	5	1	2	3	—	—	—	—					91
St. Jean														
1770	512	162	115	40	51	34	20	3	4	5	2	5	1	955
1775	424	158	139	57	43	37	25	10	8	3	7	1	2	913
1780	426	151	81	49	45	45	13	10	8	5	3	1	5	842
1785	521	159	89	73	56	40	16	11	11	4	2	—	5	987
1789	541	152	94	69	60	48	12	4	4	3	4	3	7	1,007
St. Jean—Women only														
1770	132	16	11	4	3	4	1	—	—					171
1775	108	11	11	5	5	—	2	1	—					143
1780	98	14	9	6	3	7	—	1	—					138
1785	143	17	7	3	5	6	—	—	1					182
1789	172	18	7	7	6	8	—	—	—					218
Elbeuf as a whole														
1770	785	268	154	64	79	58	30	10	9	7	2	7	8	1,481
1775	642	290	191	75	68	63	31	15	13	11	12	2	8	1,421
1780	705	261	126	65	71	67	23	15	11	9	7	4	13	1,377
1785	826	245	127	89	78	58	30	17	17	7	3	2	14	1,513
Elbeuf as a whole—Women only														
1770	213	25	15	10	7	6	2	—	—	—				278
1775	183	19	16	4	10	3	2	1	—	—				240
1780	173	24	12	8	5	8	—	—	1	—				231
1785	229	22	10	6	7	6	6	—	1	1				282

Note: The categories are divided as follows: (1) up to 6 livres; (2) 6 livres, 1 sol to 9 livres, 19 sols; (3) 10 livres to 14 livres, 19 sols; (4) 15 livres to 19 livres, 19 sols; (5) 20 livres to 29 livres, 19 sols; (6) 30 livres to 49 livres, 19 sols; (7) 50 livres to 74 livres, 19 sols; (8) 75 livres to 99 livres, 19 sols; (9) 100 livres to 149 livres, 19 sols; (10) 150 livres to 199 livres, 19 sols; (11) 200 livres to 249 livres, 19 sols; (12) 250 livres to 299 livres, 19 sols; (13) 300 livres and over.

TABLE 2–9a

Professions Represented on the List of 100 Most Highly Taxed Individuals
in Elbeuf, 1770–85

	1770	1775	1780	1785
Men				
Manufacturer	54	66	57	60
Rentier	5	1	4	4
Merchant	12	12	11	10
Horse dealer	2	2	1	—
Cultivator	4	3	3	3
Grain merchant	2	4	2	2
Dyer	3	3	3	2
Tool grinder	3	2	2	2
Farmer of the tithe	1	—	3	—
Old clothes dealer	1	1	1	1
Grocer/drysalter	2	2	1	1
Linen maker	1	1	—	1
Carder	1	1	2	2
Candlemaker	1	2	2	1
Baker	1	—	—.	2
Miller	1	1	—	—
Butcher	1	2	1	1
Caterer	1	—	1	—
Tavernkeeper	1	—	—	—
Papermaker	1	—	—	—
Sizer	1	—	1	1
Worsted maker	1	1	1	1
Locksmith	—	1	2	1
Innkeeper	1	1	1	—
Surgeon	—	—	1	1
Gardener	—	—	—	1
Dressmaker	—	—	—	—
Apothecary	—	—	—	—
Mason	—	—	—	1
No profession listed	1	—	1	1
Women				
Manufacturer	5	3	2	2
Rentière	—	—	1	—
Farmer of the tithe	—	—	—	1
Merchant	1	—	—	—
Miller	1	1	—	—
Farmer of the duchy	1	1	1	1
Butcher	—	—	1	—
Innkeeper	—	—	1	1
Total	110	111	107	104

be misleading if it were concluded from this that there was a near total reassignment of places in the monetary elite to an entirely new group of individuals during this period. Nothing could be further from the truth, and the illusion is dispelled by our knowl-

TABLE 2–9b

Name	1770	1775	1780	1785
Grandin	9	9	9	10
Flavigny	6	6	5	6
Delarue	7	6	7	6
Beranger	6	6	2	2
Lefebvre	5	5	4	3
Godet	5	6	5	4
Quesné	4	5	6	6
Duruflé	4	5	5	5
Dupont	3	2	2	2
Bourdon	3	3	3	4
Sevaistre	3	4	4	2
Guilbert	3	2	1	–
Hayet	2	1	1	1
Dubuc	2	2	–	–
Guenet	2	1	1	1
Leroy	2	2	1	1
Maille	2	2	2	2
Frontin	2	1	1	1
Vedic	2	1	1	2
Lejeune	1	1	1	2
Lemercier	1	1	2	2
Patallier	1	2	1	2
Louvet	1	2	3	3
Dugard	1	2	2	2
Delacroix	–	1	2	3

The names in Table 2–9b are a selection from the 193 persons and 85 families that were represented on the lists of one hundred most highly taxed individuals between 1770 and 1785. They represent the twenty-five families that had plural representation at one time or another.

edge that the 193 persons represented only 85 families, no more than 60 of which were on the list in any given year. Moreover, 37 families were on the list in every one of the four years studied. To be sure, individuals struggled to improve their financial situations, to displace one another at the top of the heap, but this in no way indicates a change in the class structure or an open, mobile society. A nucleus of families continued throughout this period to dominate the social structure from above.

The evidence for this conclusion is even greater when we look at the families represented, at one time or another, by more than one member. They number 25, but no more than 19 in any year. Twelve of them appear on the list with plural membership at all times. In 1770, 19 families were represented by 72 individuals; in 1775, 18 families by 71 individuals; in 1780, 16 families by 63 individuals, and in 1785, 19 families by 66 individuals. This means that, on the average, 31.3 per cent of the families accounted for 62.9 per cent of the individuals on the list. The great majority of these families were engaged in the manufacture of woolen cloth.[50]

An investigation of property holding in Elbeuf will now be undertaken. Of 95 declarants for the Forced Loan of Frimaire-Nivôse II, 59 were manufacturers or ex-manufacturers. All of them except 8 manufacturers and 7 others had invested in real property, and all of them save 5 manufacturers and 5 unidentifiable individuals drew an income of more than 300 livres from these investments. Of the 27 persons who had an annual income of more than 1,000 livres from real property, 22 were manufacturers. It seems correct to say that persons whose main occupation was commercial (there is only one *cultivateur* on the list) also had considerable real property investments, and that the manufacturers were first among them.[51]

Was this true throughout this period? In order to answer this question, several documents were used, especially the *vingtièmes* of the old regime and the *contribution foncière* of the Revolution.

The *vingtième* roll [52] available for use was first drawn in 1759, but it was corrected annually until 1780. The dating is, however, vague, so that it is impossible to measure changes in property holding during this twenty-one year period. Indeed, if information is used at all, it must be assumed that it is valid for the year 1780.

Total estimated annual revenue in Elbeuf from all types of property, including houses, was 208,263 livres, 15 sols. Of this amount, religious and communal institutions held a total of 5,054 livres, and the Prince de Lambesc leased out his feudal dues (for the duchy as a whole) worth 51,200 livres. This left 152,009

---

[50] See Tables 2–8, 2–9.   [51] *Arch. Mun.*, Series G.   [52] *Arch. Dép.*, C 560.

TABLE 2–10

Distribution of Landed Property by Income Categories, 1759–80

Revenue per person	Number of persons in this category	Per cent of taxpayers	Total revenue (in livres & sols)	Per cent of all proprietors	Per cent of all property held
1,000 +	22	1.5	32,536	4.6	21.4
300 +	129	9.0	85,412	26.5	56.2
200–299	59	4.0	13,315.10	12.2	8.8
150–199	45	3.1	7,222.10	9.3	4.8
100–149	52	3.6	5,572	10.8	3.7
50– 99	87	6.0	5,384	18.0	3.5
Less than 50	90	6.2	2,567.15	18.6	1.6
Totals	484	33.4	152,009.15	100.0	100.0

Source: *Arch. Dép.*, C 560—Vingtième Roll, 1759–80.

TABLE 2–11

Land Distribution by Occupation and Social Class, 1791

Occupation	Number of persons	Per cent of all proprietors	Land area in acres	Per cent of all land
Upper and middle bourgeoisie				
Manufacturers	22	20.2	54.4	22.4
Rentiers	14	12.9	39.9	16.4
Cultivators	9	8.3	67.5	27.7
Merchants	4	3.7	5.0	2.0
Dyers	1	.9	9.0	3.7
Subtotal	50	46.0	175.8	72.3
Lower bourgeoisie				
Wigmaker	1	.9	6.0	2.5
Food trades	5	4.6	4.9	2.0
Gardener	2	1.8	7.5	3.1
Usher in court	1	.9	.2	.1
Subtotal	9	8.2	18.6	7.7
Wage earners				
Textiles	8	7.3	4.2	1.7
Navvy	1	.9	.4	.2
Subtotal	9	8.2	4.6	1.9
Unidentifiable	41	37.6	44.1	18.1
Totals	109	100.0	243.1	100.0

TABLE 2-12

LAND DISTRIBUTION BY ACREAGE, 1791

Occupation	Under one acre		One-two acres		Two-five acres		Over five acres	
	Number of persons	Total surface area	Number of persons	Total surface area	Number of persons	Total surface area	Number of persons	Total surface area
Upper and middle bourgeoisie								
Manufacturers	10	3.0	4	6.0	4	9.2	4	36.2
Rentiers	7	2.2	4	5.5	1	3.0	2	29.2
Cultivators	1	0.5	1	1.1	4	12.2	3	53.6
Merchants	3	1.9	–	–	1	3.2	–	–
Dyers	–	–	–	–	–	–	1	9.0
Subtotal	21	7.6	9	12.6	10	27.6	10	128.0
Lower bourgeoisie								
Wigmakers	–	–	–	–	–	–	1	6.0
Food Trades	3	1.8	2	3.0	–	–	–	–
Gardeners	–	–	–	–	2	7.5	–	–
Ushers in court	1	.2	–	–	–	–	–	–
Subtotal	4	2.0	2	3.0	2	7.5	1	6.0
Wage earners								
Textile Workers	6	2.0	2	2.2	–	–	–	–
Navvy	1	.4	–	–	–	–	–	–
Subtotal	7	2.4	2	2.2	–	–	–	–
Unidentifiable	25	7.7	9	10.8	5	11.6	2	13.9
Total	57	19.7	22	28.6	17	46.7	13	147.9

Source: *Arch. Mun.*, Series G—Contribution Foncière, 1791.

livres, 15 sols to be distributed among 484 proprietors. As there were approximately 1,448 taxpayers in Elbeuf, this means that 33.4 per cent of the population were owners of real property. This seems a large percentage until we remember that it was common

TABLE 2–13

Composition and Value of Men's Estates, 1792–1806

Occupation	Personal effects		Rentes		Real property	
	Number of estates	Value (in livres)	Number of estates	Value (in livres)	Number of estates	Value (in livres)
Upper and middle bourgeoisie						
Manufacturers	9	35,844	12	193,767	19	495,713
Rentiers	7	13,760	9	136,789	9	78,331
Merchants	10	26,934	9	46,080	16	130,069
Cultivators	–	–	2	3,262	5	23,840
Priests	–	–	2	5,060	2	8,520
Doctors	–	–	–	–	1	6,603
Subtotal	26	76,538	34	384,958	52	743,076
Lower bourgeoisie						
Tool grinders	–	–	–	–	3	36,119
Wigmakers	–	–	–	–	5	19,589
Chandlers	1	2,019	1	640	2	15,933
Builders	1	1,200	–	–	1	12,000
Apothecaries	1	7,476	–	–	1	6,500
Artisans	27	19,703	10	20,648	31	146,219
Merchants	2	3,166	1	1,500	4	20,214
Teachers, writers	2	898	1	1,000	1	5,886
Subtotal	34	34,462	13	23,788	48	262,460
Wage earners						
Textiles	31	3,315	9	5,030	19	40,961
Foremen	1	2,290	–	–	2	8,240
Subtotal	32	5,605	9	5,030	21	49,201
Total	92	116,605	56	413,776	121	1,054,737

in a small eighteenth-century French town to own one's home, however poor.

But how was the wealth distributed? If the insufficiencies of the *vingtième* roll makes it impossible to show the distribution of land by social class, classification of property holders can be made according to income categories. Table 2–9 shows that there was a large concentration of landed wealth at the upper echelons, the lower 50 per cent of the proprietors owning only about 8.8 per cent of the property. Some evidence that upper bourgeois industrialists and merchants also had large investments in real property is contributed by the frequent appearance of names of prominent

TABLE 2–14

COMPOSITION AND VALUE OF WOMEN'S ESTATES, 1792–1806

Occupation	Personal effects		Rentes		Real property	
	Number of estates	Value (in livres)	Number of estates	Value (in livres)	Number of estates	Value (in livres)
Upper and middle bourgeoisie						
Wives of manufacturers	5	38,406	3	25,390	5	68,880
Rentières	14	133,451	13	50,636	12	132,473
Wives of merchants	4	9,149	3	12,186	4	30,350
Wives of dyers	3	6,093	1	46	–	–
Wives of cultivators	1	199	2	5,966	–	–
Wives of doctors	1	2,216	1	300	–	–
Wives of lawyers/ notaries	–	–	1	660	1	17,640
Subtotal	28	189,514	24	95,184	22	249,343
Lower bourgeoisie						
Wives of millers	–	–	1	14,000	–	–
Wives of tool grinders	1	600	1	3,216	1	4,000
Wives of chandlers	1	275	–	–	2	4,460
Wives of artisans	13	3,543	6	10,705	11	22,328
Wives of merchants	6	1,405	1	184	1	2,500
Dressmakers	2	243	–	–	1	300
Herb seller	1	120	1	100	–	–
Subtotal	24	6,186	10	28,205	16	33,588
Wage earners						
Wives of agricultural workers	1	137	–	–	–	–
Wives of textile workers	11	955	2	1,595	1	288
Textile workers	6	2,002	2	3,600	1	2,500
Subtotal	18	3,094	4	5,195	2	2,788
Total	70	198,794	38	128,584	40	285,719

Source: *Arch. Dép.*, Series Q Mutations Après Décès, 1792–1806.

manufacturing families among those who drew more than 300 livres annual revenue from land, names such as Beranger, Bourdon, Duruflé, Delarue, Flavigny, Fosse, Grandin, Hayet, Leroy, Lefebvre, Maille, Patallier, and Sevaistre.

In using the *contribution foncière* of 1791,[53] it should be noted that it lists only property in the commune of Elbeuf proper. It is, therefore, incomplete for these purposes. It is entirely possible,

TABLE 2–15

TOTAL NUMBER OF ESTATES BY PROFESSION AND SOCIAL CLASS

Men		Women	
Upper and middle bourgeoisie		*Upper and middle bourgeoisie*	
Manufacturers	22	Wives of manufacturers	7
Rentiers	14	Rentières	24
Merchants	20	Wives of merchants	6
Cultivators	5	Wives of dyers	3
Priests	3	Wives of cultivators	2
Doctors	1	Wives of doctors	1
		Wives of notaries/lawyers	2
Subtotal	65	Subtotal	45
Lower bourgeoisie		*Lower bourgeoisie*	
Tool grinders	3	Wives of millers	1
Wigmakers	5	Wives of tool grinders	1
Chandlers	2	Wives of chandlers	2
Builders	1	Wives of artisans	20
Apothecaries	1	Wives of retail merchants	6
Artisans	48	Dressmakers	3
Retail merchants	6	Herb seller	1
Writers, teachers, clerks	3		
Subtotal	69	Subtotal	34
Wage earners		*Wage earners*	
Textile workers	40	Textile workers	7
Foremen	1	Wives of textile workers	14
		Wives of agricultural workers	1
Subtotal	41	Subtotal	22
Total	175	Total	101

Source: *Arch. Dép.*, Series Q Mutations Après Décès, 1792–1806.

even probable, that all classes of the population, particularly the bourgeoisie, owned land in other parishes, both near and far. Moreover, there is difficulty in properly exploiting this tax roll, because of a lack of information on more than one-third of the proprietors. Certain conclusions can nonetheless be drawn.

If houses and gardens are excepted from the calculations, there was a total of 390.8 acres accounted for on the *contribution foncière*,

[53] *Arch. Mun.*, Series G.

besides the 1587.2 acres (1,889 *arpents*, 70 *perches*) of the forest of Elbeuf recently sold by the Prince de Lambesc to Pierre Lefrançois.[54] Of the 390 acres, 243.1 were distributed among 109 citizens of Elbeuf, and 122.9 were held by absentee owners, including 68.9 acres belonging to residents of Rouen. Church lands amounted to another 18.3 acres, and the Prince de Lambesc is listed as owning 6.55 acres. It is likely that the Prince owned a good deal more land than this, if figures can be relied on that appear in the registers of sales of national lands during the Revolution.[55]

A glance at Table 2–9 makes it clear that bourgeois *rentiers*, cultivators, and manufacturers formed a disproportionately large part of the proprietors (46 per cent) and that this group held a disproportionately large percentage of the property (72.3 per cent). Wage earners, on the other hand, were only 8.2 per cent of all proprietors and held 1.9 per cent of the land.

But this is not to say that all or even a significant part of the upper and middle bourgeoisie had substantial landed investments. The opposite seems to have been true. The median size of land holdings of all social classes (and occupational groups), with the single exception of the cultivators, was less than one acre. The statistical base of the high proportion of land in bourgeois hands is a group of ten individuals. Between them they account for 128 acres.[56] We may conclude, then, that it was more common for a bourgeois to have landed property than a non-bourgeois, but the amount was, in general, small. Nor does this in any way contradict the fact that a much larger number of persons drew a substantial income from real property, as the *vingtième* roll has shown. The exclusion from current calculations of houses, gardens, and factory buildings, all of them important revenue producing investments, explains the discrepancy. It would appear that the average bourgeois was less interested in acquiring prestigious landed property than in reinvesting in business.

Such was the situation of the land on the eve of the sale of property seized by the state. The marketing of confiscated property

---

[54] For the sake of clarity, a note about land measurements. 144 *perches* equal one acre, and a *vergée* equals one-quarter of an acre. A hectare is equivalent to 2.47 acres. The *arpent* normally equals 0.84 of an acre. Although this last figure may have been subject to some variation, we have adopted it when converting *arpents* into acres.

[55] *Arch. Dép.*, Series Q.

[56] See Table 2–12.

was of limited importance in Elbeuf. Because of the small number of *émigrés*, the greatest part of the land available for sale was that belonging to the Church and to the Prince de Lambesc.[57] Moreover, although 316.8 hectares (782.5 acres) were sequestered in Elbeuf, only 116.8 (288.5 acres) were sold by the end of the year III. According to Bouloiseau, the land sold was divided into 28 parcels and produced 1,399,600 francs in *assignats* and 494,390 francs in coin, for a nominal total of 1,833,990 francs.[58] My own investigations, which may perhaps be incomplete despite a thorough search of the sales registers,[59] show that by the end of the year VI, national lands had been sold to thirty-six individuals and had produced a revenue of 1,624,120 francs. Of the thirty-six, ten were non-residents and spent 994,035 francs, while twenty-six Elbeuvians spent 630,085 francs. The absentees, all but two of whom were domiciled in Rouen, bought approximately 2⅜ acres and 1,036 fathom lengths (*toises*) of land.[60] It was a resident of Rouen, Jacques Blard, who bought Lambesc's chateau, and a resident of Petit Quevilly, Guillaume Thillaye, who bought the mill in each of the two parishes. Twenty-two residents of Elbeuf (we have no figures for the other four) purchased a total of 32.9 acres and 2,562 fathom lengths. Eleven manufacturers purchased 25.3 (77 per cent) of the acres and 2,225 (86 per cent) of the fathom lengths. If we add the seven merchants who bought 1.3 acres and 243 fathom lengths, all but a negligible part of the land sold is accounted for.[61]

There is a reason for the small number of purchasers. Hardly

[57] Lambesc tried to save his land from confiscation. He argued that he was not subject to the laws against *émigrés,* because he was a foreign prince of the House of Lorraine in the Holy Roman Empire. He had, the argument ran, only made use of his natural right to change his residence, and did not see why he should suffer on that account. His plea failed to impress the revolutionary authorities, and it was his property that made up the largest part of the national lands sold in Elbeuf. *Arch. Mun.,* Délib., Vol. II (April 29, 1792).

[58] Marc Bouloiseau, *Le Séquestre et la Vente des Biens des Emigrés dans le District de Rouen* (1792–an X) (Paris, 1937), pp. 105, 256.

[59] *Arch. Dép.,* Series Q, Registers of Sales of National Lands, 1791—year VI.

[60] It is impossible to convert fathoms, a measure of length, into acres, a square measure, because we lack the dimensions of the land parcels in question.

[61] The other purchasers are: a cultivator (4.5 acres), a court usher (1.5 acres), a butcher (0.3 of an acre), and the owner of the transport franchise (97 fathom lengths). Two purchasers cannot be identified, and we do not know how much was bought by the gardner and the rentier who appear on the list. See also Sion, *Paysans,* p. 406.

any attempt was made to cut up the land into pieces sufficiently small as to be within the reach of the peasant or wage-earning population. The Revolutionary government did pass a law on September 13, 1793, enabling propertyless heads of families to apply for 500 livre certificates applicable to the purchase of national lands, but it met with no success. Because 500 livres was only an infinitesmal sum when the average price paid is considered, people were unwilling to go through the formalities required to receive the money. One had, for example, to ask for and get a certificate of good citizenship from the municipality before proceeding further.[62] According to Bouloiseau, bourgeois, artisans, and small businessmen got 61.8 per cent of the land and all of the buildings sold in Elbeuf and Rouen.[63] My own research indicates that in Elbeuf an even larger proportion went to the upper bourgeoisie, but it is possible that this is merely a reflection of differences in definition of terms.

III

All estates of deceased persons had to be reported to the local *bureau d'enregistrement*, where a property transfer tax was paid. The records of these transactions, which have survived in Elbeuf for the years 1792–1806, provide evidence on the division of wealth among social classes and on the structure of individual fortunes. There is a fault in these records that must be borne in mind: they contain property located within the district of the bureau only. Transfers of property belonging to the same persons but located elsewhere were carried out separately. It is also impossible to distinguish between land and houses, for the capital value of both is usually given together. Moreover, it was general policy not to declare liquid assets belonging to the deceased at the moment of his death.

The statistics that follow are based on a sample of 276 estates, 175 belonging to men and 101 to women. Men left a total of 1,585,218 livres, and women, 613,097 livres.[64] For men, we find the following percentages:

---

[62] Bouloiseau, *Séquestre*, pp. 215–17, 248–53; *Arch. Mun.*, Délib., Vol. IV (5 Messidor II).

[63] Bouloiseau, *Séquestre*, p. 254.

[64] These figures cover a period when inflation was running rampant. They are, therefore, valueless as absolute numbers, and it would be useless to compare an estate of 1792 to an estate of 1806. But as inflation is a constant in all cases across time, percentages of property distribution remain unaffected.

Class	Estates	Total wealth	Personal effects	All real property	Rentes
Men					
Upper/middle bourgeoisie	37.2	76.0	65.6	70.4	93.0
Lower bourgeoisie	39.4	20.2	29.6	24.9	5.8
Wage earners	23.4	3.8	4.8	4.7	1.2
Total	100.00	100.0	100.0	100.0	100.0
Women					
Upper/middle bourgeoisie	44.6	87.0	95.3	87.3	74.0
Lower bourgeoisie	33.6	11.2	3.1	11.7	21.9
Wage earners	21.8	1.8	1.6	1.0	4.1
Total	100.0	100.0	100.0	100.0	100.0

The disproportionate amount of wealth in the hands of the upper and middle bourgeoisie stands out clearly, and it is also evident that the wage earners held only a minimum amount of property. Indeed, fifteen out of the forty textile workers died possessed only of a small bundle of personal effects whose worth ran from 9 to 150 livres.

We come now to the study of individual fortunes. The following statistics show in percentages the part played by personal effects, *rentes* (most of which are based on land, as governmental obligations are a negligible quantity at this time), and real property in the fortunes of each social class:

Class	Personal effects	Rentes	Real estate	Total
Men				
Upper/middle bourgeoisie	6.4	32.0	61.6	100.
Lower bourgeoisie	10.7	7.5	81.8	100.
Wage earners	9.4	8.4	82.2	100.
Women				
Upper/middle bourgeoisie	35.5	17.8	46.7	100.
Lower bourgeoisie	9.1	41.5	49.4	100.
Wage earners	27.9	46.9	25.2	100.

Among the men, the only significant difference in the investment pattern of social classes is the high percentage of *rentes* in the fortunes of the upper and middle bourgeoisie. This may perhaps be accounted for by the common bourgeois practice of putting money out at interest. Otherwise, we note that real property still made up the bulk of the fortunes.

Among the women, the composition of individual fortunes varies more according to social class than in the case of men. Thus, lower bourgeois women have fewer personal effects in their fortunes than do the other classes. Upper and middle bourgeois women held fewer *rentes*, and wage earners held less real property than their neighbors. In general, women had more *rentes* (pensions and annuities given them by their husbands) and personal effects and less real property than men.

IV

We have now seen that the upper (and middle) bourgeoisie of Elbeuf dominated the economy of the town in every way. Never more than 10 per cent of the population, this class nonetheless provided a livelihood for more than 50 per cent of the inhabitants. The bourgeoisie also held far and away the greatest part of the accumulated wealth. It does not appear, however, that the bourgeois made a great show of their affluence. Perhaps they were afraid of the inquiring eyes of the tax collector, or perhaps they had not yet broken away from the old French peasant tradition that dictates a relatively ascetic way of life while money is put away for a rainy day. Certainly, the bourgeois had good reason to keep their personal expenditures down, for that was one way (however minor) to accumulate capital for reinvestment. Whatever the reason, it appears that their style of life in no way reflected a need for obtrusive and conspicuous consumption. The bankruptcy records for 1786–1807 show the annual personal expenditures of sixteen individuals: eleven manufacturers, three wholesale merchants, a dyer, and a butcher. Although the sample is too small to warrant drawing general conclusions, the results are indicative. The manufacturers spent 800, 1,500, 1,800, 2,000, 2,328, 3,000, 5,000, 8,000, 9,000 and 14,500 livres per year. The merchants spent 875, 2,000, and 4,080. The dyer spent 1,800, and the butcher, 800.[65] In Rouen at this time the average yearly household expenditure of an export-import merchant was 3,000–

---

[65] *Arch. Dép.*, Series Q, Statements of Bankruptcy, 1786–1807.

3,500 livres, signifying a life of ease if not great wealth.[66]   In Elbeuf, only four manufacturers and one merchant appear to have lived on a higher scale.

It is probable that the income of many bourgeois of Elbeuf was not commensurate with their high social position. As a result, their style of life was less affluent than that of the bourgeois of great cities like Paris and Bordeaux. The Parisians, in particular, would perhaps have been reluctant to recognize them as equals, not only because of their relatively low economic standing but also because they bore the stigma of provincialism. But the fact that they were not easily accepted elsewhere in no way keeps us from treating the bourgeois as the dominant class in Elbeuf, the more so as we are not concerned here with the subjective status evaluations but with objectively defined social role.

Having now established the social structure of Elbeuf, we turn to a study of the effect of economic and political events of the revolutionary period on the several classes of the population, and of the role of those classes in shaping these events.

[66] Pierre Dardel, " Importateurs et Exportateurs Rouennais au XVIIIe Siècle, Antoine Guymonneau et ses Opérations Commerciales (1715–1741)," *Bulletin de la Société Libre d'Emulation du Commerce et de l'Industrie de la Seine-Inférieure* (1949–52), p. 127.

CHAPTER 3

ECONOMIC PROBLEMS AND INDUSTRIAL DEVELOP-
MENT DURING THE REVOLUTION

I

The seventeen-seventies were a period of relative prosperity for the manufacture of Elbeuf between the crises of the seventeen-sixties and the end of the old regime. Unfortunately, I have been unable to find production statistics for this period, but complaints about the economic situation during the Revolution usually made a point of referring to it as a golden age of prosperity. Even so, all was not without shadows.

An investigation made under the auspices of the Archbishop of Rouen in 1774 found that as many as one-half to two-thirds of the inhabitants of certain parishes had no other resources than their day-to-day wages. This meant that in periods of economic difficulty they had immediately to fall back on charity. And because charitable institutions were practically non-existent outside the cities, the result was beggary and brigandage. The problem was so serious that in 1780 the Académie de la Conception of Rouen sponsored an essay contest on how to wipe out beggary in the Province. The winning essayist, Demandolx, lieutenant-général of the *sénéchaussée* of Marseille, suggested several procedures. It would be necessary to stop the influx of " gens oisifs, vagabonds et pervers " that resulted from the easy access to Normandy from the sea. Industry of all sorts would have to be encouraged and charitable aid provided in time of need. He called for the establishment of workhouses in the hospitals for children and the aged, who would, in so far as possible, contribute to their support by working, and for the creation of public works projects to employ able-bodied beggars. A social insurance plan to which the workers would contribute during prosperous periods was to finance the scheme.[1]

Elbeuf possessed none of these means of dealing with economic difficulty. And it suffered from this lack, particularly in 1779, when trade was " sans activité," and in 1785, when the municipal officers spoke of " l'anéantissement total de la manufacture." The latter year marked the beginning of the pre-Revolutionary crisis and was scourged by the double pestilence of an extremely cold winter and high grain prices that caused the greatest damage to " la plupart d'ouvriers chargés d'enfants et qui n'ont d'autre ressource que le travail de leurs bras." Had it not been for the generosity of certain wealthy inhabitants, the greatest part of them would have died of starvation.[2]

This sort of charity, at best a stop-gap measure, filled the need even in so difficult a year as 1785. Soon, however, the crisis was to grow so great that nothing but government intervention could deal with it. Realizing this, the Elbeuvians in 1789 followed Demandolx's suggestions and asked for the creation of a workshop-hospital in the city. The plan was to employ children between the ages of five and fourteen, as well as elderly people, in the production of cloth lists. In return, they would receive food, shelter, and a small salary equivalent to one-third that of a regularly employed worker. The plan, no doubt valid so far as it went, failed to deal with the essential problem of securing employment for the mass of the labor force. It met with no success. Necker referred the petition to the Commission Intermédiaire of the Provincial Assembly, which rejected it for lack of funds. Elbeuf was to get its hospital only much later in the Revolution.[3]

The existence of a crisis is one thing, its explanation is another. Contemporaries and historians have been arguing about its causes ever since its outbreak, and the argument still goes on. The Anglophobia of the Normans made them quick to blame the English Commercial Treaty of 1786 for all their troubles. The Chamber

---

[1] Georges Coeuret, L'Assemblée Provinciale de Haute Normandie (1787–1789), (Paris, 1927), pp. 185–87; Demandolx, Discours sur les Moyens . . . de Faire Cesser la Mendicité dans la Province de Normandie (Avignon, 1780), pp. 11–14, 20, 23–24, 38–40.

[2] Arch. Dép., C 202; C 193.

[3] Arch. Nat., H¹ 1420; St. Denis, Histoire, VI, 175–83.

of Commerce of Rouen argued that the English would shortly inundate the French market and would be successful in capturing it, because they could, for a variety of reasons, sell their goods more cheaply than the French. They had excellent raw materials including coal and wool in England and could obtain additional wool from Spain and cotton from the colonies at cheap rates. The French, on the other hand, had none of these advantages, importing almost all of their wool from Spain and their coal from England. The English also reduced their costs through the use of machinery, while the accumulation of capital in the hands of manufacturers and a benevolent government fiscal policy enabled them to avoid economic crises or to pass through them with a minimum of damage, all things which the French could not do.[4] Even Du Pont de Nemours, a partisan of the treaty, had to admit that in Normandy " depuis le traité, la concurrence anglaise est certainement très fâcheuse," although he attributed the fact to the non-enforcement of the treaty which, he said, would have adequately protected French industry if properly applied.[5]

The extremely harsh judgment directed against the treaty by its Norman contemporaries was taken up in the early part of this century by Charles Schmidt who, basing his work on the reports of the Inspectors of Manufactures, believed that the treaty was one of the major factors in turning the industrial bourgeoisie against the old regime.[6]

Certainly, there is good reason to believe that the Eden Treaty aggravated the pre-Revolutionary economic situation, without establishing a cause and effect relationship between the two. First of all, we know that the crisis had already begun in 1785, a year before the treaty was signed and two years before its effect could be felt. Moreover, the Chamber of Commerce itself seemed in 1788 to fear, in so far as Elbeuf was concerned, the future more than the present. It wrote:

---

[4] *Observations de la Chambre de Commerce de Normandie sur le Traité de Commerce entre la France et l'Angleterre* (Rouen, 1788), *passim*; see also Henri Sée, " The Normandy Chamber of Commerce and the Commercial Treaty of 1786," *Economic History Review*, II (1930), 308–13.

[5] Du Pont de Nemours, *Lettre à la Chambre de Commerce de Normandie: Sur le Mémoire qu'Elle a Publié Relativement au Traité de Commerce avec l'Angleterre* (Rouen, 1788), pp. 11, 48.

[6] Charles Schmidt, " La Crise Industrielle de 1788 en France," *Revue Historique*, XCVII (1908), 91–94.

Elbeuf fabrique annuellement 18 mille pièces de draps et étoffes de laine. Les fabriques de cette ville offrent, du premier aspect, un état de prospérité qui séduit; mais elles n'ont pas la ressource de trouver, comme les fabriques anglaises du même genre, d'excellentes laines nationales, à bon compte, & propres à leur fabrication. Nous estimons que, dans les draps ordinaires de cinq quarts de large, & du prix de 15 à 16 livres l'aune, les fabriques d'Elbeuf ne pourront soutenir la concurrence des draps de Leeds, appellés draps de Bristol, qui, dans la même laize, ne coûtent pas 11 livres tournois l'aune. Les fabricants d'Elbeuf ont plus de confiance dans leurs draperies fines; mais pour peu qu'ils négligent les moyens d'en modérer le prix, celles des anglais qui en approchent déjà beaucoup par la qualité, les supplanteront dans les marchés de l'Europe, et même en France.[7]

In short, although there was reason for apprehension, Elbeuf industry had thus far been able to remain in competition with the English.

What, then, did cause the crisis?

It seems to be splitting hairs to at once deny the causal effect of the treaty as such and to attribute the depression to the backwardness of French industry, wool production, and commercial or fiscal policy, as do Gaillardon and Cahen.[8] It is obvious that none of these factors would have come into play had it not been for competition. If it was indeed the state of affairs here described that provided for a potential crisis, then the English treaty, by providing the context in which the potential could become actual, must be blamed for the crisis. But we reject this thesis, if only for lack of coincidence in the dates, and so must look elsewhere.

Elsewhere in this case means to the Labrousse thesis, which makes of the depression of 1785–89 basically an agricultural phenomenon. One begins with an excessively bad harvest, the result of which is high grain prices. All but the wealthiest cultivators not only do not profit from rising prices but suffer therefrom because they are grain consumers. There is, thus, a general decline in rural purchasing power, first, because the rise in prices does not compensate for the fall in volume and, second, because the peasant is obliged to spend a greater share of whatever income he has

---

[7] *Observations de la Chambre de Commerce*, pp. 41–42.

[8] Leon Cahen, "Une Nouvelle Interprétation du Traité Franco-Anglais de 1786–1787," *Revue Historique*, CLXXV (1939), 257–85, especially pp. 273–85; Charles Gaillardon, "L'Industrie et les Industriels de Normandie au Moment de la Convocation des Etats-Généraux de 1789." *Revue d'Etudes Normandes*, III (1908–9), 22–23, 133–53, 258–69.

on food. This movement is accentuated by farm unemployment due also to smaller harvests. Because the majority of the population is rural, a general decline in the demand for industrial goods sets in. Urban centers are doubly affected by the drop in rural demand and by the impact of high grain prices on the expenditures of the city poor. The struggle between urban and rural poor for employment in industry may permit the manufacturers to cut their expenses by reducing wages, but whatever they may save in this way not only aggravates the situation of the populace but is ineffective as a measure against the crisis. Sooner or later, they must reduce production as markets close and industrial prices fall. They thus cut their losses, but the resulting unemployment only intensifies the overall difficulties. A remedy is found only when a good harvest restores the incomes of the majority of the population.[9]

As Labrousse himself admits, this schema must be subtly applied in order to explain validly the economic variations of different industries and regions. It is in this regard that Landes' criticism of the theory must be considered.[10] He offers two basic criticisms. The first, that the proposition according to which farm income and farm prices are, for the majority of cultivators, inversely proportional, is not absolutely proved, is well taken. However, in the case of Elbeuf this does not invalidate Labrousse's thesis, for we have abundant evidence to prove that the peasant population of the Elbeuf hinterland were, by and large, marginal producers of grains and other foodstuffs, always dependent on the industry for an income which enabled them to eke out a meager living. They would thus be the first to be affected in the way Labrousse suggests by a crop failure, even if we adopt Landes' formulation of a middle range of cultivators who did not necessarily suffer. We can thus affirm that it was, in fact, the agricultural crisis that was responsible for the poverty of the Elbeuf countryside and for that of the urban workers, to the extent that the latter's misery was also due to high grain prices.

[9] E. Labrousse, *Esquisse du Mouvement des Prix et des Revenus en France au XVIII⁰ Siècle* (Paris, 1933), especially pp. 615–17, and *La Crise de l'Economie Française à la Fin de l'Ancien Régime et au Début de la Révolution* (Paris, 1943), general introduction.

[10] David S. Landes, " The Statistical Study of French Crises," *Journal of Economic History*, X (1950), 195–211; Danière, " Feudal Income and Demand Elasticity

There is a second term to the proposition: that the woolen industry was directly affected by the agricultural crisis, that the fall of rural purchasing power caused a crisis of relative industrial over-production. Landes is right in saying that this hypothesis depends on the assumption of large rural cloth consumption before the depression, which he does not believe existed. Danière, on the contrary, believes that the countryside did constitute an important textile market. We are not in a position to settle the argument.

One observation is, however, necessary. We know for a fact that the industry in Elbeuf did decline at this time and thereby re-enforced the poverty of those who depended on it for a living. But its original decline may not have been entirely caused by the agricultural crisis, although it no doubt had a role therein. In other words, the mediate causes of the twin phenomena of the general crisis may have been different, and the first might theoretically have occurred without the second. For this to be true, it would have to be shown that the second, the industrial crisis, was caused by something else, the most notable possibility being a decline of foreign markets. It does appear that Elbeuf exports declined at this time. The German states had placed duties on French cloth, and orders from Spain were on the downgrade. It is here that English competition no doubt made itself felt, more so than in France itself. After all, there had always been considerable imports of contraband English cloth before the treaty, and there is no reason to believe that the quantity increased significantly just because the procedure was now legal. It was just that it was now more obvious and provided an excellent scapegoat.[11] In the foreign markets, on the other hand, the English did enjoy considerable advantages due to their technical improvements and lower manufacturing costs. Du Pont de Nemours believed, moreover, that Elbeuf manufacturers had, instead of trying to meet their competition, fallen into the trap of their own cupidity when they raised their prices some 20 to 25 per cent in a period of a few years. For him, this price rise was " le fruit de l'esprit de monopole, & des facilités que lui donnent les règlements & les privilèges

---

for Bread in Late 18th Century France," *Journal of Economic History*, **XVIII** (1958), 317–31.

[11] *Observations de la Chambre de Commerce*, p. 42; Schmidt, " Crise," pp. 91–94.

exclusifs des corporations." [12] We have seen that this spirit did exist and may well have had the effect Du Pont attributed to it.

Although complaints over the state of the woolen industry start as early as 1785, it is in 1788 that they become almost daily. In 1787, Goy, then Inspector of Manufactures of the Generality of Rouen, wrote that the industry had remained stable until that time, 5,255 bales of wool having been used in 1786 to manufacture 18,301 pieces of cloth work 9,621,396 livres. It was only recently that the sales of solid color cloth, the immense majority of the cloth produced in Elbeuf, had begun to fall off. Several manufacturers had begun to make striped woolens on which the profit was large, but they were few in number, and Goy predicted that their career would be short-lived.[13] In any case, the signal of alarm had been sounded.

The investigation ordered by the Provincial Assembly of Rouen in the spring of 1788 uncovered the great extent of the crisis. The municipalities or syndics were asked to fill in a table showing the number of poor, the ill, the old, and the unemployed. They were also required to indicate charitable aid available in their communes. Can their figures be trusted? There was an evident interest in swelling the ranks of the needy and in minimizing available charitable assistance, in order to obtain government aid. On the other hand, there may have been a tendency to lessen estimates of the needy and of money needed to support them for fear of being forced to pay a poor rate. Thus, while the exactness of the figures cannot be guaranteed, there is reason to believe that conflicting pressures may have neutralized one another so that the figures that have come down to us represent at least reasonable orders of magnitude.[14]

The communes surrounding Elbeuf, in all of which numerous workers were employed in spinning wool for the manufacture, were in a bad way. The municipal officers of Orival wrote:

Il serait trop long de donner la liste de ceux qui manquent de travail dans ce moment. On prie seulement de se souvenir que six cents personnes

---

[12] Du Pont de Nemours, *Lettre à la Chambre*, pp. 62–64.

[13] *Arch. Nat.*, F 1365—MS volume entitled " Mémoire général sur les bureaux de visite et de marque établis dans la ville et généralité de Rouen, sur ses différentes fabriques et sur ses principaux établissements de commerce, avec quelques observations en conséquence des tournées de l'inspecteur des manufactures . . . en 1787," pp. 31–34.

[14] *Arch. Dép. de l'Eure*, C 43 (October 10, 1788).

au moins sont occupées dans les fabriques d'Elbeuf et de Rouen et comme ces fabriques souffrent beaucoup, grand nombre d'ouvriers sont dans ce moment sans ouvrage et ceux qui sont occupés gagnent fort peu par la modicité des salaires. On compte 600 personnes parce-que les femmes et filles sont occupées pour la filature.

At Oissel, 200 persons who normally worked for the factories of Rouen, Elbeuf, and Darnetal were un- or underemployed. At Petit Couronne, there were numerous women and girls who spun for Elbeuf and Darnetal " dont beaucoup manquent d'ouvrages par la diminution des fabriques et d'autres gagnent fort peu." Similarly, more than 200 men, women, and children of Grand Couronne worked in the woolen industry, the men at carding, the others at spinning. Of them it was said: " de jour en jour le prix de leurs travaux diminue; et . . . pour comble de misère, ils sont menacés d'être absolument et incessament privé de tout travail. . . ." [15] For the city of Elbeuf the municipal officers estimated in April, 1788, that there were 500 unemployed, but because of the " languishing state of the manufacture," there would be 2,000 within three months.[16] There was some reluctance on the part of the central administration to believe these pessimistic forecasts, and on October 31, 1788, the Minister of the Interior wrote to Maussion, the Intendant of Rouen, asking him to check on the situation, as he had been informed that shipments of cloth from Elbeuf to Paris were currently larger than ever before.[17]

Such a challenge to the honesty of the city's administrators could not go unanswered. Three times in the month of November the municipal officers or the mayor individually wrote to defend themselves. The figures cited in the letters do not always coincide with one another, but they are all in the same range. In the average year of the last ten, the city used 5,100 bales of wool to manufacture 13,000 pieces of cloth. To manufacture one bale of wool a year's work by a man, woman, and child was necessary, which meant that 15,300 people were normally employed in a radius of three leagues around the city. But in the year running from October 1, 1787, to September 30, 1788, only 3,683 bales

---

[15] *Arch. Dép.*, C 2211, C 2212; see also E. Le Parquier, " Une Enquête sur le Paupérisme et la Crise Industrielle dans la Région Rouennaise en 1788," *Bulletin de la Société Libre d'Emulation du Commerce et de l'Industrie de la Seine-Inférieure* (1935), pp. 141–42, 157, 177.

[16] *Arch. Mun.*, Délib., Vol. I (April 8, 1788).

[17] *Arch. Nat.*, F¹² 1366.

were used and consequently only 11,049 persons had been employed, or 4,251 fewer than usual. Among other reasons cited for this state of affairs was that in the previous few months Elbeuf manufacturers had lost 300,000 livres in bankruptcies suffered by their clients, a fact which naturally discouraged them from wanting to keep their businesses operating at a normal rate.[18]

The description of the municipality was seconded by the Inspectors of Manufactures who found 1,500 workers in Elbeuf unemployed. Goy thought the fault lay in a lack of orders and the bankruptcies, while the itinerant Inspectors could do no better than to state " de science certaine que la stagnation des fabriques d'Elbeuf . . . provient de la concurrence Anglaise." [19]

Measures proposed to deal with the crisis or, more correctly, to provide for starving humanity were diverse. The municipality could not resist the opportunity to ask for a year's suspension of taxes including the *tarif*, which constituted a surcharge of 18 livres a year on the food of the average worker. Together with Goy and Blin, the *bailli*, the municipal officers wanted an *atelier de charité* to employ workers to build a road from Elbeuf to Pont-de-l'Arche. The itinerant Inspectors thought it more advisable simply to give a bounty of two sols per pound of wool put out to spin by the manufacturers, but the latter preferred the more direct method of a public works project. To support this suggestion, they wrote:

Les apparences sont fausses, les travaux manquent absolument aujourd-'hui; et l'on peut assurer qu'au moment présent au lieu du tiers des ouvriers sans travail, il y en a plus de moitié qui, quand même le commerce sortirait de son état léthargique tout à l'heure, ne pourrait avoir un travail reglé que dans 2 à 3 mois, par la raison qu'il faut 3 à 4 mois pour la fabrication d'un drap, que la première opération est la filature et qu'aucun fabricant n'ose s'en trop charger vû les circonstances.

Moreover, if help were not forthcoming, the worst was to be feared: " Un esprit de révolte & de sédition produit par le défaut de travail et par la cherté des vivres s'est déjà manifesté dans notre enceinte et il aurait pu avoir les conséquences les plus funestes si la prudence du magistrat chargé de la police de la ville n'y eût apporté obstacle." [20]

In the face of the overwhelming evidence Necker was finally constrained to grant 6,000 livres to the city for use in road work. The funds were sufficient to employ 150 workers for a period of

[18] *Arch. Mun.*, BB⁸.   [19] *Arch. Nat.*, F¹² 678.   [20] *Arch. Mun.*, BB⁸.

somewhat more than six weeks, after which new aid was solicited
and granted in the sum of 4,000 livres on May 28, 1789. A third
grant of 4,000 livres was made in April, 1790. The total was so
small that it could not do more than alleviate the misery of a very
small section of the population.[21] This was the more true as the
winter of 1788–89 was one of the worst in Normandy since the
legendary one of 1709. The thermometer had reached a low of
— 17.4° centigrade, enabling the *Journal de Rouen* to write
that " L'histoire ne fournit pas d'exemple d'un hiver aussi long,
aussi rigoureux & aussi constant que celui qu'on éprouve en
cette année . . . ce degré de froid est le plus considérable qu'on
ait éprouvé en Normandie." [22] Still, Elbeuf was fortunate to have
even this aid, the government having shown itself close with its
money in refusing other requests from less important towns such
as Tourville-la-Rivière in the Elbeuf hinterland.[23]

It is not surprising to find continuing concern over the (unim-
proved) state of the industry in 1790. New factors were soon to
aggravate the crisis. The manufacturers greeted the new threats
to prosperity with a call for government aid, saying that despite
the continuing crisis, they had not sought to shelter their capital,
but instead had given work to as many people as possible " afin
d'alimenter les habitants pauvres de leur ville et de vivifier à
l'entour une infinité de campagnes que nourissent les travaux
de cette fabrique." Their success had been indifferent, although
money had been available to pay the workers. What would they
do if the supply of coin dried up? [24] As Harris points out, the
need to pay a premium in order to obtain coin to meet a wage
bill would be a particular burden to manufacturers, unless they
could compensate by increasing the price of their goods. Faced
with a declining demand, it is hardly likely that the manufacturers
would have this recourse open to them. The result would be to
force a slowing down of production, as manufacturers strove to
protect their investments.[25] Because of money hoarding and exportation of capital that resulted from unsettled political and economic conditions, the 60,000 livres in small coin needed by the

[21] *Arch. Mun.*, BB[8]; Délib., Vol. I (March and April, 1790) ; see also *Arch.
Dép. de l'Eure*, C 41 (April 3 and June 5, 1789).
[22] *Journal de Rouen* (January 7, 1789), p. 6; (January 14, 1789), p. 17.
[23] *Arch. Dép. de l'Eure*, C 41 (July 3, 1788).
[24] *Arch. Nat.*, F[12] 652.
[25] S. E. Harris, *The Assignats* (Cambridge, 1930), pp. 4–5.

manufacturers to pay their workers each week was no longer available by the middle of 1790.[26] In July, 1790, the manufacturers and municipal officers asked the National Assembly to consider the problem. Shortly after this, the municipality, remembering Law's failure, found that the proposed issue of legal tender paper money (*assignats monnaie*) would be "infiniment dangereuse à l'état et leur subdivision encore plus funeste aux manufactures et aux campagnes puisqu'ils seraient donnés en paiement à des ouvriers qui ne pourraient les échanger sans un grand sacrifice contre les denrées de première nécessité qui doubleraient infailliblement de prix." On the other hand, they had no such objection to *assignats domaniaux* "qui ne seraient négociables que de gré à gré et qui seuls seraient admis dans l'achat des biens nationaux. Ce serait un moyen sûr d'accélérer la vente et de faire reparaître le numéraire." [27] Despite these protests, the assignat, still backed by the national lands, became legal tender in September, 1790. Still, it is hard to see how these assignats could have threatened the stability of prices, as they were issued in large denominations and therefore did not fall into the hands of the majority of the population. Not until May, 1791, were 100 million livres of 5-livre assignats issued, to which were added 300 million livres of 50, 25, 15, and 10 sous notes in the following December.[28]

Because the early assignats did not fill their need, the manufacturers resorted to another expedient, the *billets de confiance*. Backed theoretically by the property of the manufacturers, but in reality only by their good name, they were granted a large measure of support by successive governments, which saw in them a means of providing a much needed means of exchange.[29] They were eventually reimbursed with 5 livre assignats but some continued in circulation until early in 1793.

The first association to issue *billets de confiance* was created by a few manufacturers on June 4, 1791. By July the *procureur* of the commune was saying that the *billets* were the "cause de la fermentation non seulement parmi les citoyens livrés aux travaux de la fabrique mais encore dans toutes les autres classes des habi-

---

[26] It does not appear that payment in truck was common in Elbeuf. At least, we have not met with a single instance of it during our period.

[27] *Arch. Nat.*, D^vi 51; *Arch. Mun.*, Délib., Vol. I (September 13, 1790).

[28] Harris, *Assignats*, p. 26.

[29] *Ibid.*, p. 25.

tants." As a result of this complaint, the *caisse de confiance* was reorganized on September 6, this time with all the manufacturers participating. The preamble of the association stated that its founders " las de lutter contre les difficultés qui accompagnent la disette du numéraire qui est l'aliment, et la vie de leurs ateliers, et le premier moyen de toute entreprise, se sont enfin réunis en association légalement approuvée pour concerter entr'eux les moyens de rémédier aux maux dont ils sont menacés." They therefore resolved to issue paper up to a limit of 600,000 livres and declared themselves mutually responsible for it. In reality, 525,187 livres were put into circulation. Originally, the association was supposed to last only until July 31, 1792, but circumstances forced its continuation until at least January 31, 1793, when an inspection revealed 325,235 livres and 15 sols in bills still outstanding. They were shortly to be replaced by assignats.[30] In the final analysis the operation was successful, for it permitted the manufacturers to continue in business when the lack of ready cash might have hindered them.

The woolen industry was in distress during most of the Revolution and Empire, and the wails of self-pity are often heard. So much so, indeed, that one comes to be extremely critical in the face of them. The greatest attention must be paid to the nuances of the situation, as well as to its causes.

It would appear that 1791 constitutes a breathing space between the grave crisis of 1785–89 and the depression of 1792—year VIII.[31] In that year, the departmental administrators were able to write: " Nos fabriques ont éprouvé, cette année, la plus grande activité, et la consommation a été considérable." They thought that the most notable cause of this upward movement was inflation. The English manufacturers, they said, had withdrawn from the French market because of the difficulty of transferring French money without a high percentage of loss, thus leaving the way open for native products.[32] (The theory presupposes a growth of the internal market due to the effects of better harvests in

---

[30] *Arch. Mun.*, Délib. (July 14, 1791) ; *Arch. Dép.*, L 2495.

[31] Robert Schnerb, " La Dépression Economique sous le Directoire après la Disparition du Papier Monnaie," *Annales Historiques de la Révolution Française*, No. 61 (1934), p. 47.

[32] *Procès-verbal des Séances de l'Assemblée Administrative de la Seine-Inférieure aux Mois de Novembre et Décembre, 1791, Seconde Session* (Rouen, 1791), pp. 119–20; Henri Sée, *Histoire Economique de la France* (Paris, 1942), II, 43–44.

1790 and 1791.) There is yet another reason for the prosperity of 1791. Depreciation of foreign exchange, the result of the lack of confidence of foreigners in the Revolution and of the export of capital, proceeded more rapidly than depreciation of currency on the domestic market. Exports were thus stimulated, since Elbeuf woolens were now cheaper in terms of foreign money.[33] On the other hand, this depreciation brought about an increase in the price of Spanish wool (from 6 livres, 2 sols to 8 livres, 5 sols the pound), a change which in turn forced cloth prices up and reduced the consumption thereof within France.[34]

But it was the wars, civil as well as foreign, that ruined the industry of Elbeuf. It was inevitable that a city such as Elbeuf should suffer particularly, because of the trade it carried on with Spain, Italy, and the South of France. First, there was the British blockade, second, anti-republican agitation at home. The needs of national defense called for tight control of foreign trade. During the early part of 1793, this took the form of an absolute prohibition of exports, a resurgence of mercantilism. Then, from October, 1793, to Germinal II, trade picked up but under the close control of the Commission des Subsistances. From Floréal to the beginning of the year III, private individuals were again encouraged to participate in foreign trade with neutral nations, but this authorization was made less attractive by the requirement that merchants turn in foreign exchange received through these transactions for assignats, that is, that they accept a 50 per cent loss on their trade. They were also required to sell any imports at prices set by the maximum. It is only after Thermidor that foreign trade once again becomes a private matter.[35]

The Elbeuvians blamed governmental measures for their distress. That they should have taken the effect for the cause is not surprising in the light of their general attitude toward the Revolution. A readily available scapegoat is a tempting thing. Thus, when Elbeuvians were asked to file reports of income in 1793 at the time of the Forced Loan of Frimaire-Nivôse II,[36] only four persons (two manufacturers, one tool grinder, and one wood mer-

[33] Harris, *Assignats*, pp. 238–40, 242.
[34] Sée, *Histoire Economique*, pp. 43–44.
[35] Georges Lefebvre, "Le Commerce Extérieure en l'an II," in his *Etudes sur la Révolution Française* (Paris, 1954), pp. 170–98.
[36] *Arch. Mun.*, Series G.

chant) declared profits. All the rest claimed to have suffered losses, and they explained their plight by a common formula: " Bénéfices: nuls à cause du maximum." It is repeated almost as many times as there are persons on the list. But the declarants ignored the real problem: the revolt of Lyon. Because Lyon merchants acted as agents for Elbeuf's trade with southern Europe, the revolt was a hard blow to trade. Not only were markets closed but debt collection became impossible. The length of the revolt (July–October, 1793), and the subsequent process of re-establishment and repression explain the losses of the Elbeuf manufacturers. Indeed, the largest part of these losses was attributed by them to their clients at Lyon. Nonetheless, the manufacturers persisted for a long while in blaming the crisis on " les désastres qu'enfanta le règne de la terreur," as is shown by the comments of one of their number, Hayet, as late as 1822.[37]

This is not to say that the Elbeuvians were entirely wrong when they blamed things other than war for their distress. A lack of raw materials did re-enforce the effects of the war on the woolen industry. Something or other was always lacking. In May, 1793, it was combustible wood. In Ventôse year II, it was hemp used in the making of cards. A month earlier, the Société Populaire was drawing up petitions, looking hither and yon for oil and soap, the absence of which " peut préjudicier infiniment aux travaux de la fabrique." The problem was a continuing one. On 1 Germinal, the municipal officers estimated the needs of the manufacture as follows (in pounds):

Oils	260,000	Sulphur	4,000
Soaps	160,000	Cochineal	2,000
Potash	100,000	Nitric Acid	6,000
Indigo	40,000		

—and this for an eleven-month period. They had little success in obtaining what they asked for, at least in sufficient quantities. On 17 Vendémiaire III, the Société Populaire protested that 60 quintals of soap accorded to the city were so insufficient as to be derisory. Here again, the blame may be laid not on the reluctance of the government to comply with the petitioners' request (it had, on the contrary, every interest in so doing, given the fact that

[37] Pierre Henry Hayet, "Notice Historique sur la Ville d'Elbeuf" (MS. in Bibliothèque de la Ville de Rouen, Ms. g. 1).

the Elbeuf manufacture was at this time almost exclusively employed in making uniform cloth for the army), but to the interruption of commerce by the war. It was, for instance, impossible for the soap manufacturers of Rouen to import animal fat from Russia and potash or pearl ash from America or the northern European countries.[38]

Among the other items in short supply in Elbeuf were candles, again because of the unavailability of animal fat that was their basic ingredient. The municipal officers attributed the shortage to the butchers, who, they said, sold fat outside the regular market in order to avoid the maximum. At various times during the year II, it was impossible to procure coal and pitch. In Ventôse, only 160 pounds of cotton were available for the stocking industry that used 6,000–7,000 pounds a year.[39] Worst of all was the shortage of wool itself. Despite a considerable increase in the use of domestic wools in Elbeuf, the greatest part of its supply still came from Spain. In Thermidor II, 611,650 pounds of wool (38 per cent of the 1,600,000 used annually) were on hand. Moreover, only 138,450 pounds had been washed and were ready for use.[40]

To the pressure on the manufacture caused by a dearth of raw materials was added the opposite but quite as annoying one of requisitions for the army. The *levée en masse* came to Elbeuf on 21 Ventôse II, with the requisition of 10,000 pieces of cloth. On 17 Germinal, the General Council of the commune urged the manufacturers " de ne s'occuper que des besoins de la République." A month later, fine cloth was added to the requisition, perhaps as one of the luxury goods with which to pay neutral traders for their grain imports.[41]

Despite the variety of measures (right of pre-emption, prohibition of dying wool in any but the national colors) taken to ensure the delivery of woolen cloth, the government had trouble in getting the manufacturers to conform to its desires. Johin, the representative of the *Comité d'Approvissionnement* in Elbeuf, often complained of the manufacturers' lack of patriotism, shown

[38] *Arch. Mun.*, Délib., Vol. III (May 2, 1793); *Arch. Dép.*, L 5618, 30 Pluviôse and 14 Ventôse II; L 5619, 26 Pluviôse and 1er Sans-culottide II; L 5620, 17 Vendémiaire III; L 2401; *Arch. Nat.*, F[12] 1389–90.

[39] *Arch. Dép.*, L 5621, L 2401, L 2405; *Arch. Mun.*, Délib., IV (7 Brumaire II).

[40] *Arch. Dép.*, L 2401.

[41] *Arch. Mun.*, Délib., Vol. III (21 Ventôse and 17 Germinal II); Délib., Vol. IV (22 Prairial II); Lefebvre, *Etudes*, pp. 179, 182.

by their slowness in making deliveries and by their attempts to
defraud the Republic by maintaining that their cloth was of a
higher quality than it really was. The Committee wrote:

> De quelle nation sont-ils donc ces égoistes! Quelle est donc leur patrie?
> Ont-ils le malheur de n'être pas pères? Ne comptent-ils pas de fils parmi
> les zélés défenseurs de la République, qui combattent pour eux, et qui
> aient besoin de vêtements qui les garantissent de l'intemperie des saisons?
> Ah, puissent-ils périr s'ils ne se meuvent que par le plus sordide intérêt,
> s'ils ne connaîssent d'autre bonheur que le leur propre et s'ils concentrent
> la patrie dans leurs familles, de tels êtres ne sont pas dignes des jouissances
> que promet notre glorieuse révolution, puisqu'ils n'ont pas rempli la tâche
> obligatoire des français qui l'aiment et la soutiennent.
> . . . Nous vous invitons [les citoyens de la Société Populaire], au nom
> de la patrie plaintive, de nous seconder de tous vos moyens dans nos
> pénibles travaux. Nous vous adjurons d'électriser les fabricants malévoles
> de votre commune, de les surveiller continuellement, de ne pas permettre
> . . . que les matières premières soient mal filées, mal fabriquées parce
> qu'elles se trouvent perdues; de ne pas permettre qu'il soit fait un usage
> criminel de la rame, par le moyen de laquelle les draps [sont] tout énervés
> et qui rend au soldat son habit inutile lorsqu'il a été mouille, puisqu'il lui
> devient trop court et trop étroit.
> Gardez-vous de souffrir que ces draps soient expédiés des fabriques
> sans avoir reçu les apprêts dont ils sont susceptibles. Veillez aussi à
> ce que les ouvriers n'imposent pas de loix aux fabricants, instruisez-les,
> premiers de tous, que la fabrication des draps de luxe doit être remplacés
> exclusivement par celle des draps des troupes, et que ces draps doivent
> être corsés et de longue durée.
> Ayez l'oeil vivant sur toutes les manoeuvres de leur part dont l'objet
> serait d'obtenir une augmentation de salaire disproportionée au cours
> ordinaire.
> Faites entendre cet avertissement salutaire et terrible: La Loi révolu-
> tionnaire punit quiconque peut servir son pays et n'en fait rien.[42]

Even before the arrival of this letter, the Société Populaire had
taken up the question and had ordered that the names of manufacturers of unsatisfactory cloth be posted in its meeting rooms,
where they might be the object of a just scorn. One member took
the occasion to attack the workers of the commune who, he said,
preferred getting drunk to working. His remarks caused " quelques petits murmures dans la Tribune," but the Société " applauded
his energy." [43]

Six weeks later the Société was in a less co-operative mood. It

---

[42] *Arch. Dép.*, L 5621—5 Prairial II; see also *Arch. Mun.*, Délib., Vol. IV (28
Prairial II).

[43] *Arch. Dép.*, L 5618—1 Prairial II.

asked Johin why he wanted its members to redouble their efforts
to supply the Republic with cloth. "Notre société n'est point
particulièrement composée de chefs de manufactures. Ceux-là sont
en plus petit nombre," it wrote. But this statement is untrue. We
know that not only were many manufacturers members of the
Société, but also that they enjoyed an influence in it even greater
than their numbers would indicate.[44] Undiscouraged by this lack
of co-operation, the government continued to enforce its requisitions, although with more suppleness after Thermidor. So it was
that permission was granted manufacturers to work on fine Spanish
wool for their own purposes, if they had none suitable for the
production of uniform cloth. The latter was still to have priority.[45]

Why the reluctance of the manufacturers to co-operate? One
might suppose that it was not entirely their fault, given the shortage of raw materials, were it not for the fact that a survey made
in Vendémiaire III showed more than enough wool available to
fill the orders placed by the government.[46] It is perhaps true that
shortages nevertheless did play a role. A more important reason
was the manufacturers' wish to avoid the maximum.

In October, 1793, the District of Rouen, in accordance with the
law of the maximum of September 29, set the following price
schedule for Elbeuf cloth:

Type of cloth	Price in 1790	Maximum price
	(in livres & sols)	
Fine cloth:		
First quality	30	—
Second quality	27	—
Third quality	24	—
Ordinary cloth:		
First quality	22	29.6.9
Second quality	20	26.13.9
Third quality	18	24
Poor quality cloth	15–16	—
5/8 Cloth ("ci-devant royales")	12	16
Cloth "Façon de Louviers"	15–16	20/21.6.9

[44] *Arch. Dép.*, L 5619—16 Floréal II; see also Chapter 5 below.
[45] *Arch. Mun.*, Délib., Vol. IV (3 Sans-culottide II, 23 Vendémiaire III).
[46] *Arch. Mun.*, Délib., Vol. IV (17 Vendémiaire III).

These prices, which conformed to the rise of one-third over prices of 1790 prescribed by the law, were for ordinary colors, adjustments being allowed for more expensive dyes such as blue and green. It will be noticed that no maximum was set on fine cloth of the sort made in Louviers.[47] The manufacturers, despite their dislike of the maximum, continued to demand that fine cloth prices be set as well, for fear that if this were not done they would be unable to sell any at all.[48]

To blame the maximum for the vicissitudes of economic life in Elbeuf is unwarranted by the facts. The fault lay with the war and consequent needs of national defense. This fact did not stop the manufacturers from having their own opinions on the matter.

According to the manufacturers, it cost 767 livres, 16 sols, 8 deniers to produce a piece of ordinary cloth of the fourth quality. It was made up of 32 *aunes* (ells) sold at 22 livres each, or a total of 704 livres. The manufacturers thus claimed a loss of 63 livres, 16 sols, 8 deniers per piece. The maximum would not have been effective had it not been for the requisitions. Without them, the manufacturers might have escaped the maximum altogether, through fraud, as did the other merchants.[49]

The situation was, from the manufacturers' point of view, intolerable and could not continue. Attempts made throughout the year II to get the *agents généraux de l'habillement* to raise maximum prices were constantly interrupted by walk-outs and a general lack of intelligence between the negotiators. After Thermidor, the new regime was more understanding and permitted a price rise that put ordinary cloth at between 26 and 33 livres the *aune* according to quality in Frimaire III, when a new increase was refused.[50]

The maximum was abolished in Ventôse III, but abolition did not automatically put an end to all of Elbeuf's problems. For a long while, the manufacturers had claimed for themselves the 5 per cent over and above maximum prices allowed wholesalers for transport costs and profit margin, and their claim had been

---

[47] *Arch. Dép.*, L 2401.

[48] *Arch. Dép.*, L 5618—22 Germinal II.

[49] Lefebvre, *La Révolution Française*, pp. 393–94; *Arch. Dép.*, L 5621.

[50] *Arch. Dép.*, L 5621—19 and 25 Fructidor II; Fernand Gerbaux and Charles Schmidt, *Procès-verbaux des Comités d'Agriculture et de Commerce de la Constituante, de la Législative & de la Convention* (Paris, 1906–10), IV, 602–3.

honored. In Pluviôse III, however, the *Comité d'Approvisionnement* tried to recover this money on bills paid between Nivôse and Floréal II. The manufacturers refused to comply, and the commissioners decided to bring the case before the courts. At the same time, they refused to honor new bills carrying this 5 per cent surcharge. It took an order of the Committee of Public Safety on 7 Floréal III to put an end to the legal action against the manufacturers.[51]

Despite the difficulties to which the industry was subject under the Revolutionary government and Thermidorean Reaction, there were no bankruptcies in Elbeuf from 1792 to the year V. This may well have been due, as Dardel suggests, to the overall economic paralysis of the period. That is, capital may have gone into hiding and production fallen off.[52] However much of a burden government requisitions may have been, they apparently did not cause the losses the manufacturers' complaints would indicate. It is even possible that the government provided a market to replace those that were lost through war and blockade. In the year VII, when they no longer enjoyed this resource and were on the point of ruin, the manufacturers asked for government orders " au nom de l'humanité et de la justice." [53]

The restoration of economic liberty under the Directory did not much help Elbeuf industry. The war and the blockade continued, although the end of the civil war and the partial reopening of the Mediterranean commerce may have caused some mild improvement.[54] The only figures we have show that in the year III the Department of the Seine-Inférieure, which had produced 36,866 pieces of cloth annually before the war, now produced 24,550 or one-third less. There had been a replacement of 31,385 workers and 1,901 looms by 20,762 workers and 1,227 looms, figures which indicate a decline commensurate with that of the number of cloths manufactured.[55] S. B. J. Noel, editor of the *Journal de Rouen*, noted that Elbeuf normally exported 4,000 pieces of cloth annually in peacetime, but then proceeded to sidestep the obvious conclu-

---

[51] *Arch. Mun.*, Délib., Vol. IV (22 and 28 Pluviôse, 14 and 21 Ventôse, 3 and 21 Germinal, 5 and 25 Floréal III).

[52] Pierre Dardel, " Crises," *Revue d'Histoire Economique et Sociale*, XXVII (1948), 53–71.

[53] *Arch. Nat.*, F[12] 1391.

[54] Henri Sée, *Histoire Economique*, II, 47.

[55] *Arch. Nat.*, F[12] 1344.

sions by attributing the decline of the industry, on the one hand, to the impossibility of obtaining Spanish wool and, on the other hand, to " l'inobservance des règlements, . . . l'introduction d'artisans étrangers à la fabrique, ou de simples ouvriers, qui, satisfaits de leur honnête médiocrité, s'estimaient heureux, avant cette époque, de consacrer leurs bras à la prosperité des manufactures, ont eux-mêmes élevé des ateliers, monté des métiers, etc." [56]

The statistical investigation of the year VI showed a certain improvement in the economy of Elbeuf. Still, the industry was producing only 12,000–14,000 pieces of cloth totaling 400,000 *aunes* annually as compared with 18,000–20,000 pieces and 700,000 *aunes* before the Revolution. And in the year IX it employed only 5,000 persons, about one-third the pre-revolutionary number.[57] Everyone hoped that things would get back to normal once peace had been restored.

Peace, peace, but there was no peace. On 29 Ventôse VIII, the departmental administrators wrote that " depuis que l'Europe en armes voit balancer les destinées de toutes les puissances, l'industrie si florissante est frappée d'une inértie funeste que la paix seule peut changer en activité." Already in Vendémiaire, Delaistre, the last commissioner of the Directory attached to the departmental administration, had written: " le commerce anéanti, les manufactures abandonées, les fabriques interrompues, le numéraire disparu de la circulation, les ouvriers nombreux sans ouvrage et sans pain, annoncent un hiver infiniment difficile à passer." Later in the same year the Conseil Général of the Department corroborated this view by stating that: " L'agriculture est languissante, l'industrie est nulle, les manufactures sont sans produit, le commerce sans activité." It attributed this state of affairs to " une diminution très sensible de consommation dans l'intérieur, . . . le défaut de circulation des matières premières, . . . celui de l'exportation des objets fabriqués, . . . la cherté des divers combustibles, . . . l'insuffisance des loix relatives aux vols secrets et aux banqueroutes frauduleuses." [58]

---

[56] S. B. J. Noel, *Second Essai sur le Département de la Seine-Inférieure* (Rouen, 1795–year III), pp. 189–90. On the question of new manufacturers, see below, Section III.

[57] *Arch. Dép.*, Series M—Statistiques, Enquête de l'an VI, and Enquête de l'an IX.

[58] *Compte Rendu de l'Administration Centrale du Département de la Seine-Inférieure depuis le 1er Brumaire an IV jusqu'à l'Organisation du Nouveau Système Administratif, Établi par la Loi du 28 Pluviôse an VIII* (Rouen, year VIII), p. 252;

The year IX saw no improvement. During Frimaire, Beugnot called for the establishment of a series of *ateliers de charité* within the woolen industry and proposed Elbeuf as the best city in which to give his plan a try. He wrote: " La mendicité qui y est effrayante céderait aux premiers secours parce que le pauvre qui n'a pu quitter le travail, mais que le travail a quitté, n'en a pas perdu l'habitude et ne demande qu'à le reprendre." The departmental administrators remained pessimistic at the end of the year and complained particularly about the lack of coal and wool and the fraudulent imports of English products.[59]

The peace that followed on the Treaty of Amiens allowed the manufacture to move forward on the road to prosperity. But it took some time before the full effects of the new political developments could be felt. We find the Prefect asking once again for government aid, this time in the form of orders for cloth. The request was refused in turn by the Ministers of the Interior, Navy, and War, who said that the prices of Elbeuf woolens were too high, and, moreover, the city had other markets open to it. In general, production *was* up, and, if industry was relatively slow in getting started again, Beugnot thought this should be attributed only " à l'attente incertaine de la paix ou de la guerre, et à l'espèce d'inquiétude qu'on éprouve même dans les premiers mois de paix, sur l'influence d'un si grand changement et sur les relations." [60]

The optimism was well founded. " La paix a ravivé nos fabriques," wrote the departmental administrators. If manufacturers did not find the state of the industry entirely satisfactory, they nevertheless stated that they were currently using 6,000 bales of wool a year, half French and half Spanish, to make 18,000 pieces of cloth, 8,000 Spanish and 10,000 French, that sold for a total of 13,750,000 francs and gave them a profit of 1,666,000 francs.[61]

Etienne Dejean, *Un Préfet du Consulat, Jacques-Claude Beugnot* (Paris, 1907), pp. 102–31; *Arch. Nat.*, F^{1c} V Seine-Inférieure I—Mémoire du Conseil-Général, Session de l'an VIII, pp. 1–2, 8–10.

[59] *Arch. Nat.*, F^{20} 256—Mémoire joint à l'état statistique du mois de Brumaire, an IX (signed by Beugnot). Another copy may be found in 40 AP 3; F^{1c} V Seine-Inférieure I—Mémoire du Conseil-Général, Session de l'an IX.

[60] *Arch. Nat.*, F^{1c} V Seine-Inférieure I—Conseil Général, Session de l'an X; *Arch. Dép.*, Series M; *Exposé Sommaire de son Administration Présenté par le Préfet du Département de la Seine-Inférieure au Conseil-Général à l'Ouverture de la Session de l'an X* (Rouen, year X), p. 16.

[61] *Arch. Nat.*, F^{1c} V Seine-Inférieure I—Mémoire du Conseil Général, Session de l'an XI; *Arch. Dép.*, Series M—Mémoire of Parfait Grandin and Mathieu Fronton on commerce of Elbeuf.

When Napoleon visited the city in Brumaire, he was pleased with what he saw, and the city in turn thanked him for bringing the peace that allowed it to flourish. Beugnot went along on this trip and reported the industry to be in " le meilleur état," its

TABLE 3–1

NUMBER OF BANKRUPTCIES IN ELBEUF, 1786–1813

1786	5	(3 manufacturers, 1 grain merchant, 1 tanner)
1787	0	
1788	1	(a mercer)
1789	4	(1 manufacturer, 1 grocer, 1 joiner, 1 milliner)
1790	6	(2 manufacturers, 2 merchants, 1 butcher, 1 tin-smith)
1791	1	(a manufacturer)
1792–year IV	0	
Year V	2	(1 dyer, 1 tavernkeeper)
Year VI	3	(all manufacturers)
Year VII	4	(2 manufacturers, 2 merchants)
Year VIII	0	
Year IX	1	(a manufacturer)
Year X	0	
Year XI	6	(5 manufacturers, 1 merchant)
Year XII	6	(4 manufacturers, 1 mercer, 1 dyer)
Year XIII	7	(5 manufacturers, 1 merchant, 1 weaver)
Year XIV	5	(4 manufacturers, 1 merchant)
1806	6	(5 manufacturers, 1 merchant)
1807	6	(4 manufacturers, 1 innkeeper, 1 butcher)
1808–10		No information available
1811	12	(5 manufacturers, 1 grocer, 2 merchants, 1 dyer, 1 tanner, 1 builder, 1 spinner)
1812	7	(2 manufacturers, 3 merchants, 1 baker, 1 builder)
1813	2	(1 manufacturer, 1 joiner)

The records are incomplete for 1812.
Source: *Arch. Dép.*, Series Q-Statements of Bankruptcy, 1786–1806. *Arch. Nat.*, F[12] 871[a] (1811–1813).

" prosperity " having increased by one-third since 1788—a fact which made for complete political loyalty on the part of the population, even of the rich who had been suspected of aristocratic leanings during the Revolution.[62]

This prosperity, somewhat less than general if we are to believe the bankruptcy statistics,[63] nonetheless marked a new departure in

[62] Guilbert, *Voyage Fait par le Premier Consul en l'an XI de la République dans les Départements de l'Eure et de la Seine-Inférieure* (Rouen, n. d.), First Part, pp. 66–68; Dejean, *Beugnot*, pp. 322–33.

[63] See Table 3–1. There were eighty-one bankruptcies in Elbeuf from 1786 to 1813, not including the years 1808–10, for which no information is available. Although it is certain that crisis in the economy is generally reflected in the

Elbeuf. If in the year XIII the manufacture was far from being as prosperous as it would have been in peacetime, it was at least not inactive—far from it. There appears to have been little unemployment. Unfortunately, the situation was to deteriorate as the maritime war continued. In 1806 the departmental administrators affirmed that all branches of commerce and industry were suffering and were obliged to dismiss their workers.[64]

As though the war were not enough to burden the industry,

bankruptcy statistics, there is no one to one relationship between them. There are too many factors operative, factors that may depress the economy but not cause bankruptcies on a large scale, as we have seen in the case of the year II. Moreover, there is the question of the stability of individual enterprises that may be influenced by a whole set of variables of which we have no knowledge.

If the bankruptcy statistics cannot provide a picture of the general economic situation, they can tell us something about capital investment. The sixty-three bankruptcies for which figures are available break down as follows:

Profession	Number	Total Debt (in livres)
Manufacturers	36	4,175,102
Merchants	15	2,138,321
Dyers	2	79,054
Mercers	2	38,737
Butchers	2	35,987
Joiners	1	3,945
Tanners	1	21,192
Pedlars	1	12,879
Tavernkeepers	1	10,514
Weavers	1	6,523
Milliners	1	22,590
Total	63	6,544,845

The distribution of debts is as follows:

Amount (in livres)	Manu-facturers	Merchants	Dyers	Mercers	Butchers
Under 5,000	1	–	–	1	–
5,000–10,000	–	4	–	–	1
10,000–20,000	4	–	1	–	–
20,000–50,000	7	3	–	1	1
50,000–100,000	10	5	1	–	–
100,000–500,000	12	–	–	–	–
Over 500,000	2	3	–	–	–

No single debtor owed as much as one million livres. The highest single failure involved 626,000 livres, owed by a manufacturer. The tables show the great difference in capital investment between manufacturers and wholesale merchants, on the one hand, and the artisans and shopkeepers on the other.

[64] *Arch. Nat.*, F1c V Seine-Inférieure I—Situation du Département de la Seine-Inférieure au 1er Floréal, an XIII (By Beugnot) and Mémoire du Conseil-Général, Session de 1806; F20 256.

other problems arose at the same time. Money went into hiding during the year XIV to such an extent that in Brumaire there was not enough available to meet the payroll. This fact, added to unemployment and reduced salaries, excited the workers and caused the mayor of Elbeuf to fear the worst, if a remedy were not found. He asked that a credit be accorded by the Bank of France to meet this need. In addition, Spain raised its tariff on woolen cloth by 5 francs, 15 centimes per meter. The Chambre Consultative de Commerce of Elbeuf wrote: "Si le surcroît d'impôts persiste, il faudra considérer comme nulle la consommation de ces draps en Espagne . . . ce qui achevera de faire au commerce, déjà très affaibli, un tort réel, lors surtout que le débouché de ces marchandises en Espagne est regardé comme d'un intérêt majeur." [65]

The short respite that followed on the conclusion of the peace was obviously over. The question is: Did the continental system restore war-threatened prosperity? We can give no answer to that question, for statistics are either completely lacking (for the most part) or contradictory. So it is that in 1807 the Prefect wrote that only 5,000 to 6,000 persons were employed in the industry, but a survey of the same year showed 18,380 workers producing goods to a value of 12,000,000 francs, indicating a fairly healthy economy. Under the circumstances all we can do is to fall back on Sée's affirmation that the continental system favored the prosperity of the woolen industry until 1810.[66]

The situation becomes clearer starting in 1810. The crisis that started then was tied to two phenomena: poor grain harvest and the vicissitudes of war. The troubles in Spain were surely no stranger to a lack of raw materials that made itself felt in Elbeuf, but the more general cause was the ever-changing situation of commerce, following on political events, that brought with it first a great expansion of speculation and later a forced and ruinous contraction. As the President of the Rouen Tribunal of Commerce wrote in 1811:

Cet état funeste [de commerce] a pour cause principale la continuelle mobilité des lois qui le régissent aujourd'hui, cette alternative de prohibitions et de permissions qui s'entredétruisent, ce changement journalier dans

---

[65] St. Denis, *Histoire*, pp. 157–58, 164.
[66] *Arch. Nat.*, F^{12} 1568; Henri Sée, *Histoire Economique*, II, 85.

le tarif des droits, ces perpétuelles vicissitudes qui font que le commerçant, après avoir conçu une opération sur les données du jour, la voit devenue impossible ou ruineuse par les dispositions du lendemain.

According to St. Denis, the crisis of 1810 caused a loss of 25 per cent of the capital of the textile industry. This cannot either be confirmed or denied but the great rise in the number of bankruptcies in 1811 would seem to point to the truth of the statement.[67]

The manufacturers were pessimistic about their future, which they felt would be compromised by the lack of ready cash and of a firm public credit. At the beginning of 1811, they expressed themselves through the medium of the *Chambre Consultative de Commerce:*

On ne vit jamais l'argent plus rare, plus difficile à se procurer. Toute négociation devient presque impossible, et les paiements ne se font qu'avec une peine extrême. La méfiance générale, qui fait réserver les capitaux, fermer toutes les bourses, menace nos manufactures d'une stagnation effrayante et, déjà, les marchandises s'y accumulent. Les faillites se multiplient et deviennent plus ruineuses que jamais. C'est certainement de la disette d'espèces que provient la cause immédiate de cet état désastreux.

In 1812 the situation was complicated by a disastrous rise in grain prices that cut deeply into the internal market.[68]

The contraction of the market did not immediately affect the production of woolen cloth. Statistics for the period 1810–16 show that production decreased from a norm of 18,000 pieces in 1810 to 15,500 in 1811, the figures for the first half of the year being particularly low. In 1812 and 1813 production was satisfactory (17,900 and 19,400 pieces, respectively), but in the first half of 1814 the manufacture fell into utter ruin, producing only 2,800 pieces. The cause is not hard to determine. A departmental administrator wrote with complete justice that " pendant le trimestre de janvier, [l' industrie] est rapidement tombée dans une nullité absolue. On ne peut s'en étonner, puisqu'il n'y avait plus partout que trouble et incertitude." Only with the coming of the first Restoration did the situation improve well enough even to resist the disturbance of the hundred days, 23,000 and 25,300 pieces of cloth being produced in 1815 and 1816 respectively.[69]

In general, then, this crisis was one of relative overproduction

[67] *Arch. Nat.*, F¹² 871ᵃ; St. Denis, *Histoire*, VIII, 251.
[68] *Arch. Nat.*, F¹² 871ᵃ; St. Denis, *Histoire*, VIII, 240–43.
[69] *Arch. Dép.*, Series M; *Arch. Nat.*, F¹² 1585.

and, as such, a crisis of the new type. Although agricultural difficulties played a role, we are no longer in the presence of an economic downturn due to high grain prices aggravated by a cut in industrial production as markets close. Capital is not withdrawn in an effort to cut losses, at least not in the first phase.

TABLE 3–2

NUMBER OF WORKERS IN ELBEUF TEXTILE INDUSTRY, 1810–16

Date	Workers in machine spinning	Workers in hand spinning	Number of weavers	Other workers	Total
1810[1-2]	450	7,000	1,800	3,000	12,250
1810[3-4]	675	5,600	1,800	3,000	11,075
1811[1-2]	900	1,600	1,200	2,000	5,700
1811[3]	900	1,600	1,200	2,000	5,700
1811[4]	1,000	1,600	1,300	2,200	5,100
1812[1]	1,000	1,600–2,000	1,300–1,400	2,200–2,500	6,100–6,900
1812[2]	1,000	2,500	1,550	2,750	7,800
1812[3]	1,500	2,300	1,950	3,300	9,050
1812[4]	1,500	2,300	1,950	3,300	9,050
1813[1]	1,500	2,300	1,950	3,300	9,050
1813[2]	1,500	2,300	1,950	3,300	9,050
1813[3]	1,800	2,300	2,050	3,500	9,650
1813[4]	1,800	2,300	2,050	3,500	9,650
1814[1]	300	400	300	500	1,500
1814[2]	900	1,200	900	1,500	4,500
1814[3]	1,500	2,300	1,950	3,300	9,050
1814[4]	1,800	?	2,150	3,800	?
1815[1]	1,800	600	2,150	3,800	8,350
1815[2]	1,800	600	2,150	3,800	8,350
1815[3]	1,800	600	2,150	3,800	8,350
1815[4]	1,800	600	2,150	3,800	8,350
1816[1]	2,000	600	2,400	4,300	9,300
1816[2]	2,000	600	2,400	4,300	9,300
1816[3]	2,000	600	2,400	4,300	9,300
1816[4]	2,000	400	2,400	4,300	9,100

Source: *Arch. Dép.*, Series M—Etat de situation des fabriques et manufactures de draps, drawn up by Pierre Henry Hayet, mayor.

Instead, production continues while sales drop, leading to overproduction. Of course, old habits still persist and consequently may come to the surface in the face of some event particularly frightening in its economic consequences, as witness the first quarter of 1814. But if it would be silly to apply schema valid for the crises of 1846–47, 1873, or even 1929 to the years 1810–14, it is nonetheless necessary to mark the birth of a new trend.

Yet another measure of the prosperity of the manufacture is the number of workers employed. The figures coincide with what we already know of the economic situation. So it was that in 1810 their number was already down from a pre-Revolutionary high of 16,000–18,000 to 12,250 in the first half of the year and 11,275 in the second. The real recession came in 1811 when the corresponding figures are 5,700 and 6,100. Low at the beginning of 1812, an increase in employment manifested itself in the second half of the year and went as high as 9,650. The first quarter of 1814, the high point of the crisis, brought the number down to 1,500, after which there was a slow recovery to 4,500 and 9,050 in the succeeding quarters. In 1815 the number was 8,350 and in 1816, 9,300. Lest it be thought that the last figure does not indicate as high a level of prosperity as in 1810, it should be added that the explanation lies in the change of the organization of the industry. Between 1810 and 1816 the number of workers spinning wool on machines increased about five times, while those spinning by hand decreased by eleven-twelfths. The number of spinning machines had grown from 200 in 1810 to 900 in 1816, and there were 900 weaving looms as opposed to 600 in 1810. Power required to use these machines was furnished by horses, which had doubled in quantity from 120 to 250. The greatly increased productivity of a worker running a machine as opposed to a hand worker explains the reduction in the total labor force.[70]

II

Troubles in the industry were usually accompanied, when not caused, by high grain prices, the result of shortages. The question of the grain supply was critical for Elbeuf for two reasons: first, because it had a large industrial population to feed, and second, because it was a grain distribution center for a large part of the Department of the Seine-Inférieure, including even the southern suburbs of Rouen. The largest part of the Canton of Elbeuf was a forest amounting to 1,486 acres, while there was only 168 acres of arable, 72 acres of garden (*masure*), and 40 acres of pasture

[70] *Arch. Dép.*, Series M: see Table 3–2.

land, according to an estimate of the cantonal administrators made in 1798. In Messidor II, a similar investigation ordered by the Representative of the People Siblot reported 47.3 acres of wheat, 15.1 acres of mixed rye and wheat (*méteil*), 11.5 of rye, and 9.4 of barley under cultivation in the commune, not enough to feed the city much less supply the market for outsiders.

This meant that Elbeuf was dependent for its supplies of grain on the neighboring parishes of the Department of the Eure, wherein lay the rich grain lands of the *Vexin Normand* and the *Lieuvin*. Grain was shipped in from as far away as Pont-Audemer and Bernay until 1793, and in the year IV we find that no fewer than twenty-six communes of the Eure were habitual suppliers of Elbeuf.[71] This was certainly one of the reasons for which Elbeuf had solicited its transfer from the Seine-Inférieure to the Eure in 1789. In that year the municipality asked the National Assembly:

que vous ne ternissiez pas notre lustre, que vous ne ruiniez pas notre commerce et nos propriétés, que vous n'enleviez pas à ces paroisses leurs correspondances avec une ville qui répand dans leurs communes l'abondance, fait fleurir l'industrie, alimente une partie des habitants en même temps qu'elle est le dépôt de leurs productions dont elle procure la consommation et le débit et devient pour chaque cultivateur une ressource avantageuse qui encourage son zèle et le dédommage de ses sueurs. . . .

The truth was that the cultivators were also a resource for Elbeuf. Elbeuvians were not unconscious of the fact that the transfer of grain between departments would be no easy matter, even though their right to free circulation of grain was theoretically guaranteed, as had been proved by the recent famine.

The rampant parochialism of the French countryside, aided by fears of a repetition of the celebrated *pacte de famine*, would continue to act as a brake on the grain trade for a long time to come. The division of France into smaller administrative areas than had been customary under the old regime would, it was feared, re-enforce this localism—hence the Elbeuvians' petition

[71] *Arch. Mun.*, F⁴; F. Evrard, " Les Subsistances en Céréales dans le Département de l'Eure de 1788 à l'an V," Commission de Recherche et de Publication des Documents Relatifs à la Vie Economique de la Révolution, *Bulletin Trimestriel* (1909), pp. 2–15; Charles de Robillard de Beaurepaire, *Renseignements Statistiques sur l'Etat de l'Agriculture vers 1789* (Rouen, 1899). For the location of the communes, see J. Vernier, *Répertoire Numérique des Archives Départementales— Seine-Inférieure-Période Révolutionnaire—Série L* (Rouen, 1914), Appendices 2 and 3.

to the National Assembly. They got no satisfaction, although the Assembly did allow them to present the matter to the departmental administrators. In the end, nothing at all came of the request.[72]

Elbeuf was thus particularly open to the calamities occasioned by a lack of grain. The disturbances of 1788–89 were only the beginning of a movement that was to exercise its pressure on the city during a good part of the Revolution and Empire. All the measures taken by the government, none of them strikingly original, were unsuccessful in coping with the crisis.

In September, 1788, Necker suspended the export of grain and, in November, revived the old regulations that ordered grain to be sold only in markets and required that the inhabitants of the market towns be supplied before the merchants and bakers. In April, 1789, local judicial officers were authorized to force cultivators to bring grain to market and to inspect grain supplies within their jurisdictions.[73] Still grain did not reappear in sufficient quantities, and the people began to be exasperated. During the *grande peur* of the summer of 1789, armed bands roamed the countryside setting grain prices and attacking convoys going from La Havre or Rouen to Paris. Coincident with the fall of the Bastille, Rouen was the scene of a veritable revolt on the part of the city poor who also attacked and destroyed cotton spinning machines whenever they could lay their hands on them. In September the Commission Intermédiaire of the Provincial Assembly, while protesting against the presence of commissioners of the Paris Commune in the Province and proposing to fix grain prices, spoke of the need to " faire cesser une anarchie funeste et d'établir un régime qui puisse nous garantir des effets de la cupidité et de la licence." In October it had given up all hope of restoring order, because " l'anarchie, soutenue par la force active des milices bourgeoises dans les villes et les paysans armés dans les campagnes ne nous laisse même pas l'espoir de faire écouter nos représentations. . . . Toutes les têtes fermentent: le désordre est dans toutes les villes

---

[72] Vernier, *Archives*, pp. xxxiv-xxxv; *Arch. Nat.*, D^{iv} 17 dossier 283; *Procès-verbal de l'Assemblée Nationale Imprimé par son Ordre*, Troisième Livraison, VII (Paris, n. d.), No. 189 (February 1, 1790), p. 7.

[73] Georges Afanassiev, *Le Commerce des Céréales en France à la Fin du XVIIIe Siècle* (Paris, 1894), pp. 491, 511–13; Charles Desmarest, *Le Commerce des Grains dans la Généralité de Rouen à la Fin de l'Ancien Régime* (Paris, 1926), pp. 24–25, 223–24.

et la famine nous menace. Notre récolte généralement mauvaise
ne nous laisse pas l'espoir de nous alimenter pendant la totalité
de l'hiver." [74]

Whatever may have been the reluctance of other bourgeois
militias to protect the free flow of grain, Elbeuf's Volunteer
Patriots were open to no criticism on this point. On July 27 a
detachment of eleven of them went out to the neighboring village
of Poses on the road to Louviers where an angry crowd was, with
the complicity of the soldiers assigned to guard it, holding up the
dispatch of a boatload of grain for Paris. They succeeded in
mastering the tumult and sending the ship on its way. This adven-
ture did not sit well with the municipality of Louviers, which
arrested a certain Guilbert, one of the Elbeuvian guards, for having
participated in the operations. The municipal officers of Louviers
later claimed that they had done so only to protect him from an
angry mob that had wanted to lynch him. A detachment of the
Elbeuf guard together with members of their Rouen counterpart
and some dragoons of the Penthièvre regiment went to Louviers to
release Guilbert. They met with resistance from the Louviers
militia, a resistance that was supported by what appears to have
been a majority of the population, a large part of which had participated in the pillage at Poses. A massacre was avoided only
by a last minute compromise that allowed the Elbeuvians and their
allies to honorably withdraw to the faubourgs to await a deputa-
tion of municipal officers who would discuss with them ways and
means of setting Guilbert free without running the risk of a lynch-
ing. The conference was held, but without result. Guilbert was
not released until August 4 and only then as a result of pressing
demands made by the Rouen municipality. The affair did, however, give Elbeuf the occasion to write to the Paris Commune about
its exploits and to receive praise for the city's "firm and wise"
conduct. [75]

Precious little good these exploits did. Only a few days later
the municipality wrote that strong precautions would be necessary
to prevent interference with Paris-bound grain convoys. Rumors

[74] Ernest Lebègue (comp.), *Procès-verbal de la Commission Intermédiaire de
l'Assemblée Provinciale de Haute Normandie, 1787–1789* (Paris, 1910), pp. 118,
120–21, 126–27 n.

[75] *Arch. Nat.*, D^{xxix} 37; *Intrépidité de Onze Volontaires Patriotes de la Ville
d'Elbeuf Qui . . . Ont Attaqué Quatre Mille Furieux Qui Pillaient un Bateau de
Bled Destiné pour l'Approvissionnement de la Capitale* (n. p., 1789).

of revolt were everywhere, the people calling for wheat and declaring that they would not be satisfied with barley as a substitute. On September 9 "un nombre très considérable de personnes" had demonstrated their discontent in front of the city hall, and the municipal officers were obliged in the days that followed to "invite" cultivators to bring as much grain to market as possible and to order the closing of the market to bakers during the first two hours of each market day.[76] In October they wrote of the famine that had been raging for six months and said that only a miracle had preserved the city itself from the disorders of the countryside. They were unable to cope with the situation because the *bailli* refused to aid them in enforcing market regulations. The city had undertaken to procure flour and to sell it to bakers, but the bakers were unsatisfied and claimed that the flour assigned them was both bad and high priced. They refused to bake. The city ordered them to provide bread, and they appealed the order to the *bailli*, who ruled in their favor, thus quashing all municipal efforts in this field. At this time only 120 sacks of grain were being brought to the Elbeuf market weekly, instead of 1,400–1,500 as in the previous year. The municipality turned to the government for direct aid in the form of grain allocations and was refused. On November 27 Necker wrote that it was very likely that the municipality itself was responsible for the desertion of the market "en voulant y faire venir par la force les laboureurs et décimateurs de votre canton." He invited the administrators to obey the decree of the National Assembly guaranteeing free trade in grain and at the same time expressed the opinion that persuasion rather than constraint was the proper course of action to adopt. Specifically, why not establish a bounty of 20 sols per quintal on all grain brought to market?[77]

The first action taken by the municipality when it assumed police powers in 1790 was to set the price of *pain bourgeois* at 2 sols, 9 pence the pound and that of white bread at 3 sols, 3 pence, an increase of 3 pence over the prices of 1789. It also ordered the bakers to "garnir leurs boutiques [de pain], de le vendre au jour et de se conformer aux règlements de la police." Several times during the year it ordered bakers, millers, and grain merchants to desist from buying at the market until the citizens had

---

[76] *Arch. Mun.*, Délib., Vol. I (August 7, September 10 and 12, 1789).
[77] *Arch. Mun.*, BB⁸; Délib., Vol. I (November 27, 1789).

made their purchases, setting the hours when the former might be served.[78] As this sort of action indicates, the problem here and throughout 1790 and 1791 was less one of high prices than of short supply, although prices did shoot suddenly upward beginning in July, 1791—for two reasons, according to the *Procureur* of the Commune. The first was that the circulation of paper money was finally making itself felt, and the second, " l'affluence des boulangers de Rouen et autres qui se meunissent pour le temps de la moisson où les halles sont désertes." The result in both cases—high prices and/or short supply—was the same: the *menu peuple* could not procure enough grain to meet their needs. Inevitably when this happened they rioted, and it was several times necessary to call out the National Guard to restore calm. On one occasion a riot assumed much greater proportions. In February, 1791, two persons held in jail in Elbeuf and accused of having participated in a bread riot of the previous October were to be transported by boat to Rouen. Just as the boat was about to weigh anchor, a crowd ran wild and attacked the soldiers guarding the prisoners. The soldiers opened fire and killed two of the attackers while wounding several more. Two soldiers were gravely wounded. On the following day a detachment of national guards and regular cavalry were sent from Rouen to keep the peace. Five arrests were made.[79]

From July, 1791, prices started on a slow upward climb. Cultivators were reluctant to bring their grains to market for fear of being forced to sell at low prices. On March 7 there were riots and forced sales at the neighboring market of Neufbourg in the Eure. On the request of the Elbeuf municipality, the Directory of the Department of the Seine-Inférieure ordered a group of 400 national guardsmen and troops of the line to go to Elbeuf to protect the market scheduled for the following Saturday. But before they started out reports were received from the Department of the Eure stating that the attacking bands had been broken up. The order was therefore countermanded. Still, just to be sure, fifty cavalrymen were dispatched to the city, but no disturbance occurred.[80]

[78] *Arch. Mun.*, Délib., Vol. I (April 9 and 24, August 24, and September 24, 1790).

[79] *Arch. Mun.*, F[4]; Délib., Vol. I (September 2, 1790) ; *Arch. Nat.*, D[xxix] 37.

[80] *Arch. Mun.*, Délib., Vol. II (March 7, 1792) ; *Arch. Nat.*, F[7] 3689[1].

It was in the summer and autumn of 1792 that, despite a brief reprieve following the harvest in September and October, the shortage of grain began to assume the proportions of a famine. Prices ceased their slow upward climb to shoot sky-high, reaching 15 livres the quintal in July and August, 14, in December and in January, 1793. In order to meet the crisis, the municipality sent commissioners and national guardsmen into neighboring grain growing regions to persuade cultivators to furnish the market, at the same time taking measures to fix the price of bread and to forbid bakers to make white bread. To farmers who complained that they did not have enough manpower to thresh grain help was offered. This policy encountered three sorts of resistance: first, from the farmers themselves, who simply refused to conform to the requisitions addressed to them; second, from wage-earners of the city, who found the procedures employed too slow and inefficacious and favored more direct action. In November they went so far as to invade the city hall to demand that the municipality sound the alarm and call a general mobilization. The third source of opposition was the District of Louviers and others of the Department of the Eure who fought toe-to-toe with Elbeuf against the latter's requisitions of grain grown in the areas of jurisdiction. In the first case the city was more or less powerless. All it could do was to insist as persuasively as possible, but without marked success. Vis-à-vis the protesting wage earners, more effective action could be taken. There was the prohibition of unauthorized assemblies and the punishment of those who showed a propensity for rioting. Such conduct, said the municipality, could only worsen the situation, and those who indulged in it were " mauvais citoyens et ennemis de toute ordre et de tout bien." Finally, the city appealed to the Ministry of the Interior against Louviers' pretentions. At the end of 1792, Roland ruled in Elbeuf's favor, authorizing it to continue its requisitions and to send out the National Guard to do threshing " chez les recalcitrants." To justify his decision he wrote: " Le marché d'Elbeuf est un de ceux qui contribuent le plus à la subsistance des habitants de Rouen. Comment cette ville s'approvisionnera-t-elle si, par des mesures dictées par l'intérêt particulier d'un département voisin, on réduit au nécessaire absolu les habitants des lieux où se tiennent les marchés? " [81]

[81] *Arch. Mun.*, Délib. (August 30, September 22, October 4, 9, 11, 16, and 20,

During all this time little help was forthcoming either from the departmental administration or the national government, although Elbeuf was continuously appealing for aid. When the Elbeuvians asked for grain, they were offered money or given vague promises that they would have a part in the next shipment, a shipment that was eagerly awaited but rarely arrived. Occasionally a small quantity sent by the government did arrive, but it was hardly sufficient to meet the need. Suggestions were more common than grain, like the one made by the District of Rouen in November urging the city to borrow money in order to be able to import grain from abroad. The municipality replied that this was not necessary, for there was grain available, and it was just a question of making it come out of hiding.[82]

How to get the grain out of the granaries and onto the market? The Elbeuvians had some very concrete ideas on the matter and expressed them in a petition to the Minister of the Interior in October, 1792. Blaming a vicious avarice for the shortage of grain, they asked that cultivators be obliged to bring their grain to the market nearest their domicile every market day or pay a 500 livre fine for non-compliance. If they refused to thresh or bring grain to market, the municipalities should undertake the execution of these operations. In order to avoid disturbances in the markets, each parish attached to a market should furnish a detachment of five men to guard it. Price fixing was also envisaged at 8 livres the quintal (24 livres the sack) in a good year and 10 livres (30 livres the sack) in a bad one, the corresponding prices of bread to be 2 sols and 2 sols 6 pence the pound. In order to more adequately control grain supplies, each cultivator would be forced to declare the amount of his harvest to the municipality and would thereafter have to provide receipts of delivery of the grain to market. A 500 livre fine would be imposed, together with corporal punishment, should he sell his grain elsewhere. If the farmer refused to bring a part of his grain to market, he would be fined 50 livres only. Finally, the petitioners asked that " défenses soient . . . faites aux laboureurs de faire battre leurs grains et d'en faire des lits avec leurs pailles sans les vanner pour les garder plus longtemps, qu'au contraire il soit ordonné au laboureur

November 4 and 23, 1792) ; Evrard, " Subsistances," p. 38. The quintal was equal to 2 bushels or approximately 100 pounds.

[82] *Arch. Mun.*, Délib., Vol. II (October 28, November 10, 13, and 14, 1792).

de ne battre qu'à fur et mesure de ce qu'il lui faudra pour garnir la halle. . . ." This was the only way to " arrêter ce désespoir [du pauvre] qui n'est occasionné que des spéculateurs qui s'efforcent de le priver de sa nourriture," and thus avoid possible revolts.[83] Although no immediate satisfaction was granted the petitioners, the municipality enforced many of these provisions before it had legal authority to do so.

It would seem that nothing that was done in the realm of grain supply was destined to succeed. While prices continued to climb, quantities continued to diminish in 1793 and until the end of the year IV. Statistics of grain available are complete for only a few of these months in 1793 and the year II. The Elbeuf market had to be supplied with a minimum of 150 sacks of 6 bushels each of wheat (450 quintals) per week or 2,000 quintals a month in order to feed the city population. An idea of the extent of the deficiency is gained when it is seen that in January, 1793, only 753 quintals were brought to market. In April the figure is only 255, although, admittedly, the figures for two market days are missing. It is unlikely that the additional amount made any significant difference, for only 50 quintals were available at an average market. In October, immediately following the harvest, it is true that the 2,620 quintals of wheat for sale were more than enough for the city of Elbeuf alone. It is another story when it is noted that no fewer than 24,000 people from the surrounding area were attempting to buy grain at the market. In November the quantity available suddenly fell to 1,624 quintals and in December, with the harvest exhausted, to 156 quintals supplemented by 109 quintals of flour.[84]

The arsenal of weapons at the municipality's disposal was, as we have seen, small. Moreover, it was often forced to compromise in order to obtain any results at all. Thus it fixed bread prices in accordance with the maximum at 2 sols, 6 pence the pound of *pain bis*, but the bakers simply refused to bake until they were accorded a subsidy. Farmers, upheld by the village municipalities, refused to obey regulations, and when, rarely, they did obey, they ran the risk of their shipments being pillaged en route. For the Elbeuvians the explanation was simple: it was all a gigantic conspiracy directed against them,

---

[83] *Arch. Nat.*, F⁷ 3689¹.   [84] *Arch. Mun.*, F⁴.

un concert fomenté par la malveillance entre les laboureurs soutenus des manouvriers qu'il excitent à les empêcher de porter à la halle, au point qu'il n'est que trop à craindre que les habitants des campagnes ne prennent les armes comme ils en menacent tous les jours pour repousser la force armée que pourraient requérir [les commissaires aux grains des représentants du peuple], ce qui est malheureusement arrivé au Bourgtherould, et avec impunité au point que ce peu de laboureurs qui defferent à ces réquisitions sont arrêtés sur les routes, au point enfin que les authorités constitués des campagnes, loins de punir ces excès y applaudissent et les encouragent.[85]

No possible means were neglected in an effort to solve the problem thus presented. A loan of 30,000 livres was contracted by the municipality to be used in purchasing grain, and a petition for aid was sent to the Convention on the occasion of the publication of the Constitution of 1793. The commissioners sent to Paris by the municipality stressed especially the usefulness of the cloth industry to the Republic and the danger that valuable production would be lost in the time spent by workers in running about the countryside looking for grain. They asked also that Elbeuvians be permitted to buy directly from the cultivators without going through the markets. This last demand was motivated by the fact that, because Elbeuf's suppliers were not located in its arrondissement, it was impossible to compel them to supply the city's market under the terms of the maximum of May 4, 1793.[86] And the famine continued, increasing in virulence every day. The " fraternal invitations " issued by the Société Populaire to the neighboring communes to bring grain to market and not to interfere with the free circulation of foodstuffs were of no avail.[87]

From time to time, small supplies of grain were granted to Elbeuf by the Department. They were always insufficient. The city tried to stretch whatever supplies it did have by refusing the bakers the right to bake anything but bread, to the exclusion of cakes or pasta. The planting of potatoes was also encouraged.[88] But you can only stretch a given quantity of grain so far—and that was not far enough. At the end of its rope, the municipality sent commissioners to Paris to ask that the law of 18 Brumaire

[85] Arch. Mun., Délib., Vol. III (May 18 and 20, July 9, 17 and 25, September 5 and October 24, 1793).
[86] Arch. Mun., Délib., Vol. III (June, 1793), passim.
[87] Arch. Dép., L 5619–28 Frimaire II.
[88] Arch. Mun., Délib., Vol. III (4, 27 and 29 Ventôse, 23 Germinal, and 14 Prairial II).

II forcing farmers to ship grain to their usual markets be enforced. The commissioners received a somewhat niggardly encouragement, being told to enforce the law themselves. Accordingly, they sent out requisitions to the Districts of Louviers, Pontaudemer, and Bernay. The first never even bothered to reply, the last two answered that they had transmitted the order to the communes under their jurisdiction but they were afraid nothing would come of it. They were right. In the ten-day period from 13 to 22 Ventôse II, only 309 quintals of wheat reached the market where 650 constituted a minimum requirement. The workers who went into the countryside to buy bread, and thus lost precious time and money, were forced to pay up to 10 sols per pound, instead of 3 sols 6 pence they would have paid on the market had any been available. Even then the bread thus obtained was not enough to meet the demand. During the month of Prairial the Société Populaire twice petitioned higher authority for a supplementary ration for the workers of the woolen industry. It appears that they had only 13 ounces of bread daily, whereas the workers of Rouen under similar requisition to work for the government were guaranteed a pound and a half a day. Children under the age of six and old people over the age of sixty were given a half ration, presumably because they were considered to be unproductive members of society. The workers were half-starved, said the Société Populaire, and they would not go on working unless something were done to remedy the situation.[89]

What was done about this request is not known. But it was symptomatic of a long rivalry between Rouen and Elbeuf in the matter of grain supply. Elbeuf, in direct competition for grain with the Army of the Côtes de Cherbourg, was in a bad enough position already without having to supply Rouen. At the same time, supplying of Rouen was one of the market's traditional functions. That a conflict should develop was natural. Rouen requisitioned grain, Elbeuf refused to obey, Rouen accused Elbeuf of hoarding—and so it went. The situation was the worse because Rouen chose to call for grain at times when shortages were at their high point, as in Fructidor II, when the price in assignats at Elbeuf had reached 42 livres the quintal. Even allowing for the depreciation of the assignat, which then stood at about 40 per cent of its face value, the price had gone up tremendously. The maximum obviously could not be enforced.[90]

We know further that famine continued to rage in Elbeuf through the years III and IV. The repeal of the maximum of 4 Nivôse III and the general relaxation of government authority under the Thermidorean Reaction helped matters not at all. By the end of the year III, the price for a quintal of wheat had reached 617 livres, 17 sols, while the assignat had fallen to 7.5 per cent of its face value. In Ventôse IV, the assignat of 100 livres was worth 1 livre, 5 sols, 6 pence. For a good part of the year IV the market reports of Elbeuf carry no mention of prices at all, stating only that of wheat " il n'en est point venu." It was only in Fructidor IV, when 2,007 quintals were delivered to the market, that the situation began to get back to normal.[91]

During this period all the old measures for ensuring the grain supply were renewed many times.[92] Any detail added here would be only to repeat what already has been said. One new method was, however, employed. On 21 Nivôse III, the District of Rouen announced that the Convention had ordered an end to the requisitioning of grain, the order to take effect in a month's time. Upon hearing the news, the Elbeuf municipality decided to open a subscription to raise money with which to buy grain to distribute to the citizens. At the beginning, 8 pounds of wheat per period of ten days was the ration accorded. This was quickly reduced, in Ventôse, to 7 pounds. In order to make supplies go further, the " gens aisés " were no longer to be given their rations, starting at the end of Ventôse. But that helped not at all. In Germinal rations were again reduced, first to 5 pounds and then to 1 pound of wheat and 1 pound of rice. In Floréal the grain supply was so short that another reduction, to as little as half a pound, was introduced—and this while the price was going up from 6 sols

---

[90] *Arch. Nat.*, AF[iii] 262—*Tableau des Valeurs Successives du Papier Monnaie dépuis le 1er Janvier 1791 (vieux style) jusqu'au 6 Thermidor, an IV (Rouen, year V–1797)*, (a printed brochure) ; *Arch. Mun.*, Délib., Vol. IV (1 Fructidor II) ; George Dubois, " Les Subsistances dans la Seine-Inférieure de 1793 à 1795," *Bulletin de la Société Libre d'Emulation du Commerce et de l'Industrie de la Seine-Inférieure* (1935), pp. 226–27.

[91] *Arch. Dép.*, L 421; Evrard, " Subsistances," p. 95; Dubois, " Subsistances," p. 222.

[92] *Arch. Nat.*, AF[ii] 142 carton 1107; *Arch. Mun.*, Délib. Vol. IV (29 Frimaire, 28 and 29 Germinal III).

to 80 sols and finally to 100 sols the pound, after the demoneti-
zation of the 5-livre royal assignat on 27 Floréal III.[93]

The same policy was continued in the year IV for lack of any
other possibility. The price charged by the city to the indigents
it supplied with grain fell to 30 sols the pound in Brumaire, the
rest of the cost being absorbed by the city through the use of money
earned from the sale of surplus soap. Difficulties in procuring
grain were so great, however, that the departmental Commissaire
du Directoire, F. N. Augustin, wrote on 16 Pluviôse that unless
something were done, "ce département sera dans une famine
complète." Indeed, there were only 1,220 pounds (12 quintals)
of wheat and 500 pounds of rice on hand on 18 Messidor. In
Thermidor it was noted that beggary was tolerated because no
public assistance was available.[94]

The year V saw the end of the years of misery and famine in
Elbeuf. By Frimaire prices had become fairly well stabilized in the
10–11 livres per quintal range out of which they did not move,
except for seasonal fluctuations, for several months. In the year VI,
prices fell still further to between 8 and 10 livres and remained
stable through the years VII and VIII. Shooting upward in the
year IX, a year of extreme difficulty for the manufacture, grain
doubled in price by Floréal X, before starting on a downward
slide that brought prices back to normal a year later. The year
XII saw abundant supplies and normal prices as well. When the
intensity of the war increased in the year XIII, prices began to
fluctuate between 12 and 15 livres the quintal, staying in that
range until the beginning of 1806. From then until May, 1810,
prices varied between 9 and 13 livres, the last figure being high but
not excessive. June, 1810, was the beginning of a new cycle of
high prices that, after a brief respite in the first months of 1811,
brought prices up to over 20 livres at the end of 1811. The real
year of crisis was 1812, the lowest price never falling below 20
livres and going as high as 32 livres, 13 sols, 4 pence in April.
In 1813 prices slowly declined, but it was not until the end of
the year that they returned to normal (9–13 livres). The year

[93] *Arch. Mun.*, Délib., Vol. IV (23–30 Nivôse, 8 Pluviôse, 9, 24 and 28 Ventôse,
7, 14, 21 and 28 Germinal, 8, 12 and 29 Floréal, 19 Prairial, 9, 26 and 28 Messidor,
6, 10, 17 and 30 Thermidor, and 5ᵉ jour complémentaire III).

[94] *Arch. Nat.*, F¹ᶜ III Seine-Inférieure 7; *Arch. Dép.*, L 231; *Arch. Mun.*, Délib.,
Vol. V (10, 15 and 17 Brumaire, 18 Messidor IV).

1814 presented no grain supply problems, despite political and industrial disturbances; neither did 1815, although prices did increase somewhat toward its close.[95]

Although high prices in this period sometimes caused concern on the part of the administration, it was only once judged necessary to enact regulatory measures, the fixing of bread prices in Messidor X. For the rest, no real fears about the possible consequences of high prices were expressed before the crisis of 1811–12. On November 18, 1811, the sub-prefect of the arrondissement of Rouen wrote that the mayors of the region blamed high grain prices not only on the bad harvest but also on " la cupidité des riches cultivateurs et [des] blatiers et marchands de farine," who indulged in speculation. When grain came to market, it was grabbed up by the merchants who also bought directly from the farmers in the countryside. In order to end speculation, the sub-prefect recommended the application of the law of 7 Vendémiaire IV, which forbade grain sales outside of the markets, and that no merchants should be admitted to the markets until local consumers' needs has been satisfied. On second thought, he said, it might be dangerous to enforce this sort of measure, for it would alarm the people. Why not just arrest some speculators and let the government enter the grain business as a market supplier. This last should be, according to the sub-prefect, " la mesure la plus efficace," given the fact that " la classe ouvrière et nombreuse dans l'arrondissement est peu occupée, et que la modicité des salaires qu'on lui accorde ne suffira pas à ses besoins. Il est donc naturel de redouter les excès auxquels elle se livrerait infailliblement si le prix du pain continuait a s'élever. . . ." [96]

The sub-prefect was right to express these fears, for they had a real basis, although it took several months for them to be realized. Normal supply of grain to the Elbeuf market was 1,500 to 4,000 hectoliters every two weeks. In early March, 1812, only 900 arrived. The response of the crowd was immediate. On March 7 a group of women in the market harassed one seller to such an extent that he consented to sell them a sack of grain well below the going price. This was the signal for a general uproar. The same demand was made of other cultivators, and their refusal touched off a riot that neither the National Guard nor the Gen-

---

[95] *Arch. Mun.*, Délib., Vol. V (12 Thermidor V) ; *Arch. Mun.*, F⁴.
[96] *Arch. Nat.*, F⁷ 3639; *Arch. Mun.*, Délib., Vol. A, (23 Messidor X).

darmerie was able to control. In short, what happened was the
forced sale of grain at prices fixed by the buyers, by this time an
old tradition in the Norman countryside. To re-enforce their
position, the attackers started a rumor that the mayor had fixed
prices at the level they wished, an allegation the former stoutly
denied. The commotion eventually went so far that some grain
was taken and never paid for. Fifteen arrests were made. The
popular nature of the riot is proved by the social standing of
those arrested. Nine of them can be identified, including one cloth
merchant (*not* a manufacturer), a butcher, a tanner, a gardener,
a woodcutter, and four workers in the textile industry: two
shearers, a carder, and a weaver. Everyone escaped without punishment, because the families saw to it that the cultivators were
paid for the grain taken on condition that they would not testify
against the accused. This ruse excited the anger of the commander
of the Gendarmerie who feared a new outbreak of rioting once
the ringleaders had been let go.

By April calm had been restored in Elbeuf, and there were no
further incidents, despite the high prices that continued to prevail.
Prices set by the Prefect in May were only a little lower than the
free market prices that had provoked the rioting and too high for
most consumers—40 francs the hectoliter of wheat (26.70 francs
the quintal) and 55 to 65 centimes the kilo of bread, depending
on its quality. Grain also remained scarce. In April 1,200 quintals
were brought to market, in August, 613, the seasonal shortage
of the harvest time re-enforcing the cyclical phenomenon. Immediately following the harvest, an adequate supply was available for
a month beginning in the second half of September. But the time
of plenty was short-lived, as the Prefect wrote in December that
the supplies of the department would fall 577,089 hectoliters
short of its yearly needs. The monthly figures for grain that reached
Elbeuf from March to August, 1813, are: 1,000, 1,220, 1,800, 920,
1,120, and 680 hectoliters. Only in September, 1813, when 4,100
hectoliters were available for sale, did the situation improve
definitively, to remain good for the next two years. All was calm
until the end of our period.[97]

[97] *Arch. Nat.*, F[7] 3639; *Arch. Mun.*, F[4].

III

Before the late eighteenth century, the only machinery used in the woolen industry were fulling mills, consisting of mallets moved by a water wheel.[98] Even when, on the eve of the Revolution, machinery began to penetrate into Normandy, its spread was slow, despite the efforts made by the Provincial Assembly to propagate it. In Rouen, where cotton manufacturers wanted to use machines to help meet English competition, there were riots and machine breaking.[99] That this did not occur in Elbeuf was due only to the relative unimportance of machinery there.

Why this slowness in adopting modern techniques? One reason was certainly the imperfection of available machinery. Cotton was less fragile than wool and therefore more easily adaptable to machines. Perhaps even more important was the essential conservatism of the Elbeuf manufacturers. They were immensely proud of the quality of their cloth and therefore reluctant to adopt any procedures that might harm it. This was a characteristic they and their successors were to exhibit throughout the nineteenth century and into the twentieth, with the result that the industry of Elbeuf is now almost extinct.

Machines were used in certain minor processes of the woolen industry before the major ones. In 1787 Cherel was using them to card wool, a process which, according to the Inspector of Manufactures, produced a product of good quality. A machine to shear wool had been invented as early as 1778 by Everet and improved upon by Delarche in 1784. It too was run hydraulically.[100]

The first major operation to which machinery was applied was that of spinning. There were ninety-six spinning jennies in Elbeuf in 1787. Opinion as to their usefulness was divided. Goy in 1787 wrote that they were " d'autant plus intéressantes qu'en procurant un fil égal et une économie dans le main d'oeuvre, on n'est point exposé à être volé par des fileurs étrangers, ce qui est arrivé trop souvent." But Brinon, another Inspector of Manufactures, thought they were " dans leur état actuel plus propres à donner de l'économie et de la célérité dans le travail qu'elles n'y donnent de perfection. Le filage qu'elles produisent est inégal." [101]

[98] Ballot, *Machinisme*, p. 162.
[99] Lebègue, *Procès-verbal*, p. xlvii; Coeuret, *L'Assemblée Provinciale*, pp. 215–17.
[100] *Arch. Nat.*, F[12] 1365; Ballot, *Machinisme*, pp. 180–81.
[101] *Arch. Nat.*, F[12] 1365.

In the long run mechanical spinning became an economic necessity, especially under pressure of the crises of the Revolutionary period. The machines available at that time had forty to fifty spindles and each produced 8–9 pounds of thread measuring 3,000–4,000 *aunes* to the pound daily. Four spinning women were required to run the machines, and they earned three francs a day between them. By hand the work would have cost double the amount. These facts impressed manufacturers all over France sufficiently to make them realize that the introduction of machinery might be one way to circumvent the crisis of the year III, for it was a time when there was a shortage of manpower due to army recruiting and a loss of productivity because of time spent in procuring grain supplies.[102] The statistical reports of the year VI showed that " dupuis 12 à 15 ans, on obtient une assez belle filature par le moyen de mécaniques à filer la laine. Ces mécaniques conduites par des femmes donnent une économie de gros qu'on évalue à peu près à moitié." The manufacturers regretted that they did not have enough money to accept the offer made by two English entrepreneurs to install a water frame " qui devait fournir toute la filature de nos manufactures." [103] Such a machine had existed in Louviers since 1786 and in Lillebonne since 1793.[104]

The next advance in spinning machinery was made with the introduction by Flavigny and Sons in the year XIII of a gamut of machines invented by Douglas. Hayet and Sons and Amable Delaunay also installed them in their factories. The installation cost 20,054 francs; they could process 50 to 60 kilos of wool daily, and included machines for sorting and separating raw wool, for carding, spinning, shearing, and teaseling cloth. The system had several disadvantages, however. First, the machines were run by manpower and required great care to keep thread from breaking. Second, they could spin reliably only the carded wool used in making coarse cloth. But carded wool was only used for a small part of Elbeuf's production. More and more, the industry specialized in the manufacture of smooth-napped cloth (*à poil ras*),

[102] Ballot, *Machinisme*, p. 176; Robert Anchel, " Une Enquête du Comité de Salut Public sur les Draperies en l'an III," Commission de Recherche et de Publication des Documents Relatifs à la Vie Economique de la Révolution, *Bulletin Trimestriel* (1913), pp. 381 ff.

[103] *Arch. Dép.*, Series M—Enquête Statisque de l'an VI.

[104] Sion, *Paysans*, p. 298.

for which combed wool was needed. Moreover, while carded wool could be spun immediately after carding, combed wool had first to undergo several intermediate processes, for which machines were not yet available. The machines invented by Cockerill and sold in France beginning in 1812, although better than Douglas', did not solve this problem.[105] These difficulties, no doubt, go far to explain the reluctance of many Elbeuf manufacturers to buy Douglas' machines, even when the government offered to finance their acquisition by granting long-term loans.[106]

Despite the difficulties, these machines were ever increasingly adopted in Elbeuf. In 1811, four hundred of them were already in use, and the Chambre Consultative des Manufactures could write: " Il est constant qu'à l'aide de ces machines, l'entrepreneur aura le moyen d'augmenter de beaucoup les produits de sa fabrication, mais il ne cherchera à fournir de cet avantage que lorsque des temps plus heureux le lui permettront. Car à quoi lui servirait cette surabondance," given the economic crisis of the moment. With the coming of the peace and the re-establishment of prosperity, the number of spinning machines reached eight hundred in 1811 and nine hundred a year later.[107]

Other operations were in the process of being mechanized at the same time as spinning. Shearing machines made by Leblanc of Reims were installed in Elbeuf between 1803 and 1806 and were improved upon by two Elbeuvians, Fouard and Gancel, in 1808. Their machine did the work in three-fifths of the time required by hand and produced better quality goods.[108] But the combing problem remained unsolved. A primitive combing machine had been invented by Cartwright in England in the seventeen-eighties, but it was not used in Elbeuf before 1825. It was not until 1845 that Heilman constructed a really efficient machine of this sort.[109]

Weaving was mechanically backward. The flying shuttle invented in 1733 and known in France since 1747 did not come into general use until the Empire. In 1810 an improved version in-

[105] Sion, *Paysans*, pp. 298–99; Ballot, *Machinisme*, pp. 183–93, 203.
[106] *Arch. Mun.*, Délib., Vol. B (September 28, 1808) ; St. Denis, *Histoire*, VIII, 205.
[107] St. Denis, *Histoire*, VIII, 242.
[108] St. Denis, *Histoire*, VIII, 195–96; Ballot, *Machinisme*, pp. 211–12.
[109] Ballot, *Machinisme*, p. 203.

vented by Jean Despraux de Condom was brought by the Elbeuf manufacturers. But mechanization was extremely slow, and it did not become general until after the Franco-Prussian War. By that time the manufacture of Elbeuf was dominated by immigrants from Alsace, while most of the manufacturers of this period had left the industry. Domestic hand-loom weaving even increased during the Revolutionary era.[110]

The introduction of machinery had the greatest of consequences for the organization of the industry. The changes may be summed up under three headings: integration, urbanization, and proletarianization.

Integration itself implies two separate but related phenomena: the grouping of the various processes of wool manufacture under the control of one man and the establishment of factories. Both were favored by mechanization and the consequent need for large amounts of capital. It is in spinning that we have the first examples. Although the introduction of a low-cost jenny enabled some domestic spinners to survive for a relatively long period of time, the greater efficiency and lower cost of Arkwright's waterframe and Crompton's mule doomed them to extinction. They were replaced by machines in factories, the latter numbering thirty in 1811 and fifty-five in 1815. Although output did not rise very greatly between the beginning of the Revolution and 1811, capital investment went up from 10 million to 15 million francs, which indicates the cost of machinery as well as the increased number of manufacturers in Elbeuf. In 1806 the Prefect of the Seine-Inférieure wrote that " en général, l'homme industrieux ne borne ses spéculations à un genre de travail qui lorsqu'il n'a ni assez de capitaux ni assez de crédit pour réunir sous sa main les diverses parties de son genre de fabrication." [111]

Integration meant urbanization, at least in the case of Elbeuf. It would theoretically have been possible to create factories in the fields, as sometimes happened in England, but the prior existence of workshops for preparing and finishing the wool in the cities did not favor them. Rather, the old workshops formed the nuclei into which the newly mechanized processes were fitted. Except for

[110] Ballot, *Machinisme*, pp. 249–51; Sion, *Paysans*, 301 ff., 317; G. Olphe-Galliard, *Les Industries Rurales à Domicile dans la Normandie Orientale* (Paris, 1913), p. 8.
[111] Sion, *Paysans*, p. 298; St. Denis, *Histoire*, VIII, 243; *Arch. Nat.*, F[12] 1568.

weavers, the workers now came daily into the city from outlying communes to work. If in the year XI the majority of workers of St. Aubin and Orival employed by Elbeuf manufacturers still worked either in their homes or at factories established in their communes, those of Grand Couronne went to " travailler à la ville à la journée." Moreover, we know that in 1807 a sufficient number of workers from St. Aubin, Cléon, and Freneuse commuted to the city to justify the establishment of a ferry on the Seine for their use. It was specifically stated that the boat was to be used to " ramener les ouvriers travaillant à la fabrique d'Elbeuf." From November 1 until the end of February, the boat left the left bank of the Seine between 7 A. M. and 8 A. M., in March, April, and September at 6 A. M., and from May through August at 5 A. M. It returned from Elbeuf at 8:15 P. M. from March 1 to September 15, and at 9:15 P. M. from then until the end of February. This meant a twelve to fourteen hour working day depending on the season, the latter figure applying from May until October.[112]

The movement toward the city appeared irreversible. Of 5,700 workers employed in Elbeuf in the crisis year of 1811, 3,130, or slightly less than 55 per cent, were domiciled in the city. Others came daily to work in Elbeuf, but no precise figure is cited for them. It was stated that some worker dyers " demeurent dans les communes environnantes; mais ils se rendent chaque jour dans leurs ateliers, où ils sont employés pendant l'année entière." Again for spinners, " un très grand nombre se rend chaque jour dans les ateliers établis en ville," although they lived outside it. In 1815 one-half of the spinners employed in the industry came to work from the " suburbs." For the moment, the phenomenon of urbanization was evident only in the woolen industry. Tanners and saddle makers worked in workshops in the surrounding villages, while locksmiths and hosiers worked independently on a domestic basis.[113]

In 1788, Messance had written:

Quand un habitant des villes est obligé d'aller végéter à la campagne, il faut au moins deux générations pour que ses descendants soient capables des travaux de l'agriculture.

---

[112] Ballot, *Machinisme*, pp. 223–25; St. Denis, *Notice Historique sur la Ville de St. Aubin-jouxte-Boulleng* (Elbeuf, 1888), p. 365; *Arch. Dép.*, Series M.

[113] *Arch. Dép.*, Series M—Statistiques Industrielles de la Ville d'Elbeuf, 1811 and 1815.

Un habitant des campagnes, dès qu'il entre dans une ville, réussit à ce qu'il entreprend.

D'où vient cette différence? Le campagnard est porté à la ville par un certain génie, et le citadin ne va à la campagne que parce qu'il y est forcé.[114]

The third paragraph is an incorrect explanation of the first two. If peasants went to the city, it was because they had to earn a living—and this was the only way open to them.[115]

We have seen that the agricultural difficulties to which peasants were subject in the course of the eighteenth century had made them turn more and more to industrial work on a domestic basis; no longer as a supplement to their income, but as its basis. In so far as they were dependent upon the sale of their labor power for their exclusive source of income, these peasants were playing the social role of proletarians—even while still on the land. No quantitative statement can be made as to how many peasants had been deprived of land and/or were entirely occupied in industrial pursuits before coming to the city. But if they needed to do some industrial work in order to survive, and industry was moving to the city, they would have to follow it. Little by little they would cease to have any agricultural occupation and become full-fledged proletarians.

This movement is quite independent of any wage differentials between town and country. Whether or not the peasant stood to increase his income by becoming an urbanite is irrelevant. He moved when two conditions were fulfilled: (1) when agriculture could no longer give him a living, and (2) when the industry upon which he depended became urbanized. We have seen the development of the second phenomenon. As concerns agriculture, the Revolution aggravated the situation of the poorer peasants, particularly by continuing the enclosure movement that had already made so much progress in Normandy. In an area most of whose acreage was in forest land, the prohibition against allowing animals to wander in the woods was a hard blow. A peasant's income might be substantially reduced by such a prohibition, along with the suppression of *vaine pâture*, the enclosure of common

[114] Messance, *Nouvelles Recherches sur la Population de la France* (Lyon, 1788), p. 29.
[115] We have discussed this problem in Chapter 1 above, pages 20 ff.

lands, and the loss of the right to gather the sticks and branches for use as fuel.[116]

The only workers in the labor force of Elbeuf who succeeded in slowing down their conversion to proletarians were the weavers, and that was because of a relative lack of technological advance in their branch of the industry. There was as yet no economic need to integrate weavers into the factory system. There was no negative sanction against the weavers, so that they were able, with the relatively high wages they received (as compared to spinners), to accumulate money with which to buy land and thus re-enforce their independence. In 1834 the Elbeuf Chamber of Commerce reported that one-half of them were land owners.[117]

Did proletarianization mean pauperization of the mass of the workers? This question cannot be answered in so far as it concerns the transition from agricultural to industrial worker, for there is no information on farm incomes, except for wages paid to agricultural day laborers. The latter seem to have earned about the same as a teasler at the beginning of the Revolution.

Information on wage levels is scanty, and the existence of both the maximum and the assignats makes it difficult to draw any conclusions therefrom. The maximum raised wages by one-half and prices by one-third over 1790, but this proves nothing, as prices in 1790 were already inflated. It is likely that the purchasing power of the wage earner did suffer in this period; and it is certain that it did so after the repeal of the maximum and the onset of uncontrollable inflation. For instance, a weaver's wage had, according to Caron's statistics, gone up slightly less than four times between 1790 and Germinal III. But grain prices went up nine to ten times during the same period, depending on the quality of the grain. The pound of beef went up from 8 sols, 3 deniers to 3 livres, 8 sols, 6 deniers, or eight times. Only cider, a favorite drink in Elbeuf, did not outrun the wage movement, its price rising only three and one-half times. In general, then, wages lagged behind prices from 1792 until the end of the year IV, even

---

[116] Albert Soboul, "La Communauté Rurale (XVIIIe–XIXe Siècles). Problèmes de Base," *Revue de Synthese*, 3e Serie, VII (1957), 283–315; Alun Davies, "The New Agriculture in Lower Normandy, 1750–1789," in Royal Historical Society, *Transactions*, 5th Series, VIII (1958), 141–43; Sion, *Paysans*, p. 406; *Arch. Mun.*, Délib., Vol. III (March 2 and April 30, 1793); Délib., Vol. V (18 Floréal IV); *Arch. Dép.*, L 5618–24 Floréal and 16 Thermidor II.

[117] Sion, *Paysans*, pp. 316, 406.

during the maximum, when the government was more concerned with, and more successful in, holding the line on wages than on

TABLE 3–3

WAGES IN ELBEUF, 1790–YEAR III

Occupation	1790	1791	Year II	Year III
Teasler	20	20[a]	30	–
Dyer	20	18	30	–
Spinner	9 per pound	20–25[a]	13.6 per pound	5.15.0
Gardener	25	–	37.6	–
Shearer	10 per cloth	15 per cloth	15 per cloth	–
Mason	30	30	45	4.7.1
Carpenter	30	28	45	4.10.0
Joiner	35	30	48	–
Locksmith	35	30	52	5.0.0
Unskilled worker	18	16	27	3.14.3
Burler	6 livres per cloth	–	9 livres per cloth	–
Agricultural worker	20[b]	–	30[a]	–
Female agricultural worker	12[b]	–	18[a]	–
Roofer	30	–	45	–
Stonecutter	30	–	45	–
Carter (of cloth)	40 per cloth	–	60 per cloth	–
Fuller	40 per cloth	–	60 per cloth	–
Thresher	12 per cloth	–	18 per cloth	–
Female woolsorter	10 per 12 pounds of wool	–	15 per 12 pounds of wool	–
Female warper	10 per warp	–	15 per warp	–
Women who tied broken threads	12 per piece	–	18 per piece	–
Blacksmith	18.8	–	–	3.10.0
Woodcutter	28.10	–	–	6.16.8

Note: In the first three columns all figures are given in sols and pence, unless otherwise indicated. In the fourth column all figures are given in livres, sols, and pence and represent assignats. The third column contains the official figures, according to the maximum. All wages are for one day's work, unless otherwise indicated. The letter a indicates that this wage included payment for overtime. The letter b indicates a food ration was given each employee over and above the money wage.

Sources: Arch. Mun., Series G; Délib., Vol. III (6 Frimaire II); Délib., Vol. IV (19 Messidor II); Pierre Caron, " Une Enquête sur les prix après la Suppression du Maximum," Commission de Recherche et de Publication des Documents Relatifs à la Vie Economique de la Révolution, Bulletin Trimestriel (1910), pp. 384–87. All figures in this article are given in assignats.

prices. Later, between the years V and VIII, wages resisted a fall longer than did prices.[118]

[118] Pierre Caron, " Une Enquête sur les Prix après la Suppression du Maximum," Commission de Recherche et de Publication des Documents Relatifs à la Vie

In 1804 the mayor of Elbeuf declared that labor in the city was one-third dearer than in 1789.[119] At the time he wrote, the quintal of first quality grain stood at 12 livres, approximately one-third more than at the end of 1790. This would indicate that wages and prices were advancing at about the same rate. Such a conclusion is, however, too hasty. For one thing, the price of grain was subject to excessive variation and cannot, therefore, be adopted as our sole measure of the price level. For a second, we do not have price indices on commodities normally consumed by wage earners in this period. Again, we know that the average textile worker earned 1.25 francs a day in 1811 and 2 francs a day in 1815,[120] but the meaning of these figures is obscure. The question of pauperization must, for the moment, remain moot.

The perennial sickness and troubles of which the Elbeuf woolen industry was the victim during the Revolution should not be allowed to conceal the fact that this was also a period of foundation building and development. The introduction of machinery, the changes in the organization of the manufacture, the proliferation of entrepreneurs (their number increased from approximately 70 in 1782 to 130 in 1811 and 140 in 1815, while others had been in and out of the business in the interim) all testify to the importance of this period for the future of Elbeuf textiles.[121]

Several things indicate the strength of the industry at this time. First of all, a new confidence in its ability to meet competition. If in the year IV the departmental administrators could write only that France was capable of producing cloths as fine as any available with only a little effort, by the year VI the manufacturers themselves were saying that their cloth was in fact superior to that of their English and German competitors. Not only was it beautiful, they said, but it had " la solidité et le moelleux qui . . .

Economique de la Révolution, *Bulletin Trimestriel* (1910), pp. 384–87; Robert Schnerb, " La Dépression Economique sous le Directoire après la Disparition du Papier Monnaie," *Annales Historiques de la Révolution Française*, No. 61 (1934), p. 47.

[119] Prosper Delarue, "Notice sur la Ville et sur les Fabriques d'Elbeuf en Brumaire an XIII (October, 1804)" (Unpublished MS. in Bibliothèque de la Ville de Rouen, MS. g. 1 [supp^t 709]), p. 8.

[120] *Arch. Dép.*, Series M—Etat de Situation de la Commune d'Elbeuf, 1811, 1815, signed by Pierre Henry Hayet, mayor.

[121] *Ibid.*; see also *Arch. Mun.*, HH 11 and 14; Mathieu Bourdon, *Etude sur l'Importance Commerciale et Manufacturière de la Ville et du Canton d'Elbeuf* (Caen, 1863), pp. 6–7.

assurent la superiorité." [122] These were new words in their mouths; previously it had been most common to complain of the disadvantages under which the industry was laboring, so as to be able to justify appeals for government aid.

The optimism seemed to be justified by the results of the industrial expositions of the years IX, X, and 1806. At the first of these, Elbeuvians were awarded one bronze medal and one honorable mention. At the second, they received two bronze and two silver medals, and in 1806 one silver medal and a general citation in which the judges stated: " indiquer des draps d'Elbeuf, c'est dire qu'ils sont soignés et d'une qualité suivie." It should be noted that it was always the old, established manufacturers who earned these recompenses and almost never those whose names were unknown before the Revolution.[123]

Another and much more important recognition was granted Elbeuf industry by the governments of the Revolution and Empire: it was asked to give its opinion on the negotiation of various commercial treatises under consideration in the year V, a request that was never made under the old regime, as we know from the history of the English treaty of 1786. Moreover, the idea of according industrialists at least an advisory role in the establishment of economic policy was institutionalized in the year IX with the creation of a Commission de Commerce and later of a Chambre Consultative de Commerce.[124] The members of these two bodies were all manufacturers, a fact that is indicative of their ever-increasing importance in the community. Once again, the names mentioned—Grandin, Flavigny, Godet, Hayet, Quesné, Sevaistre, Lefebvre, Louvet—correspond to families already well established before the Revolution.

The creation of these advisory bodies enabled the manufacturers of Elbeuf to express better their demands vis-à-vis the government.

[122] *Rapport des Travaux du Département de la Seine-Inférieure depuis le Mois de Novembre, 1792 jusqu'au Renouvellement au 1er Brumaire, an IV* (Rouen, year V), p. 62; *Arch. Mun.*, Series M—Enquête Statistique de l'an VI.

[123] *Exposition Publique des Produits de l'Industrie Française, an X. Procès-verbal des Opérations du Jury* (Paris, year XI); *Seconde Exposition des Produits de l'Industrie Française, etc., an IX* (Paris, year X); Bourdon, *Etude*, p. 13; J. Peuchet and P. G. Chanlaire, *Description Topographique et Statistique de la France* (Paris, 1811), VIII, 23.

[124] *Arch. Mun.*, Délib., Vol. V (12 Frimaire V); see also St. Denis, *Histoire*, VIII, 40–41.

They lost no time in so doing. First of all, they wanted greater control over their workers. This they sought to obtain by re-establishing the old regime system of *billets de congé*, that is, a written authorization to the worker to quit his job. Their request was granted first by local ordinance and, a year later, by government order. This order instituted the system of *livrets* or little booklets containing certificates of good conduct and discharge given by the employer to the worker upon termination of a work agreement. On 29 Brumaire XIII, women were made subject to the same system. They too had now to be in possession of these *livrets*, unless they wished to be considered beggars and treated accordingly.[125]

Of course, there were other issues, on some of which the manufacturers did not get their own way. Such was the case of their proposal to appoint three of their number to assist the justice of the peace in settling all disputes having to do with the industry, including those that set worker against employer. They wished the judgment of this body to be final and without appeal, except in cases involving the possibility of corporal punishment (*peine afflictive*), which would be referred by them, after preliminary investigation, to the appropriate court. Seeing that they could not carry the day with this request, they modified their demands to ask that all disputes between masters and workers be judged by the justice of the peace of the place in which the manufacture was set up. The reason for their insistence on this point is simply that many of the workers in Elbeuf were domiciled in the Department of the Eure and thereby escaped the jurisdiction of the local justice of the peace, over whose selection the manufacturers had some measure of control. It was in this way that they hoped to discourage the thievery of raw materials that, they charged, was practiced on a large scale by the workers. So far as we know, neither of their requests was granted.[126]

Aside from issues directly related to labor-management disputes, the manufacturers of Elbeuf regularly send recommendations to the government on all matter of things. The recommendations concerned government encouragement of wool production, of most-favored nation commercial treaties, of coal mining to provide

---

[125] St. Denis, *Histoire*, VIII, 41; *Arch. Mun.*, Délib., Vol. A, (12 Pluviôse XI, 18 Pluviôse XII); Délib., Vol. B, (29 Brumaire XIII).
[126] St. Denis, *Histoire*, VIII, 42, 63–65.

industrial fuels. Measures to be taken against bankrupts were asked so as to more effectively protect creditors. A well-justified outcry against the inadequacy of road communications with the markets continued. And there was a constant demand to put a stop to the illegal importation of English goods. In 1810 an imperial decree that ordered the destruction of all English merchandise found in France, Holland, and the Hansa towns was vigorously applauded by the Elbeuvians.[127]

One demand that may, at first glance, appear curious was that which requested the re-establishment of government regulation of industry as it had existed under the old regime. But there was a good reason for this nostalgia. According to the petitioners, the abolition of regulation had wreaked havoc on production standards and had led to indiscriminate competition that would eventually destroy the woolen industry. All sorts of people, they said, were now entering the industry, although their only qualification for so doing was their money. They were said to be entirely lacking in technical knowledge and skill. What we have here is the reaction of long established manufacturers to the invasion of their prerogatives by certain new capitalist elements, and, as might be expected, it was not limited to Elbeuf alone. But it is in Elbeuf that we find the clearly formulated desire for a return to the guild system, that is, to the status of a *manufacture royale*. Before the Revolution, the government had determined the kind of cloth that could be manufactured and had controlled the woolen trade. But despite interference by the government in various matters, as seen in Chapter 2, the manufacturers had enjoyed a good deal of autonomy. It had been possible for them to discourage competition, to protect their market against interlopers, as well as from any one of their number who attempted to profit at the expense of the community as a whole. Whatever abuses had existed might easily be corrected in the projected revival of the guild. The manufacturers were not yet so attached to the idea of laissez faire that they would reject the idea of a paternalistic government acting in their interest.[128]

---

[127] St. Denis, *Histoire*, VIII, 30–32, 42–43, 83–86, 231, 235–36; *Arch. Mun.*, Délib., Vol. A (22 Ventôse IX).

[128] *Arch. Nat.*, F[12] 2412—Printed Brochure: Louis Jourdain, *Mémoires sur les Manufactures des Draps suivi d'un Projet de Règlement Relatif à Celle de Darnetal* (Rouen, 1813); *Arch. Mun.*, Series M—Report on the Manufacture by Grandin and Frontin.

On the basis of the above information, two conclusions can be drawn about the effects of the Revolution on Elbeuf. First, economically the city's industry was, while troubled, going through an important phase of reorganization that was to have the most basic of results in the future. Second, a change can be noted in the value placed on the participation of industrialists in the life of the nation—a revaluation of the industrial bourgeoisie. We might then expect that these same bourgeois would take an ever-increasing part in the political life of their constituency. It is to that question that we must now address ourselves, so as to be able to draw a third conclusion, this time concerning politics, and thus to fix another signpost on the way to answering the more general question of changes in the social structure.

CHAPTER 4

THE POLITICAL STRUCTURE OF ELBEUF

I

The social structure of Elbeuf on the eve of the Revolution has been described. The status of the several social classes vis-à-vis one another is known, and also which individuals and families occupied the highest rungs on the social ladder. But all this is only one-half of the picture. The rest of the pieces must now be fitted into the puzzle.

What was the structure of political power in Elbeuf? Was it challenged by the Revolution? Was the challenge successful? That is, did any change intervene between the beginning and end of this period? Or did the political structure remain the same? In either case, why? It is only by asking these questions, only by studying the evolution of the social structure in the political realm that a complete understanding of the history of Elbeuf can be obtained.

The political institution par excellence of Elbeuf was its municipality. How was it organized? To what extent was there a democratic participation of the majority of the population in the administration of the city's affairs?

As was the case throughout France,[1] this participation had been in decline for some time at the beginning of the eighteenth century. Where previously all taxpayers had participated in the General Assembly of the community, they now saw their power restricted,

---

[1] Henri Babeau, *Les Assemblées Générales des Communautés d'Habitants en France du XIIIe Siècle à la Révolution* (Paris, 1893), *passim* and especially pp. 49–54, 244, 253–54; Charles Parrain, "Une Vieille Tradition Démocratique: les Assemblées de Communauté," *La Pensée*, I, No. 4 (1945), pp. 43–48.

either by disenfranchisement or by restriction of their powers. The latter was true of Elbeuf. During some earlier period, all taxpayers were responsible for the financial affairs of their parish and elected a treasurer to administer the church fabric. The treasurer was also the syndic of the parish. In other words, he was the executive officer responsible for carrying through the decisions of each parish assembly. In Elbeuf a joint meeting of the two parishes, forming the General Assembly of the community, could be held for questions concerning the city as a whole.

By the beginning of the eighteenth century, certain modifications had already taken place in this regime. The treasurer-syndic was still elected in each parish by an assembly of all the taxpayers, but the General Assembly of the city had taken on an entirely different character. It was no longer made up of all the taxpayers, but only of the syndics and ex-syndics. Because the syndics were changed every year, the General Assembly, which might more correctly be called an Assembly of Notables, was made up of fifty to sixty members.[2] On May 30, 1776, the municipality wrote:

Ces syndics déliberants, pris de tous les ordres qui composaient la communauté, c'est à dire fabricants de draps et de tapisserie, chandeliers, épiciers, serruriers, boulangers, perruquiers, etc., étaient toujours de 50 à 60 lorsqu'ils s'y trouvaient tous. Et il est essentiel d'observer que, pendant plus de 60 ans, le tableau de ces syndics qu'on a conservé apprend que dans la paroisse St. Jean qui est la plus nombreuse, il n'y avait pas plus de syndics fabricants que des autres états; et que dans la paroisse St. Etienne, où se trouve un plus grand nombre de fabricants et un plus petit nombre d'autres particuliers aptes à ces sortes de places, le nombre des syndics fabricants à 2 où 3 près ne l'emportait pas sur celui des syndics des autres ordres.[3]

It should be remembered that this statement was made by a municipality dominated by manufacturers. There was no way of verifying it, since the list of syndics had disappeared from the archives. To accept this statement as true would mean that municipal affairs were controlled by members of the lower bourgeoisie as well as of the bourgeoisie properly so called. If so, the system was to change considerably even before 1789.

In the seventy-five years prior to the Revolution, this system was alternately destroyed and re-created as a result of the venality of offices. The first creation of venal offices in Elbeuf dates from

[2] St. Denis, *Histoire*, IV, 154–64.   [3] St. Denis, *Histoire*, V, 519–20.

1702, when Louis XIV sold the offices of syndics, and lasted for about five years.[4] Other venal offices were created several times in the succeeding half-century, sometimes affecting municipal offices directly, sometimes subordinate offices such as those of tax collectors, but always designed to extort money from the city.[5]

The municipal reform of 1764 abolished, first of all, the venal offices that had not as yet been redeemed by the city and ordained that elected municipal officers should take their place. The officers were to be elected by an Assembly of Notables in which local royal or seigneurial judges were always to be included. Meeting twice a year, the Assembly was also to control the financial administration of the city by verifying all receipts and expenses before sending them to the Intendant for his approval. The mayor was to be presiding officer of the Assembly, except when a question of police or of the collection of funds destined for the royal treasury was to be discussed. In that case, the presidency fell to the seigneurial judge.

The most significant provisions of this reform were those that increased royal control over municipal disbursements. Letters patent had to approve all substantial expenditures. There could be no repairs to communal property without consultation of the notables and approval, successively, of the Intendant, the Controller-General of Finances, and the king. Acquisitions and alienations of property had to be approved by letters patent if the amount involved exceeded 3,000 livres. Under that sum, only the ratification of the transaction by the nearest royal court was necessary. The same was true for the taking of loans. All such authorizations were to carefully prescribe the use to which the money was to be put, and any breach of this discipline was to be severely punished. Any obligations undertaken by the city without having undergone these formalities were to be devoid of legal force in so far as concerns the corporate entity of the city. The contractors might have recourse only against the individual signatories.[6]

The Royal Edict of May, 1765, settled the mode of election of municipal administrative bodies. In cities of over 4,500 inhabitants, there would be a mayor, four *échevins*, six city councilors,

---

[4] St. Denis, *Histoire*, IV, 196–97.

[5] *Arch. Dép.*, C 202, 211.

[6] *Edit du Roi Contenant Règlement pour l'Administration des Villes . . . du Royaume Donné à Compiegne au mois d'Août, 1764* (Paris, 1764), *passim*.

a receiver of taxes, and a secretary recordkeeper. These twelve officers were to be elected by secret ballot in an Assembly of Notables. For the mayoralty, the electors designated three candidates among whom the king or seigneur of the city, if he existed, was to make his choice. The councilors had to be chosen from those who had been notables, *échevins* from those who had been councilors. Only those who had been *échevins* were eligible to become mayor. Councilors were elected for six years, *échevins* for two years, the mayor for three. The mayor alone was ineligible for re-election until after a period equal to his term of service had elapsed.

The Assembly of Notables was to be composed of the mayor, *échevins*, councilors, and fourteen representatives of the different orders and communities of the city. Elbeuf was divided into eight classes: the clergy (one representative), the nobles and military officers (1), the judicial officers (1), the lawyers, notaries, and *bourgeois vivant noblement* (i. e., rentiers) (2), the manufacturers (3), the surgeons and merchants (2), bakers, butchers, wigmakers, and tavernkeepers (2), and *laboureurs* and artisans (2).[7] This division took place in conformity to the Déclaration du Roi of June 15, 1766, which ordered that guilds might have a representative in the Notables only if they had eighteen voting members. Otherwise, they were to be united, for election purposes, to a guild of an analogous profession.[8] The members of the Assembly were elected for fourteen years. The Assembly thus constituted was to meet twice a year to approve the reports on finances and communal affairs made by the municipal officers. The mayor and *échevins* met every two weeks, and the councilors every month. The role of the first was the expedition of current affairs, that of the second, the supervision of finances and administration between meetings of the Notables.

Given this constitution, it would seem that the municipality of 1776 was correct in stating: " Il est donc justifié que la prépondérance des fabricants dans les délibérations publiques, soit avant, soit après le règlement de 1766, est une chimère, ou que s'il en ont eu, elle a été accordée à la confiance que les autres ordres ont eu en leurs lumières, et non pas à leur nombre." [9] But the question

---

[7] Charles Petit-Dutaillis, *Les Communes Françaises, Caractères et Evolution des Origines au XVIIIᵉ Siècle* (Paris, 1947), pp. 330–31; St. Denis, *Histoire*, V, 521.
[8] *Arch. Nat.*, AD I 14—Déclaration du Roi du 15 juin 1766.
[9] St. Denis, *Histoire*, V, 521.

remains as to whether this preponderance did exist, whatever the reason for it. The reform of 1764–66 completed the removal of the wage-earning population of the city from all participation in municipal affairs. But to whose advantage? The answer is clear: to the advantage of the bourgeoisie, which now controlled at least seven offices, not counting the clergymen or the judicial officer who were likely to be of bourgeois origin.

The changes outlined above were the beginning of an evolution in a sense favorable to the bourgeoisie and especially to the manufacturers, as we shall shortly see. But this evolution was not without its ups and downs. Whereas the Edict of 1764 had ordered that no privileges be admitted as concerns precedence in the municipalities, the letters patent of February 11, 1770, instituted " rang et séance " of the clergy and nobility over all other members of municipal assemblies.[10] Much more serious was the re-establishment of venal offices under the ministry of the Abbé Terray in 1771. A total of eight offices was created in Elbeuf, and the city was asked to redeem them at the price of 19,320 livres. The price was later raised to 45,000 livres. Given the financial circumstances of the city, which were desperate (as can be gauged by the fact that the *tarif* between 1768 and 1771 had produced only 88,284 livres revenue, while the *taille* alone for the same period was 99,602 livres), it was impossible for Elbeuf to pay the price demanded. For a short time the elected municipal officers continued to exercise their mandates. Then, a certain Dubusc, a miller's apprentice, bought the office of receiver of the municipal revenues. The municipality considered him unworthy of this high dignity and attempted to buy this single office to prevent him from getting hold of it. But its bid was refused, and the officers were told that they would have to buy all nine offices (one more had been added to the original creation), those of a mayor, lieutenant-mayor, two *échevins*, two assistant *échevins*, one *procureur du roi*, one recordkeeper, and one receiver, or none at all.[11] Still they did not buy. Fnally, this obstinacy bore fruit, but not in the way the elected officers wished. On January 3, 1773, the king appointed a mayor, two *échevins*, and a recordkeeper to hold office for an unspecified period of time.[12] And on June 14, 1774, the bargain

[10] *Arch. Mun.*, AA.
[11] St. Denis, *Histoire*, V, 428, 441–43.
[12] *Arch. Mun.*, BB[1].

between the miller's apprentice, Louis Georges Dubusc, and the government was sealed by the delivery of receipts to the value of 2,400 livres for the office of *trésorier receveur et contrôleur vérificateur*. This, it appears, was the signal of alarm for the city. The appointment of the mayor and other officers in 1773 had not disturbed the reigning calm, and there was no reason why it should have, as at least three of the four individuals appointed were manufacturers. This is to say, the power structure was in no way altered by this action of the royal government. The case of Dubusc was, however, different. By selling him the office of tax collector, the government introduced a foreign element into the fiscal system of Elbeuf. Its action seemed to indicate that it was no longer going to tolerate resistance to its will by the urban bourgeoisie. The latter was now forced to act to protect its interests.

No sooner did Dubusc enter into possession of his offices than the elected representatives of the city decided to bid for all of the venal offices. They offered 10,000 livres, half in cash and half in receipts issued at the time of the previous acquisition of venal offices in 1752. In September, 1774, the bargain was struck for 6,000 livres in cash. The problem remained as to what to do with Dubusc. A dispute between him and the municipality ensued, which was finally settled at the beginning of 1775 by the payment to Dubusc of 2,839 livres and 10 sols, 2,400 livres of which sum being deducted from the 6,000 due to the royal government.[13] On February 9, 1775, the *homme vivant et mourant* appointed by the municipality, André Gancel, was granted a receipt for the offices, and the last experiment in the creation of venal offices in Elbeuf during the old regime came to an end.[14]

The way was now open for the creation of a municipal organization for Elbeuf. On November 1, 1776, a plan of administration for the city of Elbeuf was ratified by the Conseil d'Etat and was put into effect. The new municipality was composed of a mayor, four *échevins*, a *procureur-syndic* whose duty it was to defend the community's interests and also to act as public prosecutor, a receiver of the city's revenues, and a recordkeeper . The last three persons had no vote in the deliberations. An assembly of ten notables, of whom the *bailli* was always to be the first, was also established. The notables, the municipal officers, and the former

[13] *Arch. Dép.*, C 202.   [14] *Arch. Mun.*, BB².

mayors made up the General Council of the city, which now assumed the role of the assembly of the inhabitants. The General Council now elected the city administration by a system of co-optation. Thus, the evolution begun in 1764, whose direction was toward the restriction of participation in municipal affairs to a minority of bourgeois, was continued by the plan of 1776.

The mayor was now to be elected by the General Council for three years, the *échevins* for two, the notables for five. But the mayor was not chosen directly. A list of three nominees was submitted to the Prince de Lambesc, the seigneur of Elbeuf, who was then to choose one among them.[15] The receiver, recordkeeper, and *procureur-syndic* were chosen for six years. Their terms of office were indefinitely renewable, while the mayor, *échevins*, and notables had to consent to a second term but could not be obliged to serve more than once. The mayor was chosen from among present or former *échevins*, the *échevins* from among present or former notables, and the notables themselves from among " les principaux habitants de la commune." The mayor and *échevins* were exempt from standing guard and from the boarding of troops during their terms of office.

The General Council, which had the power to make all significant decisions, was convoked by the *procureur-syndic* on the order of the mayor as often as necessary. In order to be operative, all decisions had to be countersigned by eight officers having the right to vote. The powers of the bureau (the mayor and *échevins*) were strictly limited. It could authorize expenses amounting only to 200 livres; anything above this amount had to be authorized by the General Council and approved by the Intendant. The same was true for suits at law and delegations on behalf of the city. The General Council had sole control over the accounts of the receiver of the revenues, but once again the Intendant had to give his approval.[16]

Two principal features stand out in the legislation of 1776: first, the increased control by a small section of the community over municipal affairs and second, increased supervision by the

---

[15] *Arch. Mun.*, AA. On October 7, 1775, de Rohan, Comte de Brionny and father of Lambesc, wrote to the municipal officers: " J'étais bien sûr de la solidité du titre de mon fils: c'est un avantage pour vous autant que c'est une convenance pour luy."

[16] *Arch. Mun.*, AA.

royal authority. It would seem that the bourgeois of Elbeuf were ready to accept the second term of the pair in return for the first, for the organization adopted differed in no significant way from the one they had suggested.

Table 4–1 shows that forty-six persons held municipal office under this regime. Among them were the *bailli* of Elbeuf, as provided for in the legislation, three priests, one tax farmer, one rentier, one doctor, one apothecary, one tool grinder, three merchants, three dyers, and thirty-one manufacturers. The *échevins* numbered twenty-five, of whom one was a rentier, one a tax farmer, two dyers, two merchants, and nineteen manufacturers. All the mayors were manufacturers. Moreover, of twenty persons who were promoted from the notables to the rank of *échevin*, sixteen were manufacturers, while only two were dyers, one a tax farmer, and one a merchant.

To what was this preponderance of the manufacturers among their bourgeois colleagues due? Certainly not to any formal prescription of the law, but rather to the economic and social power of this group in Elbeuf. Here we must remember a capital fact of eighteenth-century political psychology, a fact which has been demonstrated by numerous historians of the period, in particular as concerns the history of the United States.[17] Voting for one's social superiors was a well-entrenched habit for a variety of reasons, the least of which was the fear of economic reprisals. Society and its culture were, very simply, hierarchical in every aspect. From the cradle each man was taught to observe the respect due to those who stood above him on the social ladder. His education, his worship, his way of getting a living depended intimately on this prescriptive justification. It was the extraordinary man who would dare to challenge it. Even the Revolution did not succeed in destroying it entirely.

In Elbeuf it was not even necessary that these general considerations should come into play, for the law had taken care to exclude the quasi-totality of the population from any part in the electoral process. As there was no noble population of consequence in the city, only the *bailli* as representative of the Prince de Lambesc and the clergy were capable of challenging the predominance of

[17] Charles S. Sydnor, *Gentlemen Freeholders of Virginia* (Chapel Hill, 1954), *passim*.

TABLE 4–1

Municipal Officers in Elbeuf, 1776–89

Name	Profession	Notable	*Echevin*	Mayor
Beranger, Jacques	Manufacturer	e. 1780	1781–82	
Blin,	*Bailli*	Perpetual		
Bourdon, Robert	Manufacturer	1786		
Capplet, Charles	Dyer	1776–81	1786–88	
Delacroix, Jacques	Manufacturer		1777–79	1784
Delarue, Benoist	Manufacturer		1780–82	1785–87
Delarue, Bernard	Manufacturer	e. 1779	1782–84	1787–89
Delarue, Louis	Manufacturer	1779	1779–81	
Delarue, Nicolas	Manufacturer	1779		
Delarue, Henry	Manufacturer	1783–88		
Delarue, J.-B.	Manufacturer	1782–87		
Duhamel	Priest	1776–81		
Duparc	Doctor	1779–84		
Dupont, François	Rentier		1777–79	
Dupont, Jacques	Merchant		1785–87	
Duruflé l'aîné, Joseph	Manufacturer	1784–89		
Duruflé, Pierre Joseph	Manufacturer	1786		
Flavigny, Louis Robert	Manufacturer	1779	1779–83	
Flavigny, Bernard	Manufacturer		1778–80	
Flavigny, Louis	Manufacturer	1781–86	1787	
Flavigny, l'Abbé	Priest	1786		
Frontin, Mathieu	Manufacturer	1787–88	1788	
Grandin, Auguste	Manufacturer	e. 1779	1781–83	
Grandin, Louis Robert	Manufacturer	ex. 1779		
Grandin, Michel	Manufacturer			1781–84
Grandin, Parfait	Manufacturer	e. 1779	1780–82	
Grandin, J.-B.	Manufacturer	1782–83	1783–85	
Gamarre, Louis	Apothecary	1784		
Godet, Constant	Manufacturer	1782	1783–85	
Guenet, Gabriel	Dyer	1788		
Huault	Tax farmer of the duchy	1777–82	1782–84	
Join-Lambert	Dyer	1781–86	1788	
Leclerc, J.-B.	Manufacturer	e. 1780	1782–83	
Letellier, Nicolas	Tool grinder	1776–81		
Lefebvre, Jacques Nicolas	Manufacturer			ex-mayor in 1779
Lefebvre, Jean Michel	Manufacturer	1781–86	1786	
Lejeune, Pierre	Manufacturer	1783–84	1784–86	
Leroy, Constant	Manufacturer	1788		
Osmont, L'Abbé	Priest	1781–86		
Patallier, Laurent	Plaster merchant	1781–84	1784–86	
Patallier, Nicolas	Merchant	1786		
Quesné, Jacques	Manufacturer		1778–80	
Quesné, Mathieu	Manufacturer			1778–81
Quesné, Louis Robert	Manufacturer		1786	
Sevaistre, Mathieu	Manufacturer	1785		
Sevaistre, Louis	Manufacturer	1784–85	1785	

Note: Where inclusive dates are not available, I have given either the date of election (e.), or the date of the term's expiration (ex.), or where no other alternative is available, the date at which the person was found to be in possession of the office.

Sources: *Arch. Mun.*, BB³, BB⁴, HH, and Déliberations, I.

the manufacturers. It appears that the seigneur had no interest in so doing, for he chose a manufacturer as mayor every time. And the clergy was of bourgeois origin. The hegemony of the manufacturers in the administration of the city reflects the consensus that existed in a city where the bourgeoisie was secure and did not have to face the challenge of other social classes in the community.

Elbeuf was governed in this manner until August 13, 1789. On that date, three *échevins*, six notables, two ex-mayors, two ex-*échevins*, and three non-members of the municipality formed themselves into a permanent committee of the Hôtel de Ville to administer the city, under the presidency of the mayor. In this group of sixteen persons there were twelve manufacturers, one merchant, one dyer, one apothecary, and one baker or grain merchant.[18] They decided to meet every morning from 10 to 12 and every evening from 5 to 7. A state of revolutionary euphoria decreed this action, which was in no way due to the inability of the legally constituted municipality to do its job, as is proved by the participation of certain of its members in the new organization. What is much more likely is that these individuals considered it appropriate to break with the legality of the old regime, more because of the symbolic value of the break than for any other reason. On November 15, 1789, in the last elections to take place before the passage of the law on the formation of municipalities of December 14, an assembly of " taxpayers " chose, in conformity to article five of the Royal Proclamation of October 14, 1789, and to articles ten and eleven of that of October 16, three assistants (*adjoints*): a notary, a merchant, and a tavernkeeper.[19]

The law on the municipalities of December 14, 1789, formed the framework of municipal action until the creation of the Constitution of the year III.[20] It created a General Council of the commune divided into two parts: municipal officers and notables. Both were elected by primary assemblies of the active citizens. Members of the Council were chosen from citizens who paid at

---

[18] *Arch. Mun.*, Délib., Vol. I (August 13, 1789). The question as to whether the last named person, a certain Vedic, was a baker or grain merchant cannot be settled, because his first name is not mentioned in the municipal records.

[19] *Arch. Mun.*, BB[9].

[20] Jacques Godechot, *Les Institutions de la France sous la Révolution et l'Empire* (Paris, 1951), pp. 105–6.

least ten days wages in taxes. They were elected for two years, and one-half of the number was to be replaced each year. The *procureur de la commune* was elected in the same manner. He acted at once as the representative of the central government and of the taxpayers of the commune. His function was the same as that of the *procureur fiscal* of the old regime. The General Council as a whole was responsible for making all important administrative decisions, such as those regarding the acquisition or alienation of landed property, the levying of extraordinary taxes, local expenditures, the taking of loans, and the authorization of public works. Lesser affairs of an everyday nature were in the hands of the municipal officers. These included the administration of public property, the budget, execution of public works, repair and supervision of roads, and the division and collection of direct taxes. The municipality had the right to call on the army or the National Guard to enforce its decisions. Such supervision of the elected officials as was exercised by the citizens was done through the medium of the primary assemblies, which could be convoked by the General Council only. This body could not, however, refuse to convoke the primary assemblies in a city of more than 4,000 inhabitants, if the convocation were demanded by one-sixth of the active citizens.

In the six years that followed, this system was modified several times, but the basic framework was not changed. Immediately following the fall of the monarchy on August 10, 1792, the Legislative Assembly assigned to the municipalities " la police de sûreté générale pour la recherche des crimes concernant la sûreté extérieure et intérieure de l'état." On March 21, 1793, the Convention accorded them the right to deliver *certificats de civisme* and the law of March 26 imposed upon them the duty of disarming *ci-devant* nobles, priests, and suspects. The municipalities continued in possession of these powers, often exercised jointly with the *Société Populaire* and the *Comité de Surveillance* (the first formed in Elbeuf on 30 Brumaire II [21] and the second created by the law of March 21, 1793),[22] until after Thermidor.

At the beginning, then, the municipal system of government of the Revolution differed little from that of the old regime. In short, it was not revolutionary. We find in it all the traditional

---

[21] *Arch. Dép.*, L 5620.   [22] Godechot, *Institutions*, pp. 288–93.

features of the older legislation: a municipal body divided into two parts, their powers carefully differentiated one from the other. In fact, the powers were the same as those listed in the law of 1776. It was only with the establishment of the Revolutionary government in the year II that the system was significantly changed.

It is true that the law of 1789 was still based on a *cens*, a tax qualification. It was exclusive in conception. In the small parishes that had no municipalities before the Revolution, it even acted in an anti-democratic sense by restraining participation in the primary assemblies. Not so in Elbeuf, and this was what was most significant about it. This legislation replaced a system of co-optation with primary assemblies of electors.

In Elbeuf there were 1,095 active citizens in a population of 6,570 in 1790 and 1791.[23] There was no change in this number from the first year to the next, because the municipality voted on November 11, 1791, to maintain the list of active citizens drawn up in 1790, without taking into consideration the tax roles for 1791, which were not as yet completed.[24] It should be asked to what extent this system did exclude the poorest section of Elbeuf's population from participation in local affairs. If the coefficient four is adopted (which, although not entirely arbitrary, is still questionable) as constituting the size of the average family, we find that there were 1,642 heads of families. When we consider that the voting age was twenty-five, not twenty-one, a fact that affected all categories of the population in the same way, it becomes evident that the exclusiveness of this legislation has been somewhat exaggerated. Certainly, a majority was not excluded, but perhaps one-third of the population, its poorest elements, were without the right to vote. This view is confirmed by the appeal of the General Council of the city to the District of Rouen on December 29, 1791, asking that the value of the working day as a tax base be reduced to 18 sols " pour la raison que la classe des citoyens [qui] n'ont que les facultés étroites qui donnent la qualité de citoyen actif en seront soulagés." [25]

The changes that took place in municipal administration in the year II were not, at least in theory, necessarily anti-democratic, although their tendency was toward centralization. The law of

---

[23] *Arch. Nat.*, F¹ᶜ III Seine-Inférieure 1; Dⁱᵛ *bis* 38; Dⁱᵛ *bis* 52.
[24] *Arch. Mun.*, Délib., Vol. II (November 11, 1791).
[25] *Arch. Mun.*, Délib., Vol. II (December 29, 1791).

14 Frimaire II, one of those which organized the Revolutionary government, suppressed the *procureurs des communes* and replaced them with *agents nationaux* appointed by, and directly dependent on, the government.[26] Elections were also suppressed by the law of November 13, 1793, which gave the Société Populaire the responsibility for naming citizens to fill public functions, the nominations to be ratified by the representatives on mission. Examples of this occur at least twice in Elbeuf in the course of the year II. It appears, moreover, that the representative, Siblot, was confident of the loyalty of the Société of Elbeuf, for he declared himself ready to ratify any nominations it might make.[27]

Elections were in the hands of the primary assemblies from 1790 until January, 1793. The interesting thing is that by the time their electoral functions were suppressed, a general apathy had settled upon the city, and it can hardly be said that the primary assemblies were fulfilling their purpose. After the first revolutionary *élan* had passed, very few people took part in the voting, although the law in no way stopped them from doing so. Thus, in February, 1790, there were 633 voters in the mayoralty election, but by December, 1792, the number of participants had dropped as low as 48 on one of the several ballots required. And as few as 20 persons bothered to vote on one of the ballots in the election of notables of January, 1793, although on another, 216 took part.[28]

What groups and classes in the community rose to power in the revolutionary municipalities? To answer this question, it is best to consider the elections year by year. The elections of 1789–90 were, indeed, revolutionary in their results. Although the manufacturers were still the largest single group represented in the municipality, they no longer held the majority. There were now eight manufacturers, six merchants, two lawyers, and a priest, or a total of fifteen persons from the upper and middle bourgeoisie. The lower bourgeoisie was represented by six master carders, two chandlers, two old clothes dealers, and one representative each of the tavernkeepers, innkeepers, locksmiths, tool grinders, apothecaries, sizers, shoemakers, plaster merchants, writers and clerks, a

[26] Godechot, *Institutions*, p. 289.
[27] Godechot, *Institutions*, p. 300; *Arch. Dép.*, L 5618—17 Floréal II; L 5621—17 and 19 Prairial II.
[28] *Arch. Mun.*, Délib., Vol. I (February 6 and 12, 1790); Vol. II (November 15, 1790, and November 13, 1791); *Arch. Dép.*, L 6396 (November 14, 1790, November 13, 1791, and February 17, 1793).

TABLE 4–2

MUNICIPAL OFFICERS IN ELBEUF, 1790–93

Name	Profession	Notable	Municipal officer	Mayor
Lingois, Pierre	Notary			1790–91
Rousselin, Robert	Merchant		1790–91	
Tienterre, J.-B.	Merchant		1790–91	
Viard, Georges	Carder		1790	
Fouard père, Michel	Candlemaker		1790 (re-elected 1790)	
Galleran, Pierre	Manufacturer		1790	1791
Duruflé, l'aîné, Marin Joseph	Manufacturer		1790 (re-elected 1790)	
Balleroy, Francis	Lawyer	1791 (re-elected 1793)	1790	
Asse, Pierre Victorin	Lawyer		1790 (*procureur*)	
Leroy, Constant	Manufacturer		1790–91	
Dumoutier, George	Woolshearer	1790 (re-elected 1790 and 1793)		
Cherel, Nicolas	Carder	1790 (re-elected 1793)		
Leveneur, Robert	Tavernkeeper		1790 (replaced in Nov.)	
Leroy, Placide	Carder	1790		
Lefebvre	Sizer	(replaced in 1790)		
Touzé, Simon	Carder	1790		
Lebailly, Jean Pierre	Tool grinder	1790–91		
Patallier, Laurent	Plaster merchant	1790		
Bouic père, Alexandre	Merchant	1790		
Hayet, Pierre Martin	Writer/Rentier	1790 (re-elected 1793)	1791	
Lenoble, Amable	Locksmith	(replaced in 1790) (re-elected 1791 and 1793)		
Cavé, J.-L.	Candlemaker	1790		
Séjourné, Denis	Old clothes dealer	1790	1791	
Lefebvre, François	Merchant	1790–91		
Eloy, Simon	Foreman	1790–91		
Folie, Robert	Manufacturer	1790–91		
Duhamel	Priest	1790–91		
Gueroult, Philippe	Shoemaker	1790–91		
Hayet, Pierre Henry	Manufacturer		1790	
Lejeune père, Pierre	Manufacturer		1790	

TABLE 4–2 (Continued)

MUNICIPAL OFFICERS IN ELBEUF, 1790–93

Name	Profession	Notable	Municipal officer	Mayor
Osmont, Nicolas	Innkeeper	1790	1793	
Fosse, Jean-Pierre	Ex-recordkeeper at court	1790 (re-elected 1793)		
Fosse, Jean-Louis	Carder	1790 (re-elected 1793)		
Lefebvre, Nicolas Felix	Manufacturer	1790		
Fromont, Pierre	Merchant	1790		
Quenot	Old clothes dealer	1790		
Cambocal	Merchant	1790		
Gamarre, Louis	Apothecary	1790		
Delatre, Bonaventure	Locksmith		1791	
Delauné, Louis	Manufacturer		1791	
Grandin, Jacques Pierre	Manufacturer		1790 (*procureur*) (re-elected 1791)	
Fontaine, Pierre François	Usher at court	1791	1793	
Morin, Pierre	Grocer	1791 (re-elected 1793)	1793	
Duchemin, Andre	Joiner	1791 (re-elected 1793)		
Moquet, Charles	Stocking manufacturer	1791		
Passot, Pierre	Grocer	1791		
Mercier	Wheelwright	1791		
Devé	Saddle maker	(replaced in 1791)		
Mouton père	Tailor	1791 (re-elected 1793)		
Saillant, Nicolas	Perfumer			1792
Degenetes, Gabriel	Merchant		1793	
Murizon, Désiré	Manufacturer		1793 (*procureur*, and later *agent national*)	
Beranger fils, Louis	Manufacturer		1793	
Lebourgeois, L'Abbé	Priest	1793		
Lenoble	Priest	1793		
Miège, l'aîné	Stocking manufacturer	1793		
Dubuc, Noel	Thresher and forest guard	1793		
Bailly	Burler	1793		
Osmont, Nicolas	Glazier	1793		
Langlois père	Merchant	1793		

TABLE 4–2 (Continued)

MUNICIPAL OFFICERS IN ELBEUF, 1790–93

Name	Profession	Notable	Municipal officer	Mayor
Fouard, Constant	Tailor	1793		
Join-Lambert	Dyer	1793		
Jamoy, Jean-Dominique	Merchant	1793		
Heullant, Robert	Manufacturer	1793		
Fecomme	Tailor	1793		
Louvet père, Nicolas	Merchant	1793		
Gancel	Carder	1793		
Petitgrand, Benoist	Carder	1793		
Joli, Pierre Laurent Etienne	?	1793		
Chefdrue, Benjamin	Manufacturer	1793		
Delaleau fils	Manufacturer	1793		
Duval	Grocer	1793		
Grandin, Pierre Michel	Manufacturer	1793		
Delarue, François	Manufacturer	1793		

Sources: *Arch. Mun.*, Délib., Vol. I (February 6, 17, and 19, 1790); Délib., Vol. II, (November 15, 1790, and November 13, 1791); Délib., Vol. III, (9 Nivôse II); *Arch. Dép.*, L 6396 (November 14, 1790, November 13, 1791, and February 17, 1793.)

TABLE 4–3

MUNICIPAL OFFICERS NAMED BY THE SOCIÉTÉ POPULAIRE AND SIBLOT, REPRESENTATIVE OF THE PEOPLE, IN PRAIRIAL II

Name	Profession	Rank
Adam, Jean Pierre Alexandre	Manufacturer	Notable
Duruflé, Marin Joseph Mathieu	Manufacturer	Municipal officer
Flavigny, Ambroise	Manufacturer	Notable
Frémont, Modeste	Dyer	Notable
Girard, Ambroise	Private secretary	Notable
Hayet, Pierre Henry	Manufacturer	Municipal officer
Lebailly, Jean Pierre Norbert	Tool grinder	Notable
Maille le jeune, Pierre Jean Louis	Manufacturer	Notable
Menage, David Constant	Manufacturer	Notable
Sevaistre, Louis Jean Baptiste	Manufacturer	Notable

Source: *Arch. Mun.*, Délib., Vol. IV (17 and 19 Prairial II).

TABLE 4–4

MUNICIPAL OFFICERS NAMED BY CASENAVE, REPRESENTATIVE OF
THE PEOPLE IN FLOREAL, MESSIDOR, AND THERMIDOR III

Name	Profession	Rank
Saillant, Nicolas	Perfumer	Mayor
Duval, Pierre	Grocer	Municipal officer
Quesné fils, Jacques	Manufacturer	Municipal officer
Petitgrand, J.-B.	Manufacturer	Municipal officer
Boivin, Augustin	Merchant	Municipal officer
Lecalier, Jacques	Manufacturer	Municipal officer
Hayet, Pierre Martin	Writer/rentier	Municipal officer
Hayet, Pierre Henry	Manufacturer	Municipal officer
Duruflé, Marin Joseph Mathieu	Manufacturer	*Procureur*
Frémont, Modeste	Dyer	Notable
Maille le jeune, Pierre	Manufacturer	Notable
Lebailly, Jean Pierre	Tool grinder	Notable
Osmont, Nicolas	Glazier	Notable
Jamoy, Jean Dominique	Merchant	Notable
Fouard, Nicolas Constant	Tailor	Notable
Flavigny, Ambroise	Manufacturer	Notable
Join-Lambert, Bernard	Dyer	Notable
Sevaistre, Louis	Manufacturer	Notable
Girard, Ambroise	Private secretary	Notable
Cherel l'âiné, Jean	Carder	Notable
Flavigny, Joseph	Manufacturer	Notable
Vinet fils âiné, Nicolas	Milliner	Notable
Quesné fils, Mathieu	Manufacturer	Notable
Letellier fils,	Tool grinder	Notable
Leroy-Mettais, Denis	Merchant	Notable
Lecardé, Etienne	Carder	Notable
Adam, Pierre Thomas	Merchant	Municipal officer
Louvet, Nicolas	Grocer	Municipal officer
Cavé fils, J.-B.	Manufacturer	Notable
Patallier, Pierre	Manufacturer	Notable
Langlois	Merchant	Notable
Lejeune fils, Pierre	Manufacturer	Notable (refused)
Corblin, Amable	Grain merchant	Notable
Tassel, Alexandre	Merchant	Notable

Sources: *Arch. Mun.*, Délib., Vol. IV (3 Floréal, 28 Messidor, 10 and 12
Thermidor III).

TABLE 4–5

MUNICIPAL OFFICERS IN ELBEUF, YEAR III–1814

Name	Profession	Dates of Election
Adam, Jean Pierre Alexandre	Manufacturer	IV, IX, XII
Bance, J.-B. Alexandre	?	IX
Boivin, Auguste	Manufacturer	IV, IX
Bourdon, Nicolas	Manufacturer	IV
Bourdon, Pierre Constant	Manufacturer	IX
Bourdon, Pierre Mathieu	Manufacturer	1812, 1814
Bourdon, Pierre Nicolas	Manufacturer	IX, XII, 1812, 1814
Bourdon, Robert	Manufacturer	1808
Capplet, Charles	Dyer	IX
Chefdru, Ambroise	Manufacturer	V (by decree)
Chefdru, Benjamin	Manufacturer	VI (by decree)
Corblin, Amable	Manufacturer	XII, 1812, 1814
Delacroix, Henry	Manufacturer	XII, 1812, 1814
Delacroix, Jacques Pierre	Manufacturer	V, IX
Delacroix, Joseph	Manufacturer	IV
Delarue, David	Manufacturer	IV, VI
Delarue, François	Manufacturer	VII
Delarue fils, Henry	Manufacturer	IV, VI (by decree) VII
Delarue, Prosper	Manufacturer	V, IX (*adjoint*) X (Mayor)
Delaunay, Amable	Manufacturer	XII, 1812, 1814
Desgenetes, Gabriel	Merchant	VI (by decree)
Devé, Augustin	Saddle maker	XII, 1812, 1814
Durand, Prosper	Landowner	IX
Duruflé, Constant	Manufacturer	1807
Duruflé, Marin	Landowner	1808
Flavigny, Ambroise	Manufacturer	IV
Flavigny fils, Louis Robert	Manufacturer	IX, X (*adjoint*), XII 1813
Flavigny père, Robert	Manufacturer	IV
Flavigny-Gosset le jeune,	Manufacturer	IV (by decree), V
Frémont, Modeste	Dyer	IX
Frontin, Mathieu	Manufacturer	VII (Mayor), XII, 1812, 1814
Galleran, Pierre	Manufacturer	IX
Gautier, Antoine	Surgeon	IX
Glin, Jean-Baptiste	Manufacturer	1807, 1812, 1814
Godet fils, Constant	Manufacturer	1808
Godet, Joseph	Manufacturer	IX
Grandin, Alexandre	Manufacturer	IV (by decree), V, IX
Grandin, Jean-Baptiste	Manufacturer	XII
Grandin, Jean Pierre Baptiste	Manufacturer	IX
Grandin, Parfait	Manufacturer	IX
Grandin, Louis Jacques	Manufacturer	1807, 1812, 1814
Hayet, Pierre Henry	Manufacturer	IV (*Commissaire du pouvoir executif*), IX, XII, Mayor in 1808 and 1813
Henry	Manufacturer and doctor	IX, 1807
Huaut, Servant	Rentier	IX, XII

TABLE 4–5 (Continued)

MUNICIPAL OFFICERS IN ELBEUF, YEAR III–1814

Name	Profession	Dates of Election
Join-Lambert l'aîné, Bernard	Dyer	VI (by decree), IX, 1812, 1814
Lebailly, Jean Pierre	Tool grinder	IX
Lefebvre, Félix	Manufacturer	IV, and *adjoint* in X, 1808, 1812, 1814
Lefort, Jean Pierre	Manufacturer	VII, IX, 1808
Lejeune père, Pierre	Manufacturer	IX
Lejeune fils, Pierre	Manufacturer	IV
Lemercier, Louis	Wood merchant	VI
Leroy-Metais, Denis	Merchant	1808
Lingois, Pierre	Notary	IX
Louvet, Charles	Manufacturer	IV
Louvet fils, Nicolas	Manufacturer	IX, XII
Maille, Parfait	Manufacturer	XII, *adjoint* in 1808 and 1813
Menage, David	Manufacturer	1807
Murizon, Denis	Manufacturer	VI (by decree)
Patallier, Laurent	Plaster merchant	VI (by decree), IX 1812, 1814
Patallier, Pierre	Manufacturer	IX
Peton, Georges Paul	Manufacturer	1812, 1814
Quesné père, Mathieu	Manufacturer	IX
Quesné fils, Mathieu	Manufacturer	IV, VII (*adjoint*)
Saillant, Nicolas	Merchant	VI
Sevaistre, Louis	Manufacturer	IX
Sevaistre père, Mathieu	Manufacturer	IX
Sevaistre fils, Mathieu	Manufacturer	1812, 1814
Tienterre, Jean-Baptiste	Manufacturer	VI, VII
Valdampierre, Robert A. Follet	Notary	IX
Vitcoq, Thomas	Manufacturer	1807, 1812, 1814
Voranger, Charles	Maker of cards	VI

Sources: *Arch. Mun.*, Délib., Vol. V (10–13, 19, and 21 Brumaire, 4 Frimaire, 9, 21, 27, and 28 Messidor, 4 Thermidor IV; 26 Ventôse, 21 Germinal, and 22 Fructidor V); Délib., Vol. VI (22 Vendémiaire, 17, 23, and 28 Nivôse, 6 Germinal, 1, 2, and 6 Floréal VI); Délib., Vol. VII (27 Ventôse and 5 Germinal VII); Délib., Vol. VIII (29 Thermidor XII, November 22, 1807, January 26, 1809, March 14, 1815); Délib., Vol. A (25 Vendémiaire, 1 Nivôse IX, 15 Germinal X); Délib., Vol. B, May 26, 1813; *Arch. Nat.*, F[1b] II Seine-Inférieure 13; *Arch. Dép.*, L 211–1 Messidor and 7 Germinal VI; L 214-Germinal VII; L 231–22 Prairial V.

total of twenty persons. A foreman and a woolshearer represented the wage earners. The notary who was elected mayor was a member of the middle bourgeoisie. Only three of the manufacturers, one merchant, the apothecary, and the priest had been members of the pre-revolutionary municipalities. Two of the newly elected manufacturers were members of families that had been represented on the council before the Revolution.

The meaning of these statistics is clear. Although the power and prestige of the upper and middle bourgeoisie were not destroyed, both were gravely damaged. The initiative had passed into the hands of the lower bourgeoisie, newly enfranchised by the Revolution. The wage earners, some of whom still did not have the vote, remained excluded from a share in the administration. We do not have nominal voting records, but if we did, it would not surprise us to find that those wage earners who did vote placed their confidence in the lower bourgeois.

The elections of November, 1791, confirmed this trend. Those elected were three manufacturers (including the mayor), a lawyer, two wholesale grocers, two locksmiths, and one each of stocking manufacturers, joiners, saddle makers, wheelwrights, tailors, and old clothes dealers, along with a court usher. Two manufacturers, one locksmith, the lawyer, and the old clothes dealer were re-elected from the municipality of 1790. No one who had served or members of whose family had served in a pre-revolutionary municipality was re-elected. To the revolutionary movement that was progressively putting the municipality into the hands of the lower bourgeois *artisanat* was added another phenomenon: a complete break with individuals who had controlled the municipality under the old regime.

Some nuances were brought into this picture by the elections of December, 1792–January, 1793. Following is a list by profession of the members of the municipality chosen at that time: seven manufacturers, four merchants, two priests, one lawyer, one dyer, two wholesale grocers, four carders, three tailors, two court employees, and one each of joiners, locksmiths, innkeepers, writers, stocking manufacturers, glaziers, cloth threshers, woolshearers, and woolsorters. I have been unable to identify one of the persons elected. Of the above, the following were re-elected after having served in the municipalities of 1790 or 1791: two carders, two court employees, and one each of grocers, tailors, joiners, lawyers, locksmiths, innkeepers, writers, stocking manufacturers, and woolshearers. Three of the manufacturers belonged to families whose members had played a part in the municipal affairs before the Revolution.

The curious thing about these elections is the number of people who, once elected, refused to serve. For this reason, it took almost two months (December 23, 1792–February 17, 1793) and the arrival of two district commissioners, Caudron and de l'Épine, from Rouen to complete the elections. It was particularly the persons chosen to be municipal officers who refused to serve. Among them were twelve manufacturers, three merchants, two grocers, and one each of threshers, glaziers, master carders, court ushers, stocking manufacturers, innkeepers, plaster merchants, tool grinders, tanners, writers, dyers, and cloth winders. Two persons are unidentifiable. Of those who refused, three manufacturers, the dyer, and the plaster merchant had served personally in the municipalities of the old regime. Four other manufacturers belonged to families which had been represented in these same municipalities. Two manufacturers, two merchants, the court usher, tool grinder, and writer had served in the revolutionary administrations. Finally, one manufacturer was the son of a merchant who had served in the municipality of 1790.

The community, or rather the small part of it that bothered to vote, showed by its electoral action that the manufacturers and other upper bourgeois, including some of those who had been municipal officers under the old regime, had regained a certain amount of their prestige, the loss of which had been consummated by the elections of November, 1791. What brought about this change?

It is necessary to recall the nature of the conflict that divided Elbeuf in the early years of the Revolution. We can identify the protagonists with social classes, but the conflict itself was not yet class conflict in a total sense. Rather, it was limited to the political sphere. At this time, all the classes that made up the third estate were united against a common enemy: the nobility and the monarchy. If the upper bourgeoisie was increasingly class conscious, the same was not true of the classes below it in social structure. The lower bourgeoisie (if any psychological attitudes can be attributed to it) probably thought in terms of rising to the status of the upper and middle bourgeoisie.

The wage earners were not yet clearly differentiated from the lower bourgeoisie. Not yet proletarian, this class was incapable of developing the consciousness of its situation that alone would have made it an effective political force. It could not have acted on its own, independently of the lower bourgeoisie, even if more of its members than actually did had been able to participate in elections.

There were certainly occasions on which economic conflict came out into the open. Wage earners might call for higher pay, lower bourgeois might rail against the increasing control of industrial processes by the upper bourgeois. But class conflict expressed itself mainly through political channels; and here the main adversary of the upper bourgeoisie was the political class of *sans-culottes*.

The charge most frequently leveled at the upper bourgeois was that they had been associated with the old regime. The first revolutionary *élan* and the possibility that the active citizens now had of exercising some amount of power resulted, therefore, in a setback for the upper bourgeoisie. But as the Revolution advanced, consolidated its victories, proclaimed the Republic, and as the upper bourgeoisie did its best to show its loyalty to the Revolution, distrust began to disappear. It was possible for the upper bourgeois to regain the confidence of the inhabitants, in whom the habit of deferring to one's " betters " was strongly rooted. Even then, few persons directly associated with the old regime came back into prominence.

Why should so many people have refused to serve in 1792–93? Two answers are possible. First, these were the first elections to take place after the fall of the monarchy. Refusal of a place in the municipality may have been a way of refusing to co-operate with a government of which one did not approve. But there was another reason, and it was probably more decisive. Elbeuf was at this time in the throes of a food crisis, the responsibility for which would obviously have to be assumed by the city administrators. The extent of the crisis and the difficulties to which it subjected the city were hardly calculated to make these posts attractive to anyone, especially to persons who had their own business affairs to attend to. The *commissaire du directoire exécutif* for the Department of the Seine-Inférieure, F. N. Augustin, wrote to the Minister of the Interior on 16 Nivôse IV:

. . . C'est le défaut de subsistances dans ce département qu'éloigne [sic] et décourage tous les administrateurs. Un agent national est sans cesse exposé au milieu d'une commune dont le peuple meurt de faim, c'est à lui qu'il s'adresse pour avoir du pain et son désespoir, lorsqu'il en manque, s'en prend au fonctionnaire qui ne peut cependant lui en procurer s'il n'y en a pas.

He added that unless something were done, " ce département sera dans une famine complète." [29]

In the case of refusals, the government often decided to force men to fill municipal offices. This was the case in the " elections " of the years II and III. In the first instance, nominations were made by the Société Populaire and ratified by Siblot, the repretative of the people. And here the manufacturers came back in full force. Seven of them were named, along with one dyer, one tool grinder, and one private secretary. All but the last two were members of the upper bourgeoisie. Three of the manufacturers were related to men who had been municipal officers before the Revolution. This trend is confirmed by the nominations made by the representative Casenave a year later. Results: thirteen manufacturers, six merchants, two wholesale grocers, two dyers, two carders, two tool grinders, and one each of perfumers, writers, glaziers, tailors, milliners, grain merchants, and private secretaries. Among them were eight manufacturers and one tool grinder whose families had served in pre-revolutionary municipalities, and one dyer who had done so personally. Again, the upper bourgeoisie was present in great numbers.

An explanation will be attempted later as to why the Société Populaire gave its confidence to members of the upper bourgeoisie. But why should the representative, in the first case, have approved this choice, and, in the second, chosen the same group of persons on his own initiative? The answer is, I suggest, as follows: The representatives, whether of the Revolutionary government or of the Thermidorean Reaction, looked for the most solid and influential elements of the community, whom they wished to make the guarantors of their respective regimes. Other things being equal (that is, the lack of royalist sentiment being noted), nothing would then militate against the appointment of a municipality made up of the prestigious and experienced upper and middle bourgeois, one the one hand, and, on the other, of a certain number of lower bourgeois, whose advancement was due to the Revolution and whose interests were, therefore, closely linked to its success.[30]

Under the Constitution of the year III (August, 1795), Elbeuf,

---

[29] *Arch. Nat.*, F^{1c} III Seine-Inférieure 7.

[30] For lists of municipal officers giving their professions, see *Arch. Dép.*, L 5621 (July, 1793) and L 231 (Nivôse IV). Where these sources were not sufficient, I have verified the professions on the tax roles.

like all other cities of between five and ten thousand inhabitants, was provided with a new municipal system. In addition to five municipal officers elected by a primary assembly every two years, each such city had a *commissaire du directoire* named by the government and revocable by it. His role was analogous to that of the *agent national* under the Revolutionary government. One-half of the municipal officers were changed each year. They could be re-elected for a second two-year term, but there then had to be an interval of two years before they could serve a third term. If vacancies occurred between regularly scheduled elections, temporary nominations were made by the remaining municipal officers, or, in the case where a majority had to be replaced, by the Directory.

Eligibility requirements for voters were also changed somewhat, if not so radically as the municipal organization itself. The voting age was reduced from twenty-five to twenty-one, and the payment of any direct taxes at all was sufficient to grant the right to vote, instead of an amount equal to three working days as before. Voters had also to be listed on the *registre civique* of the canton, a requirement analogous to that of the *serment civique* of 1791. No mention is made of obligatory service in the National Guard as under the earlier law. The only persons excluded were domestics, non-juring priests, " émigrés radiés provisoirement," and relatives of *émigrés*. It was foreseen that from the year XII voters would have to be literate and exercise a " profession mécanique." [31] On 12 Vendémiaire IV there were 1,279 eligible voters in Elbeuf.[32]

A law of July, 1797, decided that municipalities would henceforth be recruited by co-optation, but it was never applied. The next significant change in municipal organization came with the passage of the laws that formed the Constitution of the year VIII, after the coup d'état of 18 Brumaire.

The law of 28 Pluviôse VIII (February 17, 1800) provided that in cities of five to ten thousand inhabitants there would be a mayor, two assistants (*adjoints*) and twenty-seven members of the municipal council, as well as a police commissioner. The mayor and assistants were named by the first consul on the nomination of the Prefect, who himself named the municipal councilors. The primary assemblies played no role whatsoever in this process; in other

---

[31] Godechot, *Institutions*, pp. 398–400, 411.   [32] *Arch. Dép.*, L 205.

words, elections at the municipal level were suppressed. The councilors were named for a period of three years, the mayors and
assistants for an unspecified period of time.

The Constitution of the year X again modified this system.
Municipal councilors were chosen by the government upon nomination of double their number by the Communal Assembly from
among the one hundred most highly taxed citizens. The councilors
were to serve for twenty years; the mayor and his assistants for
five. Beginning in 1812 and every ten years thereafter, the mayor
and assistants were to be chosen from among the councilors.
Administration was actually in their hands alone; for the Council
met only once a year for a maximum of fifteen days, unless convoked in extraordinary session by the Prefect.[33]

This system reintroduced some popular participation into the
Elbeuf municipality. The Communal Assembly, in which universal
suffrage was the rule, once again had a role to play. But care was
taken to preserve the system of indirect election, and it was
planned that only the one-tenth of the 1,192 eligible voters who
were communal notables would take part in the municipal elections
until the year XII.[34]

Every change in the municipal system from the year III onward
made it progressively easier for the government to frustrate any
attempt to go against its will. Voters consequently began to lose
interest. During the month of Brumaire IV, the municipality had
great difficulty in getting anyone at all to come to the primary
assemblies for the ratification of the Constitution and the election
of municipal and judicial officers, despite "l'appel des citoyens
tant au son de la cloche que de la caisse." The number of voters
varied from thirty-eight to twenty-six, and persons were elected
to municipal posts with as few as fourteen votes. On 4 Frimaire
the General Council wrote that it was "convaincu par l'expérience
combien il est désagreable d'administrer un peuple affamé et [con-
sidère] que la pénurie de subsistances où se trouve cette commune
est probablement le motif qui éloigne tous les citoyens des fonctions administratives, motif qui malheureusement ne paraît pas
prêt de cesser. . . ."[35] Indeed, resignations of elected officers continued to be frequent. They didn't care to be burdened with the

---

[33] Godechot, *Institutions*, pp. 516–20.
[34] *Arch. Mun.*, Délib., Vol. A (16 Germinal IX); Godechot, *Institutions*, p. 496.
[35] *Arch. Mun.*, Délib., Vol. V (10–13, 19 and 21 Brumaire; 4 Frimaire IV).

responsibility of a famine, and their electors were apparently indifferent as to who governed them so long as they had bread.

In the elections of the years IV to VII, twenty-eight municipal offices had to be filled in Elbeuf, not counting that of the *commissaire du pouvoir exécutif*. There were nine resignations, and nine times the Directory named temporary officers by decree. Thus there were thirty-seven nominations distributed among twenty-nine persons. Twenty-three of the twenty-nine were manufacturers. There were also two merchants, a dyer, a carder, a wood merchant, and a plaster merchant. The successive presidents of the municipal administration were all manufacturers. Moreover, fifteen of the manufacturers came from families whose members had served before the Revolution. The dyer and the plaster merchant had themselves been members of the pre-revolutionary municipalities. Only two persons, the manufacturer Jean Pierre Lefort and the wood merchant Louis Lemercier were " new men," in the sense that neither they nor any member of their families had ever served in an Elbeuf municipality.

Between the year IX and the end of the Empire, fifty-four persons shared ninety-seven municipal offices. Thirty-nine manufacturers held seventy-six offices, a plaster merchant and a saddle maker were re-elected three times each, and a rentier and a doctor were each re-elected twice. (It should be noted that the doctor was also a manufacturer.) All the rest—three dyers, two landed proprietors, two notaries, a surgeon, a merchant, a tool grinder, and one person whom I have been unable to identify—served only once. Twenty-six of the manufacturers, two dyers, one rentier, one proprietor, and the plaster merchant belonged to families that had served in the municipality before the Revolution. The only persons who were entirely new to the municipality in this period were one manufacturer, one notary, one surgeon, one proprietor and, of course, the person I have not succeeded in identifying—five in a total of fifty-four. All the rest had either served themselves or were members of families whose members had been municipal officers before the year IX. Perhaps still more important is the fact that the first nominations made under the Restoration changed nothing as to the composition of the municipality. All the persons chosen at that time had already held office under the Revolution and Empire. For this very reason, the imperial administrators experienced no difficulties or moral scruples in ratifying these same nominations during the Hundred Days.[86]

II

The citizens of Elbeuf also played a part in the election of high representative bodies: the departmental administrators and the national legislative assemblies. But their role was very indirect, similar to that of the voter in the parish assembly during the elections to the Estates General.

Under the system used for the election of the Legislative in 1791, all active citizens voted for electors who in turn chose the deputies. The electors chosen in Elbeuf had to pay at least the equivalent of ten working days in taxes and were chosen in the primary assemblies in the proportion of 1 to 100 voters.[87] Those eligible to be deputies had to pay taxes equivalent to the *marc d'argent* or 52 livres.

Although the above qualifications were used for the elections of 1791, a new law had already been enacted in August of that year altering the electoral requirements. In order to be an elector one now had to be the proprietor or farmer of land evaluated at the local equivalent of 150 working days (in the case of Elbeuf). Now, however, deputies could be chosen from among all the active citizens. This was the system employed for the election of the Convention in 1792.

The Constitution of the year III maintained the age qualification of twenty-five for electors while reducing the voting age to twenty-one. The revenue necessary was now equal to 200 working days in cities of over 6,000 inhabitants (including Elbeuf) and 150 days in other communities.

Under the Constitution of the year VIII, the primary assemblies in each commune chose one-tenth of their number to be *notabilités communales.* These notables assembled at the *chef-lieu* of the *arrondissement* to elect one-tenth of themselves as *notabilités départementales.* The departmental notables then chose one-tenth of their number to be national notables. At each level, the government chose members of the various administrations from among persons on these lists.

[86] St. Denis, *Histoire*, VIII, 365. On May 2, 1815, to be more exact.
[87] *Arch. Nat.*, D^{iv} *bis* 52.

Finally, under the Constitution of the year X, the communal assemblies with universal suffrage (although until the year XII only those inscribed on the lists of communal notables were to vote) elected the electoral college of the *arrondissement* in the proportion of 1 to 500 inhabitants, with a minimum of 120 and a maximum of 200 members. These colleges in turn elected the electoral colleges of the department in the proportion of 1 to 1,000 inhabitants, with a minimum of 200 and a maximum of 300 members. Members of the departmental colleges, elected for life, were chosen from among the 600 most highly taxed individuals of the department. The electoral college of the *arrondissement* could include as many as ten members named for life by the First Consul. The same was true up to a maximum of twenty for the departmental colleges. The task of both sorts of colleges was to elect candidates for the *Corps Legislatif*, the *Tribunat*, the Senate, and the General Councils of the *arrondissement* and department. One candidate in two had to be chosen outside the colleges themselves.

Until the enactment of the Constitution of the year VIII, the electors of the second degree chose not only deputies but sometimes other administrators as well. Justices of the peace were always named by the primary assemblies, but under the regime of the year III the electors chose the judges of the Tribunal de Cassation, the *hauts jurés*, the president, public accuser and recordkeeper of the Criminal Tribunal and the judges of the Civil Tribunal, as well as the departmental administrators.[38]

It was the means of choosing the administrators of the department that changed most frequently. Originally chosen by the electors among persons paying ten working days in taxes, they numbered thirty-six. On October 19, 1792, the hostility of these administrators to the Revolution of August 10 caused the Convention to decide that there would be a purge in the form of new elections, this time by universal suffrage. All persons aged twenty-five, resident in the department for a least one year and not employed as a domestic were eligible. The Directory of eight members, which was the really active part of the administration, was to be chosen in the same manner, instead of by the administration itself, as had previously been the case. This change did

[38] Godechot, *Institutions*, pp. 73–74, 399–400, 487, 496–97.

not stop many departmental administrators from being favorable
to, or taking an active part in, the Federalist Revolt of June, 1793.
For this reason, the *montagnards* felt it necessary to reduce them
to strict obedience. The law of 14 Frimaire II (December 4, 1793)
suppressed the General Councils of the departments, as well as
the presidents and the *procureurs-généraux-syndics*. Only the
Directories remained, and then with their powers severely limited.
Since elections were temporarily abolished under the Revolutionary
government, their members were named by the representatives on
mission. This remained the case until enactment of the new
Constitution, although their old powers of 1792 were restored to
the administrators on 28 Germinal III (April 17, 1795).[39]

Elbeuf was little represented in administrative and representative
bodies above the municipal level. No Elbeuvian was a member of
the Norman (Rouen) Provincial Assembly of 1787. On the other
hand, Joseph Grandin, a manufacturer, represented the city in the
Departmental Assembly of the Andelys and Pont de l'Arche in
1787. When he resigned because of ill health, he was replaced
by Joseph Duruflé the elder, municipal officer and manufacturer
of Elbeuf.[40] In 1790 Jean Pierre Baptiste Grandin became a member of the Departmental Assembly of the Seine-Inférieure, and,
in 1791, he was elected a member of its Directory. He eventually
rose to be its president.[41]

There were no Elbeuvians in the National assemblies of the
Revolution or Empire. Pierre Henry Hayet and Jean René Baptiste
Grandin were elected *suppléants* to the Legislative and Convention
respectively, but they never served.[42] It was only during the
Restoration that this situation was to change, and several citizens
of Elbeuf were to become members of the Chamber of Deputies.

With few exceptions, much the same people were electors as
held municipal office in Elbeuf. Those who had not been municipal officers were related to a member of the municipality. Our
list is, no doubt, incomplete, but it is nonetheless sufficient to
allow us to draw certain conclusions. Between 1791 and the year
VII, thirty persons held thirty-four posts as electors. They were
divided thus professionally: fifteen manufacturers, four merchants,

[39] Godechot, *Institutions*, pp. 98, 282–86.
[40] *Arch. Dép. de l'Eure*, C 39.
[41] *Arch. Nat.*, F^{1a} 435; F^{1e} III Seine-Inférieure 1.
[42] *Arch. Nat.*, C 138 (dossier CI 73), C 180.

a priest, two proprietors, a dyer, a woolshearer, a cloth thresher, a shoemaker, a doctor, a lawyer, a justice of the peace, and a court recordkeeper. Two manufacturers, the dyer, and one merchant

TABLE 4–6

ELECTORS CHOSEN IN ELBEUF, 1791–YEAR VII

Name	Profession	Dates of Election
Join-Lambert	Dyer	1791, VII
Grandin, Jean Baptiste Pierre	Manufacturer	1791
Hayet, Pierre Henri	Manufacturer	1791, VII
Grandin, Jacques Parfait	Manufacturer	1791
Flavigny, Louis Joseph	Manufacturer	1791
Pinel	Priest	1791
Grandin, Jacques Pierre	Manufacturer	1791, 1792
Fosse, Jacques Pierre	Court recordkeeper	1791
Balleroy, François Pierre	Justice of the Peace	1791
Duruflé, Martin Joseph	Landowner	1791
Tienterre, Jean-Baptiste	Merchant	1791, 1792
Dumoutier, Georges	Woolshearer	1792
Dubuc, Noel	Thresher and forest guard	1792
Gueroult, Philippe	Shoemaker	1792
Folie, Robert	Manufacturer	1792
Mouton fils, François	Manufacturer	1792
Fromont, Pierre Louis	Merchant	1792
Séjourné, Denis	Merchant	1792
Lefebvre, Félix	Manufacturer	1792
Hazé, Pierre	Stocking manufacturer	1792
Lingois	Notary	III
Bourdon, Pierre Nicolas	Manufacturer	III
Duruflé, Moyse	Manufacturer	III
Grandin, Alexandre	Manufacturer	III
Patallier, Pierre	Manufacturer	III
Delacroix, Jacques Pierre	Manufacturer	III
Henry, Augustin	Doctor/manufacturer	V
Durand, Prosper	Landowner	V
Bosquier, Michel Guillaume	Lawyer	V
Murizon, Désiré	Manufacturer	VII

Sources: *Liste des Electeurs du Département de la Seine-Inférieure Nommés en Exécution de la Loi du 29 mai 1791* (Rouen, 1791). A copy can be found in the Bibliothèque Nationale under the call number le[31] 29; *Archives Nationales*, AF[iii] 262; *Arch. Dép.*, L 204, L 205, L 209; *Arch. Mun.*, Délib., Vol. II (August 26 and 27, 1792).

were each elected twice. The only difference in social pattern between the elections of municipal officers and those of electors is that the break with the old regime seems to come later in the second case. Indeed, as I have shown, the first elections under the Revolution, those of 1790 and 1791, consecrated this break as concerns members of the municipality. But in the case of the electors, six of the eleven named in 1791 had either been members

TABLE 4–7

DEPARTMENTAL NOTABLES FROM ELBEUF, YEAR IX

Name	Profession
Bourdon, Pierre Nicolas	Manufacturer
Delarue, Prosper	Manufacturer (assistant to mayor)
Drevet	Secretary of the commune
Durand, Prosper Charles	Landowner
Flavigny-Gosset, François	Manufacturer
Flavigny, Joseph	Manufacturer
Flavigny père, Robert	Manufacturer
Flavigny fils, Robert	Manufacturer
Frontin, Mathieu	Manufacturer (mayor)
Grandin l'âiné	Manufacturer (member of general council of department)
Grandin, Alexandre	Manufacturer
Grandin, Louis Jacques	Manufacturer
Grandin, Jean Baptiste Parfait	Manufacturer
Hayet, Pierre Henri	Manufacturer
Henry, Augustin	Doctor
Join-Lambert	Dyer
Lefebvre, Félix-Nicolas	Manufacturer
Lingois, Pierre	Notary
Menage, David	Manufacturer
Quesné, Mathieu	Manufacturer (assistant to mayor)
Sevaistre, Mathieu	Manufacturer
Valdampierre, Nicolas	Postmaster

Source: *Arch. Nat.*, AD XVI 75–*Elections Départementales de l'an IX–Département de la Seine-Inférieure-Liste des Notables du Département Dressée d'après les Dispositions de la Loi du 13 Ventôse an IX, Concernant la Formation et le Renouvellement des Listes d'Eligibilité, Prescrites par la Constitution.* This is a printed document; another copy is to be found in *Arch. Nat.*, F¹ᵉ III Seine-Inférieure 2.

of pre-revolutionary administrations or belonged to families represented in them. It was in 1792 that the break, such as it was, came. Of the eleven electors named in that year, only two, both manufacturers, were related to old-regime administrators. Two other manufacturers and three merchants were also members of the upper and middle bourgeoisie. A shoemaker and a stocking manufacturer represented the lower bourgeoisie, and the cloth thresher and woolshearer were wage earners. It appears, then, that upper and middle bourgeois who had not been intimately associated with the old regime were at least partially successful in preserving their prestige at one level of communal affairs. More simply, the higher the post, the greater the hesitation on the part of the active citizens to turn away from their " natural superiors," even though the latter might not show great revolutionary ardor.

As in the case of the municipal officers, the later nominations of electors bring the pre-revolutionary upper bourgeoisie, together with the newer upper-bourgeois families, back into power. This phenomenon begins in the year III, but we see it most clearly on the list of departmental notables of the year IX. In that year Elbeuf citizens were twenty-two of the 1,291 notables of the Seine-Inférieure. Sixteen were manufacturers, and all of them were upper bourgeois, with the exception of two, the secretary of the commune and the postmaster, on whom we have no information. Of the twenty, fifteen were related to administrators of the old regime, and the other five had taken a part in municipal affairs from very early on in the Revolution. It is thus questionable as to whether any of them can be classified as " new men " either in a personal sense or as indicating a wider distribution of power in the class structure.

The same is true for the electoral colleges of the regime of the year X. At the *arrondissement* level, we find five Elbeuvians (two manufacturers, two landowners, and one doctor), all of old upper-bourgeois families. Two manufacturers represented Elbeuf in the departmental college. Elbeuf also had a member in both the Conseil d'Arrondissement and the General Council of the Department. In the former case, it was the ex-mayor and notary Lingois, and in the latter, Grandin l'âiné, a member of the greatest upper-bourgeois family of the city.[43]

George Lefebvre tells us that during the Revolution:

Dans les villes, l'artisanat, le commerce de détail, les arts libéraux accedèrent plus où moins nombreux au conseil général de la commune, sinon à la

---

[43] The members of the arrondissement college were: Nicolas Félix Lefebvre, Joseph Godet, Pierre Alexandre Patallier, Pierre Charles Nicolas Bourdon, and Augustin Henri. Those of the departmental college were: Jean Baptiste Pierre Grandin and Pierre Henri Hayet. See J. B. Vitalis, *Annuaire Statistique du Département de la Seine-Inférieure pour l'année 1811* (Rouen, 1811), pp. 2–11, 15, 18–24.

municipalité; en 1793, ils prédominèrent. Des hommes de professions moins relevées, d'aisance plus modeste—commis et même, en petit nombre, campagnons de métier—, s'adjoignirent à eux.[44]

This is a fair enough description of events in Elbeuf, although we may recognize the very small number of wage earners and clerks who gained access to even the General Council. The greater difference between Elbeuf and other cities lies in the timing of the change. As we have seen, it was not in 1793 and the year II that the influence of the lower bourgeoisie reached its peak in Elbeuf, but rather in the years from 1790 to 1792. After that the upper bourgeoisie regained its power.

The pre-revolutionary social structure of Elbeuf explains this difference. The thing that distinguished Elbeuf from other cities of similar size was its industry, and thus, the existence of an already highly developed upper bourgeoisie. Moreover, it was a city in which there were practically no nobles and no large clergy, there being no cathedral chapter or monastery. This meant that the upper bourgeoisie, predominantly manufacturing in its interests, had a free hand in the political affairs of the city, vis-à-vis the other social classes. This was all the more true as the city had for its seigneur the Prince de Lambesc, a member of the House of Lorraine, who was generally too occupied with court intrigues to bother being firm with his beloved subjects of Elbeuf.[45] In short, such complaints as the bourgeoisie might have were directed more against the royal government than against either the first or second estates. If this bourgeoisie participated in the Revolution, it was because of what it felt to be abuses by the monarchy rather than as an attempt to seize power (it already had) in Elbeuf.

The upper bourgeoisie had power in pre-revolutionary Elbeuf and, for that reason, had less to gain from the Revolution than its counterpart in other cities. At the same time, there were other classes in Elbeuf: a lower bourgeoisie and a class of wage earners well on the way to becoming an industrial proletariat. These were the opposing forces present. And because they existed as they did, the Revolution in Elbeuf was both rapid and short-lived. We shall now go on to see just how this happened.

[44] Georges Lefebvre, *La Révolution Française* (3rd. ed., Paris, 1957), p. 599.
[45] De La Chenaye-Desbois, *Dictionnaire de la Noblesse* (Paris, 1774), Vol. VII, article *Guise; Biographie Universelle Ancienne et Moderne, Supplément, Ouvrage Rédigé par une Société des Gens de Lettres et de Savants* (Paris, 1842), LXX, 82–85.

CHAPTER 5

POLITICS AND THE REVOLUTION IN ELBEUF

I

The Third Estate of Normandy did not exercise any great influence on a national scale in the preparation of the Estates General, as did Dauphiné under the leadership of Mounier or the Breton Club in Paris in the first days of the National Assembly. This was undoubtedly due to the fact that Normandy lacked a central co-ordinating body, such as the Provincial Estates, that could speak for it, as well as to its economic and social diversity. Nevertheless, Normans were extremely active in their cities and electoral districts during this period. In the bailliage of Rouen the name of Thouret stands out, but he was not alone. He was nothing more than a spokesman, unauthorized but representative, of the Norman Third Estate. He cannot be said to have molded Norman opinion; he merely reflected its consensus.[1]

Now, this consensus was not revolutionary, at least not in the sense that we have come to attribute to that term. There was nothing " social " in its program. At most, it sought to bring the law up to date so as to coincide with the realities of economic and political power. For the Norman bourgeoisie, this meant a constitutional monarchy in which the bourgeoisie would be assured a leading role. Essentially reformist, its demands based on principle, as distinguished from those particular to the Province, can

---

[1] E. Le Parquier, "Les Cahiers des Doléances des Paroisses Normandes en 1789," *Bulletin du Comité Départementale de la Seine-Inférieure pour la Recherche et la Publication des Documents Economiques de la Révolution Française* I (Rouen, 1914), 91–104, and "Le Rôle et l'Influence de Rouen en Normandie en Novembre et Décembre, 1788," *Bulletin des Etudes Locales dans l'Enseignement Public, Groupe de la Seine-Inférieure*, Vol. 1930–31 (Rouen, 1931), pp. xix–xxxvi.

be summed up in a few phrases: equality of representation, vote by head, common deliberations of the orders, the third estate to be represented by its own members, the inviolability of property and, therefore, equality of taxation, regular convocation of, and control of the purse strings by, the Estates General, and, finally, the re-establishment of an administrative system for the province having at its summit the Provincial Estates.

These demands were expressed by the municipalities of Normandy, as well as by individuals, in an extensive pamphlet literature published in 1788 and the early part of 1789. As concerns the Provincial Estates, the municipalities felt that the newly created Provincial Assemblies did not obviate the need for them, because the latter did not have the prerogatives attributed to the former, particularly in the voting of provincial taxes, that is, of all taxes in the Province. Several municipalities, including Rouen and Pontaudemer, based their claim on the violation of the *Charte aux Normands* issued by Louis X in 1315. In all of the calls for the re-establishment of the Provincial Estates, the Third Estate was careful to insist on applying to them the same rules of composition that it desired for the Estates General.[2]

Several arguments were used to justify the proposed changes in the Estates General, and all sought historical justification for their assertions. Clio was forced to do yeoman service. One pamphleteer started out with the assertion that under both the Franks and the Gauls, the " common people " had had the majority of votes in the assemblies of the Champs de Mars et de Mai. He then went on to trace this preponderance of the Third Estate throughout French history, attempting to show how it had always helped the growth of monarchical power. This paradise, he claimed, had been destroyed only by the increased power of the clergy and the nobility.

But rights of prescription are insufficient. The author must have felt this, for he quickly moved his argument over to more philosophical ground, taking the position later formulated by Sieyes in the famous aphorism: " Qu'est-ce que le tiers état—Tout." The Norman pamphleteer wrote:

Le peuple réside dans le tiers-état, c'est le tiers-état qui est le peuple; c'est le tiers-état qui représente les premiers francs, nos ancêtres. Donc . . .

---

[2] Camille Hippeau, *Le Gouvernement de Normandie au XVIIe et au XVIIIe Siècles* (Caen, 1864), V, 434–83.

les députés du tiers-état doivent être supérieurs en nombre aux [autres]; donc les députés de chaque ordre doivent être en raison des individus contribuables qui les composent les uns et les autres.

This argumentation leads him to a logical conclusion whereby he refuses to accept even equality of representation of the Third Estate in relation to the other two orders. The Third Estate must have a greater number of representatives than the other two combined. In fact, the author goes so far as to insist that the Third Estate itself should be broken down into orders, the first to be urban in composition and to be called *l'ordre des citoyens*, the second to be rural and to be known as *l'ordre des argronomes*. In addition, the clergy and nobles should be blended into one order, since they are both privileged. He ends up with a warning: " Vous qui gouvernez, songez que le peuple est l'abeille laborieuse qui prépare son miel avec beaucoup de soins et de peines, que le clergé et la noblesse sont les guêpes qui dévorent le produit de son travail." [3]

The radicalism of the document cited lay not in the arguments themselves but in the extent to which they were carried. The pride and self-confidence of the Third Estate is evident in all of the pamphlet literature of the day.

It is the manufacturing and commercial classes that " enliven all parts of the state, feed the public treasury by an infinity of channels, and multiply the coin of the nation by a rapid and wisely arranged [commercial] traffic." The intellectual is called the " new Prometheus," while the lawyer protects the interests of widows and orphans. The Third furnishes the soldiers and sailors to defend the nation, and the peasant provides its food. Equity demands that this heroic class of people be rewarded by a voice in the affairs of the nation—not an exclusive voice, not even a predominant one, but one which would be " equal " to that of the other two orders. Few need suffer because of this change, least of all the *noblesse de robe* devoted to the welfare of the crown. The clergy, it is true, would have to give up its fiscal privileges, the product of " la piété inconsidérée de nos anciens monarques."

[3] *Le Tiers-Etat de Normandie Eclairé ou ses Droits Justifiés* (n. p., 1789), *passim.* A copy is available in the Bibliothèque de la Ville de Paris under call number 963756.

But the Third Estate reserves its real scorn for still another group, the *anoblis*:

Jaloux à l'excès de leurs titres et de leurs privilèges, il n'est rien que la plupart des nouveaux anoblis ne fassent pour humilier et avilir l'ordre qui les a vu naître.

Méconnaissant leur origine, les ingrats déchirent le sein qui les a nourris, brisent les liens sacrés du sang, & se croiraient déshonorés d'avoir des roturiers pour leurs parents.

Au moyen de cette invention honteuse du fisc, cette classe devrait s'accroître tellement, soit par les mutations, soit par d'autres circonstances qu'elle égalerait bientôt le tiers-état, si la nature toujours bienfaisante & prompte à réparer les vices de nos institutions politiques ne se hâtait de détruire ces tiges éphémères, ou de les replonger dans l'obscurité d'où elles étaient sorties, faute de moyens suffisants pour se maintenir dignement dans leur nouvel état.

Que ces anoblis, que ceux ayant droit à la noblesse, par la possession de leurs charges, perdent donc tout espoir d'être les représentants du tiers-état, puisqu'il est évident qu'ils n'ont quitté cet ordre qui leur a fourni les richesses qui ont servi à payer leurs privilèges, que pour se soustraire aux charges imposées sur le tiers-état.[4]

This hatred of the *anoblis* is a phenomenon thoroughly typical of a class in the process of becoming conscious of itself. It is no longer permitted to wish to escape from one's class. More exactly, the bourgeoisie will no longer permit its own members to abandon their class responsibilities in the search for personal gain. One must now go up the social ladder as a member of the bourgeoisie, or not at all. This last point not only explains the hatred expressed in the above-cited paragraph, but also why the *anoblis* are even more despised than is the old nobility. A traitor is always more despicable than an enemy who will fight openly. Moreover, the stage which bourgeois class consciousness had reached at this time was such as still to admit of collaboration between classes, but not between one class and individuals of another.

This is the tenor of the message of thanks addressed by the municipal officers of Rouen to the king apropos of the Estates General. They urge him to have no fear of dissension in that body, because

les citoyens de toutes les provinces, de tous les ordres, de toutes les classes, ne sont que des français; ils composent ensemble la Nation: le titre qui

---

[4] *Considérations du Tiers-Etat de la Province de Normandie sur la Forme des Futurs Etats-Généraux* (Caen, 1788), *passim* and especially pp. 13–14.

les unit en les attachant à la patrie commune, les met en société d'intérêts, de devoirs, d'engagements. Les citoyens sont frères. Et quand il s'agit de l'affaire générale de la grand famille, les prétentions particulières des branches qui la composent, ne doivent-elles pas s'éclipser, comme les intérêts individuels de chaque tête? [5]

Suggestions such as these take on more concrete forms in the writings of Thouret himself. He starts out with a call for unity in face of adversity, such as was realized when the Parlements were suppressed in 1771. Neither the nobility nor the clergy, he assured them, had to fear for their prerogatives, for distinction of rank in a divinely ordained hierarchical society " ne cessera jamais de commander à l'opinion." Then, by an ingenious bit of casuistry, he proceeds to distinguish between prerogatives of rank and fiscal privilege, the latter of which has nothing to do with the honor of its possessors and will have to be abolished. He goes so far as to call tax exemptions an " anti-prerogative," already denounced by those to whom it belonged.

Thouret then seeks to appease fears of the infringement of the monarchical system. Royal sovereignty would not be threatened by the power of the Estates General to approve taxes any more than it had been by the fiscal prerogatives of the Parlements and the Provincial Estates. To those members of the First and Second Estates who feared that control over taxation in the hands of the Estates General would be the opening wedge in the establishment of democracy in France, Thouret replied that there was no cause for alarm. The nation, he wrote, " périrait par la démocratie, qui ne convient ni à ses moeurs, ni à la grandeur de son territoire, ni à l'étendue de sa population."

On the other hand, distinction of rank does not require the separation of the orders. Thouret suggests that the orders unite at the bailliage level to elect in common one another's deputies. Only in this way will each deputy represent the nation as a whole. Moreover, all classes within each order should be represented in the Estates General—the lower clergy as well as the bishops, the *hobereaux* as well as the court and judicial nobility, the rural as well as the urban section of the Third Estate. There

---

[5] *Adresse de Remerciment Présentée au Roi par les Officers Municipaux de la Ville de Rouen, en Assemblée Générale* (Rouen, 1789), pp. 7-8; see also *Discours à Prononcer dans l'Assemblée Générale de Tous les Bailliages de la Province de Normandie* (Rouen, 1789), *passim.*

is no suggestion to allow peasants to represent themselves. Rather, Thouret recommended: "Donnez-leur aux Etats-Généraux des patrons pleins de leur cause, qui réclament pour eux les adoucissements, l'encouragement et la protection signalée qu'ils méritent." [6]

The theme of unity combined with thorough-going reform, but not Revolution, is continued by Thouret in still another brochure of February, 1789. In order to avoid conflict between the orders, he wished the *cahiers* to be limited to demands for the enactment of the principles outlined above. It was not the role of the primary and bailliage assemblies of the Third Estate to record all their particular grievances. Instead, the deputies should be given the widest powers, and all subsidiary reforms should be left to their wisdom. "Le médecin habile s'attache-t-il à traiter partiellement les ulcères de chaque membre? Il régénere la masse de sang vicié, et le corps entier reprend sa vigueur et son embonpoint. . . . Si la France obtient une bonne constitution, par cela seul tous les abus particuliers disparaîtront, et l'impôt décroîtra par le retranchement inévitable des dépenses." Because of the great importance of the reform of the constitution, he expressed the wish

que les cahiers du tiers état soient équitables et sages; qu'en demandant justice et sûreté pour lui, il n'attaque pas les droits légitimes du clergé et de la noblesse; que sur les points fondementaux où l'intérêt de ces deux ordres est commun avec le sien, il provoque par sa cordialité leur assentiment & leur adjonction; que sur les matières ou leurs intérêts pourraient paraître contraire, s'il en subsiste encore quelques-unes, il n'emploie que le secours de la conviction par l'ascendant de l'équité naturelle, de la raison publique, et des principes imprescriptibles du pacte social; quel motif alors, quel prétexte excusable resterait-il encore à l'eloignement de la confiance, & de conciliation universel? [7]

This, then, was the climate of opinion in the bailliage of Rouen during the period of elections to the Estates General. And the bourgeois of Elbeuf were of the same mind. At the end of November and the beginning of December, 1788, all the professional groups in Elbeuf met—the manufacturers separately and the others in common—to draw up addresses to the municipal officers asking them to support a program summed up in four points: equal

[6] J. G. Thouret, *Avis des Bons Normands à leurs Frères Tous les Bons Français de Toutes les Provinces et de Tous les Ordres sur l'Envoi des Lettres de Convocation aux Etats-Généraux* (Rouen, 1789), *passim*.

[7] J. G. Thouret, *Suite de l'Avis des Bons Normands* (Rouen, 1789), pp. 6–7, 11–12, 28.

representation of the Third Estate, the Third Estate to represent itself, the division of representation by wealth and population, vote by head and deliberation of the three orders in common. Four manufacturers, six retail merchants, four master carders, two lawyers, two surgeons, two goldsmiths, two locksmiths, two bakers, two joiners, two chevaliers de St. Louis (retainers of the Prince de Lambesc), a notary, a court usher, a dyer, a caterer, a wigmaker, and a cultivator signed this petition as representatives of their professions. On December 13 the municipality endorsed their demands.

The intent of all the petitioners is made clear when we read the preamble written by the manufacturers:

> L'amour si connu des français pour leur souverain est particulièrement le sentiment inné et invariable de ses fidèles communes. L'histoire nous apprend qu'elles ont toujours été le plus ferme appui du trône. Mais aussi quel monarque méritera mieux cet amour de la Nation que celui qui la gouverne. Louis XVI, après avoir délivré ses peuples de la servitude, veut aujourd'hui en effacer jusqu'aux moindres vestiges en leur restituant les droits qu'ils avaient reçu de la nature et que de barbares préjuges leur avaient enlevés. Il ne manquera rien à sa gloire, ni au bonheur de l'état lorsqu'il aura assuré d'une manière irrévocable l'existence d'une classe nombreuse dans laquelle la patrie trouvera toujours des vrais citoyens et le roi ses plus fidèles sujets.[8]

Calm in the midst of consensus reigned in Elbeuf during the months in which elections were held and *cahiers* were drawn up. On March 28, 1789, fourteen persons were chosen by the primary assembly of Elbeuf to assist the municipality in writing the *cahier* of the city. Among the fourteen, there were two manufacturers, one surgeon, one wigmaker, two merchants, a notary, a plaster merchant, a baker, two master carders, a chandler, a stocking manufacturer, and a tavernkeeper.[9] Their work seems to have been adopted with no serious alterations.

The *cahier* began with a long preamble, which is worth quoting in full, because it well expresses the state of mind of the Elbeuf bourgeoisie:

> Le peuple réduit à la plus extrême misère, les coeurs des Français aigris par l'infortune des temps les plus désastreux, la langeur du commerce, l'inaction de toutes les manufactures, le déperissement journalier de toutes

---

[8] *Arch. Nat.*, B III 168, 116–35; *Arch. Mun.*, Délib., Vol. I (December 13, 1788).
[9] *Arch. Mun.*, Délib., Vol. I (March 28, 1789).

les fortunes particulières, une anarchie de tous les principes, le silence des loix, tout porte l'empreinte du désordre et de la confusion, tout demande à grands cris une restauration générale.

Des ministres trompés dans leurs spéculations ont, contre les plus sages réclamations, signé, par le funeste traité avec l'Angleterre, l'arrêt de mort des fabriques de France, & ont ainsi disposé de leur propre mouvement, de la subsistance d'une classe nombreuse de citoyens.

La mauvaise administration des finances, le trésor public épuisé, le dette énorme de l'Etat; les frais immenses de la perception de l'impôt, cette armée de traitants, de financiers s'engraissants du pur sang des peuples; ces gênes, ces entraves du commerce: des barrières jusques dans l'intérieur du Royaume; des obstacles sans fin à la circulation de toutes les denrées; des faillites, des banqueroutes multipliées qui restent impunies, & où tout est perte pour le créancier par le danger d'avoir recours à la justice, qui consume et absorbe tout; des arrêts de surséance accordés par la faveur à des gens de la plus mauvaise renommée, & dont le but est de dépouiller entierèment leurs créanciers; les représentations des Fabriques, des Chambres de Commerce non-écoutées & méprisées; la sorte d'indifference du gouvernement pour les manufactures, qui font le nerf et la richesse de l'Etat, & qui donnent l'âme et la vie au commerce & à l'agriculture; l'instabilité des Ministres, leur pouvoir de changer, d'innover, de tout renverser pour mettre en pratique le système qu'ils ont adopté: ces débats trop fréquents du Ministère avec les Cours Souveraines, d'où s'ensuit ordinairement la suspension de toute justice; cette ambiguité de notre constitution qui amène une sorte d'anarchie pendant laquelle naissent des désordres irréparables; des impositions sans nombre, des répartitions inégales contre lesquelles toute réclamation a été vaine jusqu'ici; les frais immenses d'une régie trop compliquée, qui, en prélevant plus d'un tiers sur les impositions, ne laisse parvenir au trésor royal qu'une partie insuffisante pour ses besoins; l'assentiment de la détresse de l'Etat, d'un déficit effrayant; cette crainte du renversement total de la fortune publique. . . . Voilà les justes motifs des doléances des Peuples. . . . Voilà ce qui couvre le plus beau royaume de l'Europe d'un crêpe funèbre, & lui imprime le sceau du deuil et de la tristesse.[10]

The first thing that comes to mind upon reading this preamble is its resoluteness. The tone is decisive, even harsh, although not threatening. The bourgeoisie is disturbed by the economic situation and the effects of general policy upon it. Practically all of the matters cited in the above introduction are linked in one way or another to the manufactures of the city. This is only natural, but it also proves that an evolution had taken place in the minds of the bourgeoisie since November–December, 1788. It is true that political and constitutional demands still found a considerable

<hr>

[10] *Arch. Nat.*, B III 168, 137 ff.

place in the *cahier*, but we shall see that these considerations have receded somewhat into the background as compared with a few months earlier. The bourgeoisie is no longer willing to sacrifice itself in the interest of national unity; it now gives firm instructions to its deputies.

If the nature of matters under discussion had changed, the philosophical basis of reform remained the same. The same justifications that we have seen in use earlier made their reappearance here. And they show that the spirit of the bourgeoisie, while demanding many changes, is, far from being revolutionary, rather conservative. The attitude of the bourgeois is similar to that of the Robe during the aristocratic revolt of the same period. Little of what they ask for is entirely new. They seem to be looking back economically, as they had politically, to some golden age. They are not trying to innovate so much as they are trying to re-establish an older and more desirable state of affairs.

It is often difficult to separate the economic from the political demands in the *cahier* of the Third Estate of Elbeuf. It is, for instance, clear that a thorough-going judicial reform cannot fail to have an effect on the economy. Still, if we care to make this somewhat arbitrary distinction, we find that fully thirty-seven of seventy-one articles or slightly more than half are predominantly economic in content.

The *cahier* begins with the already classic demands for the unification of the three orders in a single assembly and the vote by head. It then goes on to state the necessity of the enactment of a constitution as the prior condition to all other discussion. Only afterward may taxes, henceforth to be voted by the Estates General, be granted. The Estates General were to be convoked periodically every five years, and the Provincial Estates to be created in all the provinces of the realm. Curiously enough, the creation of the Provincial Estates is accompanied by a demand that all provinces give up their privileges, so that all parts of the French state might be integrated into " une seule et même famille " under a single chief, enjoying the same rights and sharing the same burdens. This contradiction becomes even more apparent— and real—when we note that the following articles wished to leave the method of tax collection and the choice of taxes to be imposed to the discretion of the Estates of each province, with the restriction, however, that the sum to be collected, as well as the amount and kinds of taxes among which the most suitable might be chosen, be fixed by the Estates General. In addition, no tax farming was to be tolerated, and the amount paid by each province was to be in proportion to its wealth, commerce, and population.[11]

The reasons behind these demands are not difficult to establish. They testify to a general distrust of the central government. It was thought that the Provincial Estates, an elective body composed of Normans, would be more sensitive to the needs of the Province. Elbeuvians felt this all the more as they were sure they were victims of a conspiracy which made of Normandy the most highly taxed province of France. The conspirators were led by the " maltô-tiers " of the general farm, who never ceased to harass the city. Thus, by striking a blow against the prevailing political and administrative organization certain economic troubles would also be obviated.

The fiscal preoccupations of the Elbeuf bourgeois were extended to indirect taxes as well. They called for the abolition of all internal customs duties, the existence of which was an obstacle to the development of commerce and industry. The *gabelle*, the lotteries, and the tax on leather should be done away with as well, they said. Finally, to replace the taxes to be suppressed and to provide a much needed revenue, a land tax should be established.[12]

It should be noted that none of these ideas were strikingly original. All had had their protagonists during the eighteenth century, notably among the physiocrats. The land tax had been proposed to the Assembly of Notables in 1787. No doubt the bourgeois of Elbeuf did not bother to justify their demands with philosophical considerations on the productivity of land and the essential goodness of an agricultural society. They would probably not have been in agreement with either of these theses. But they do not even mention them. For them, the question of taxes—and escaping them—was purely a practical matter.

The financial condition of the state also came in for criticism and remedies were suggested. A tax on bachelors over the age of thirty (with the exception of the clergy and the military) was called for. The royal demesne, including the forests, were to be sold in order to pay off the state debt. Pensions were in so far as

[11] See the *cahier*, Articles 1–6.   [12] *Cahier*, Articles 7–10.

possible to be reduced. A report of the revenue thus obtained was to be made public and " verified " every five years by the Estates General. The last provision was but another step in the direction of financial control by representative institutions, no doubt seen as the most efficient means of exercising control over public policy. The lesson of England was well taken.[13]

In the same vein, the Elbeuf bourgeois were much impressed by the idea of ministerial responsibility to the Estates General. To further ensure parliamentary control of the administration, they suggested that permanent councils be set up in each of its branches. This would avoid the breach of continuity caused by a too-frequent change of ministers. On reading this demand, one thinks immediately of the ill-fated Polysynodie of the Regency. But the essential difference is that the present demands were certainly not meant to make the government subservient to the nobility.[14]

Following these general considerations of a mixed political and economic nature, the *cahier* turns its attention to more specific matters. Article 18 demands that weights and measures be standardized throughout France. Comparative studies of the revolutions at the end of the eighteenth century have shown that this is a consideration dear to the hearts of the bourgeoisie in all countries. The example that comes to mind is that of the American Constitution, in which Congress reserves the right to make all laws in this matter. Such a provision is fundamental to the expansion of commerce—particularly in Normandy where the variety of measures was enormous, frequently varying from village to village. A measure having the same name in two neighboring towns did not necessarily have the same capacity in both. For instance, the *pot* at Elbeuf contained 1.68 liters, while that of Arques contained 1.82 liters. It was the *pot* of Arques that was used at Pont de l'Arche, and Elbeuf was part of the District Assembly of Pont de l'Arche under the regime of Provincial Assemblies of 1787.[15] Moreover, Elbeuf's commerce extended over a good deal of the territory of the realm, including Paris. The resultant difficulty in accounting procedures is not hard to imagine.

[13] *Cahier*, Articles 11–14, 17.
[14] *Cahier*, Articles 15–16.
[15] Charles LeRoy, " Mesures de Capacité en Usage en Haute Normandie aux XVIIe et XVIIIe Siècles," *Bulletin de la Société Libre d'Emulation du Commerce et de l'Industrie de la Seine-Inférieure* (1936), pp. 49–96 and (1937), pp. 155–218.

Suggestions for agricultural reform also found their place in the Elbeuf *cahier*. It appears that the doctrine that was later to be characterized as nineteenth-century liberalism had not made significant progress in the minds of the Elbeuf bourgeois as yet. We shall see later that they constantly were calling on the state to aid them in their enterprises, and that their spirit was protectionist and anti-laissez faire in nature. In this particular instance, they asked that grain exports be prohibited when certain price levels were reached. This demand would probably have gained the approval of all but a handful of innovators. Further protection for agriculture was also sought in the prohibition of the opening of dovecotes during the harvest months and in the destruction of rabbits and other herbivorous game. A desire to make the enforcement of the trespass laws more difficult is a corollary of the wish to destroy animal pests.[16]

It can be said that no particular order of importance was observed in the placing of articles in the *cahier*. One has the feeling that Elbeuvians felt it more important to get all their complaints down on paper than to create a semblance of order among them. Thus it is that we pass from considerations of agriculture to questions of military service, only to return in a moment to taxes, having considered freedom of the press in passing.

As regards military service, the hydra of provincial quasi-independence once again rears its head. The *cahier* called for the abolition of the militia and for each province to henceforth have the right to provide the state with soldiers when and as it saw fit. This was hardly the way to build the efficient army needed by the Revolution and a far cry from the nation in arms of the year II. Still, it is understandable, when we realize that the army as it then existed was to a large degree professional and too supple an instrument in the hands of the royal government. We have only to remember the fear of the National Assembly in June, 1789, that it would be encircled by royal troops in order for the *raison d'être* of this demand to become clear. In effect, this was a call for more control of the civil administration over the army.[17]

Another military question was that of lodging troops stationed in or passing through Elbeuf. The *cahier* asked only that this burden be equally divided among all the inhabitants, with the

---

[16] *Cahier*, Articles 19–22.   [17] *Cahier*, Article 23.

sole exception of widows, unmarried women, and tax collectors.[18]
The fact is, however, that this obligation was none too popular,
even though it was rare. It was government policy to avoid
burdening the city with such charges. A memoire written some-
time in the seventeen-eighties, whose source we do not know but
which is official in form, notes:

> On n'a logé troupes que dans une seule occasion à Elbeuf, M. le duc
> d'Elbeuf l'ayant lui même demandé ainsi pour réduire les habitants qui
> avaient résisté à ses volontes. Il n'est pas du service du roi de troubler
> le commerce par un logement des troupes dans un lieu semblable où les
> manufactures qui y sont entassées l'une sur l'autre ramassent vingt mil
> ouvriers qui à peine y peuvent trouver place.[19]

It is perhaps for this reason that the *cahier* was very moderate on
this subject. In practice, Elbeuvians were more exigent. In April,
1789, the municipal officers protested to the sub-delegate of Pont
de l'Arche and obtained the withdrawal of a garrison from the
city.[20]

We come now to a series of fundamental demands having to
do with the security of the person. Here the Elbeuvians demand
that the principles of individual freedom be recognized and that
any person arrested be presented to his "natural" judge within
twenty-four hours. A corollary to this was the suppression of
special jurisdictions and of the right of *committimus*, as well as
the principle of equal punishment under law without distinction
of rank.[21] The ideas expressed here are part and parcel of the
climate of eighteenth-century thought, and there is no reason to
be surprised at their appearance in this instance. One wonders if
they would not have a legitimate place in a contemporary French
cahier de doléances.

If Elbeuvians exhibited "advanced" ideas on the question of
equality before the law, the same cannot be said about their sentiments concerning the press. Of course, they were for freedom of
the press, at least *en principe*. But they wished to hedge it around
with restrictions other than libel laws. Indeed, it is hard to imagine
what freedom is left the press when the author and publisher of

[18] *Cahier*, Article 25.
[19] *Arch. Nat.*, H 1666—"Mémoire sur l'Etat cy-après des Différents quartiers de
la Généralité [de Rouen] propres au logement des troupes."
[20] *Arch. Mun.*, Series CC.
[21] *Cahier*, Articles 28, 41, 42, 51.

a book may be prosecuted for "harming morals, the state of religion." [22]

Protection of rights of individuals was only a part of bourgeois preoccupations. Equally important was the opening of the way to power for the bourgeoisie as a class. It is for this reason that Elbeuvians insist on granting accessibility to the magistracy and to military rank to the Third Estate. But they also required that this upward movement should not create another class and thus break up their own unity, such as it was. This attitude had already shown itself when the bourgeois spoke of the *anoblis*. They had already realized the truth of the statement Méhée de la Touche was to make a few years later when he wrote: "I suppose that no one can seriously argue that the ennoblement of a few bourgeois is a good thing for the bourgeoisie." [23] That is why they wished to abolish the conferring of nobility upon buyers of venal offices. Henceforth, nobility was to be granted only for personal merit, on the initiative of the king or the recommendation of the Provincial Estates.[24]

While it was necessary to provide for the future, it was equally important to deal with the present. Because the Elbeuf bourgeoisie was almost exclusively commercial, this meant dealing with economic affairs. Once and for all, the moral taint attached to interest charges had to be removed by state sanction. The distinction was finally to be made between legitimate interest and usury, the latter was to remain subject to severe punishment, especially if practiced on "enfants de famille." It may be that, as one historian has put it, the bourgeois were here opening the door to the doctrine of "universal otherhood." They were also saying: "This is necessary. So be it. We are not ashamed." [25]

It is not to be assumed that the bourgeois of Elbeuf were in sympathy with what was to become the classic capitalism of the nineteenth century. As we have said, laissez faire, and its corollary of the legitimacy of all business practices, was not their meat. Certain strict prohibitions were to be maintained or even strength-

---

[22] *Cahier*, Article 24.

[23] Méhee de la Touche, *Histoire de la Prétendue Révolution de Pologne* (1792), pp. 2, 143, cited by R. R. Palmer, *The Age of the Democratic Revolutions* (Princeton, 1959), p. 432. For a general treatment of the nobility at the end of the old regime, see Marcel Reinhard, "Elite et Noblesse dans la Seconde Moitié du XVIIIᵉ Siècle," *Revue d'Histoire Moderne et Contemporaine*, III (1956), 5–37.

[24] *Cahier*, Articles 29, 52.   [25] *Cahier*, Articles 26, 66.

ened. Stock-jobbing, which they blamed for the rarity of investment capital, was to be proscribed. Bankruptcies, which had caused them heavy losses, were to be harshly punished. From now on, places of sanctuary in which bankrupts might escape prosecution were to be done away with. No letters of safe conduct or stays of execution of judgment were to be granted them. And to make sure that no one would profit from the contemplated reform in the commercial code, the due date of all negotiable instruments was to be fixed at set times throughout the country.[26]

Hand in hand with strictly commercial reforms must go a complete overhaul of the judicial system at all levels. It would be preferable to abolish all seigneurial jurisdictions, although an exception might be made for those of ancient vintage, on condition that the seigneur consent to employ three resident judges not including " les gens du fisc," to have the court meet weekly, and to provide secure prisons. In any case, the seigneurial court, even if it were to remain in existence, would no longer have the right to hear cases to which the seigneur himself was a party. When an affair of that nature arose, jurisdiction was to be placed as a matter of right in the hands of the nearest royal judge.[27] We shall see subsequently what particular circumstances in Elbeuf prompted these demands.

The structure of the royal judicial system was to be changed as well. Justices of the peace were to be established in each city with the power to decide all cases in which sums of up to one hundred livres were at stake without appeal. Final determination of all cases was to be decided within one year of their presentation to a court, for the injurious effects of the interminable dragging of cases from one court to another had often been felt. To ensure the smooth functioning of the judicial machinery, all judges were to be prohibited from arbitrarily ceasing to exercise their functions. At the same time, although venality was to be abolished, judges would have the security of knowing themselves to be irremovable. Members of the high magistracy could be chosen by the Provincial Estates, while lower court judges would be elected. Local residents would presumably be elected to the latter posts, thus eliminating outside interference in judicial matters, at least to a certain extent. A special elective commercial court on the model of the consular

---

[26] *Cahier*, Articles 27, 32–34.   [27] *Cahier*, Articles 44, 45.

jurisdictions of the old regime was to be set up in every city, with power to decide all cases without appeal up to a certain sum. In cases where more money was involved, appeal was to be had to the commercial court of the principal city of the generality. Of course, if these changes in the form of the judicial system were to be effective, there would have to be a complete reworking of the civil, criminal, and commercial codes. The bourgeois of Elbeuf proposed that the first two be entrusted to magistrates and the last to a committee of *négociants*. Finally, so that no one might escape the workings of a now enlightened legality, they asked that extradition treaties be negotiated.[28]

Was it because Elbeuvians got along well with their seigneur that they showed themselves moderate in regard to feudal privilege? All they asked was that seigneurial rents and *corvées* be redeemed, not abolished outright, so that the feudal underling would own only " la foi, l'hommage, le treizième et l'aveu." To be sure, all exclusive fiscal privileges had to be abolished, but they were not " feudal " in the proper sense of the term. Much more important from this point of view was the demand for an end to the banalities, called " une servitude odieuse." Moreover, the important role played by water-courses in the production of cloth led the bourgeois to ask for a reaffirmation of the article of the Coutume of Normandy which rendered their use free and not subject to feudal dues.[29]

The doctrine of the sanctity of property being a fundamental tenet of bourgeois thought, it is not surprising to find certain precisions relative thereto in the *cahier*. Tithes were to be suppressed in favor of a fixed and decent salary for all clergymen. There was to be freedom to grant twenty-year leases on rural property without alienating property rights. On the other hand, clerical lands were not to be given on general leases, but all leases made had to be respected by successors of the persons who had originally granted them. Not only were enclosures to be permitted, but they were to become obligatory. Also, common lands were to be alienated, and all uncultivated and waste land was to be sold, unless, in the latter case only, the proprietors preferred to put them into cultivation. It should be noted that these last two articles

[28] *Cahier*, Articles 31, 46, 47, 49, 43, 30, and 50.
[29] *Cahier*, Articles 35–37, 39.

were included not only as measures for the protection of property but also because it was felt that their enactment would increase agricultural yield and might encourage the raising of sheep that the woolen industry needed so desperately.[30]

The improvement of domestic woolens was part of a program that included government encouragement of manufactures, deep-sea fishing and the search for, and exploitation of, coal mines. The bolstering of the French position vis-à-vis England was also the order of the day. Considering the profound hatred felt by the Elbeuvians for the Eden Treaty of 1786, they were rather moderate in expressing their opinion. They did not go so far as to demand its outright repeal but asked only that the Estates General weigh its relative advantages and disadvantages and then take appropriate action. In the interim, measures were to be taken to stop customs commissioners from allowing English goods to enter fraudulently into France, without paying the requisite duties.[31]

But man does not live by bread alone. Having ensured what nonetheless remained the staff of life by insisting on a variety of reforms, not the least of which was a prohibition on millers to accept fees in kind or to buy and sell grain, the Elbeuf bourgeois could turn to matters of the spirit. In this, it cannot be said that they were anti-clerical. What was important to them was the smooth functioning of the church—without waste. And waste was what they found when there were less than thirty regular clergy in any religious establishment. On condition of this kind of regrouping, they were ready to provide pensions for the residents—out of clerical revenues, of course. Any excess revenue belonging to the community should be applied to the establishment of workshop-hospitals, the only way to wipe out beggary. In order to ensure efficient administration, moreover, the bourgeois wished higher clerical positions to be filled only by men of experience. All *grands vicaires*, bishops, and archbishops were to be chosen from *curés* of fifteen years standing, while a curate could become a *curé* only after ten years service. Bishops and archbishops alone were to be empowered to grant all ecclesiastical dispensations, with no need for recourse to the Roman *curia*. It is possible that this last provision was a sign of Gallican nationalism as much as of anything else, but there is no way of proving it.[32]

[30] *Cahier*, Articles 40, 55, 56, 61, 62, and 65.
[31] *Cahier*, Articles 64, 67.   [32] *Cahier*, Articles 38, 54, 57, 58, and 60.

In any document of this sort there are always some clauses that seem to float about alone, without any particular relation to the whole. The *cahier* of Elbeuf is no exception. We find, for instance, a request that soldiers and sailors be pensioned when they retire from service because of wounds or old age. Another article calls for the abolition of subordinate judicial officers, such as ushers, notaries, and *commissaires-priseurs*.[33] Both are explicable: the first was perhaps meant to strengthen the merchant marine, which was so important to Elbeuf commerce, the second to do away with the petty annoyances due to the hoard of semi-judicial functionaries who flourished in the eighteenth century.

The *cahier* also asked that the Estates General confirm the Edict of Toleration of 1787. Although Elbeuf had not suffered greatly from the revocation of the Edict of Nantes and there were few Protestants in the city, the Huguenot origin of some of the manufacturers may account for the sympathy shown them by this article.[34]

Finally, the *cahier* of the Third Estate of Elbeuf came to a close by asking that all decrees of the Estates General be sent to the courts for registration and execution. It is to be assumed that " registration " in this case meant only publication and was not to entail a right of remonstrance. Even before the enactment of any law, the Estates General had the consent of the Elbeuvians to grant a temporary subsidy to the crown. In return, the crown would be well advised to refuse the evil Calonne all participation in the Estates. Under these conditions, the Third Estate was willing to co-operate to the utmost in the noble endeavor of saving the nation. Confident of success, it placed its trust in the deputies and authorized them to make whatever sacrifices might be necessary to accomplish this end.[35]

Such was the *cahier* of the Third Estate of Elbeuf. Its contents show that it was both fairly representative of the general movement of ideas of the period and that it was a clear expression of the class interests of the bourgeois who drew it up. This is not to say that its bias was not shared by other classes in the population, but certain demands which one might expect to find had

[33] *Cahier*, Articles 53, 59.
[34] *Cahier*, Article 63. See Chapter 1 above, pp. 23–24.
[35] *Cahier*, Articles 68–71.

the *cahier* been written by wage earners and peasants were conspicuous by their absence.

We have only to look at the *cahier* of a neighboring village to realize this. Les-Authieux-Port St. Ouen, situated approximately 5 kilometers from Elbeuf, was the place where much of the fulling of Elbeuf cloth was done. A part of its population was also employed in spinning wool for the manufacture. And it is apparent that these peasant workers had some say in formulating the *cahier*. To a great extent, their demands, while less elegantly and more strongly phrased, coincide with those made at Elbeuf. But there are two additional points. First: " Pour ce qui regarde les procédures concernant l'agriculture, qu'il soit défendu à tous juges d'en connaître, qu'il soit nommé dans chaque commune des experts laboureurs au nombre de trois pour être juges des différends qui concerneront les entreprises, dommages et dégradations de terres, et que ces experts soient nommés par la paroisse en général et qu'il soient remplacés par trois autres tous les trois ans." This demand translates the traditional distrust of the peasantry for legal functionaries in a field vital to its livelihood, and is paralleled by the Elbeuvians' demands for special commercial courts.

The second point noted at Port St. Ouen is even more significant and is directly against the interest of the Elbeuf bourgeoisie. It asks that: " Toutes les mécaniques de toutes espèces soient détruites et défendues." Indeed, the existence of these machines was a direct threat to the livelihood of peasants to whom spinning furnished a needed supplementary income, especially in a period of economic crisis. Luddite agitation of this sort was, then, only to be expected. But the bourgeois employers of labor needed government encouragement of machinery in order to cut their production costs and to stand up to foreign, particularly English, competition.[36] As Port St. Ouen was, like Elbeuf, part of the bailliage of Pont de l'Arche,[37] it would be up to that assembly to choose between the two conflicting points of view.

To represent itself at the assembly of Pont de l'Arche, Elbeuf had the right to choose six persons. Those chosen were Pierre Nicolas Bourdon, Parfait Grandin, and Henry Hayet, all members

---

[36] Henri St. Denis and P. Duchemin, *Notices Historiques et Statistiques sur les Communes des Environs d'Elbeuf*, Vol. III, *Les Authieux-Port St. Ouen* (Elbeuf, 1885), pp. 39–41, Articles 1 and 2 of the *cahier*.

[37] J. Vernier, *Répertoire*, pp. cxxiv–cxxvi.

of great manufacturing families, as well as Thomas François Vedic fils, a baker, Laurent Patallier, a plaster merchant, and Bosquier, a lawyer.[38] Rural parishes had the right to choose two to four deputies depending on their size. At Pont de l'Arche there were 172 deputies, and they chose twenty-four commissioners, including three Elbeuvians—Grandin, Bourdon, and Bosquier—to draw up the bailliage *cahier*. The task of the Assembly was to integrate the *cahiers* of all the parishes and then to choose one-fourth of its members to represent the area at the assembly of the Grand Bailliage of Rouen. It appears that the *cahier* drawn up by the commissioners was adopted by the full assembly on first reading without any trouble.[39]

How did this *cahier* differ from the one written at Elbeuf? First of all, because it represented a much larger area, it was considerably longer, containing 102 articles, and was a good deal more precise. It was also a more heterogeneous document, showing universal concern in almost everything. It exhibited much greater interest in legal matters, insisting, for instance, that there be three judges in all courts, and that no judge have less than ten years experience as a lawyer. Training in a law school was to be rigorously obligatory, with no dispensations possible. The status of all subordinate judicial personnel was to be closely regulated. A clear jurisdictional area was to be assigned to each court, and no parish might be divided between two courts, a practice which evidently complicated legal matters no end. There was also the request that police jurisdiction be granted to the municipalities, a request that is not to be found in the Elbeuf *cahier*, but whose absence did not stop the Elbeuvians from assuming this authority early in the Revolution.

A parallel interest, no doubt due to the presence of the representatives of the peasantry, was shown in agriculture. Where Elbeuf was far more interested in expediting business affairs, the *cahier* of Pont de l'Arche wished to settle agricultural disputes quickly by putting jurisdiction into the hands of the municipality. The peasant was to be protected against the incursion of seigneurial game by making the seigneur responsible for any damage that this might cause. And not only that: because there were predatory

---

[38] *Arch. Mun.*, Délib., Vol. I (March 28, 1789).

[39] E. Le Parquier, "Les Assemblées Electorales de 1789 dans les Bailliages Secondaires de la Haute Normandie," *La Normandie*, XIII (1906), 1–12, 32–42.

men as well as predatory animals, the law was to be changed so as to prevent the *feudistes* from being both rent collectors and drawing up the *aveux*. More land would be made available to non-privileged groups by forbidding the clergy to hold leases on rural property.

Aside from these two interests, the *cahier* of Pont de l'Arche was somewhat more firm than that of Elbeuf, although still similar in most respects. Indeed, many articles of the Elbeuf *cahier* were reproduced textually. Notable among those that were strengthened are the demands for a written constitution, meeting of the Estates General every three, instead of every five, years, the abolition of plural benefices, and the obligation of the hierarchy to reside in their dioceses. The request of Elbeuf that all judicial matters be settled within a year of the filing of a complaint is here accompanied by an article which asks that there be only two degrees of jurisdiction.

On commercial matters, what has been said above applies with equal force. Where Elbeuf asked only that customs fraud be ended, Pont de l'Arche indicates a precise system whereby this end may be accomplished. Henceforth, all cloth entering the country from England would have to be marked by a customs officer in the presence of the clerk of the manufacturers, and each bale would have to be accompanied by a certificate signed by both. Where Elbeuf asked for diverse measures against bankrupts, Pont de l'Arche was precise in demanding a special court to deal with bankruptcy cases. The Elbeuvians ask vaguely for government encouragement of manufactures, but the secondary bailliage allows its distaste for government control to be revealed by asking that the advantages and disadvantages of Inspectors of Manufactures be examined by the Estates General. Finally, another measure that may have been taken to ensure the protection of markets was that in favor of attaching the colonies to the mother country by allowing the former to be represented in the Estates.

In brief, then, conflicts between the two *cahiers* under consideration were rare. To be sure, some did exist. We find that the lawyers present in considerable numbers at the larger assembly were not so dogmatic about the abolition of special courts or of venal offices. In the first case, the assembly was willing to allow their continued existence, should they be judged indispensable, and, in the second, the request relative to venality was limited to an investigation of the question by the Estates General. It is evident that the *gens de loi* had a great deal to lose in the way of employment and influence if both items were abolished.

On economic affairs, the divergences were more marked. It is their presence which justifies the hypothesis of the more popular character of the Pont de l'Arche assembly in comparison to that of Elbeuf. Elbeuvians had asked that all common lands be sold to individual proprietors, whereas Pont de l'Arche took exactly the opposite position, for the conservation of the lands. The same was true of forests. But even more important was the refusal of Pont de l'Arche to settle the question of machinery. The influence of the manufacturers in the commission that drew the *cahier* would not permit the introduction of a statement against textile machinery. On the other hand, these same manufacturers lacked sufficient power to enforce their will on the assembly as a whole on this occasion. The result was a compromise by which the Estates were asked to look into the pros and cons of the matter, and if machines were found to be harmful, to prohibit them.[40]

It appears that the urban-rural conflict had even more serious repercussions in the assembly of the secondary bailliage when it came to the question of electing deputies to the Grand Bailliage of Rouen. Only one person was elected on the first ballot, the rest not until the third, because of this conflict. The president of the Pont de l'Arche assembly, Jacques François Houzard de la Potterie, *lieutenant particulier du bailliage*, felt it necessary to eject a certain Thélot de la Binaudière of the parish of Asseville for having accused him of conspiring to name urbanites as deputies, in preference to rural members. Thélot had wanted no more than one-quarter of the deputies to the Grand Bailliage to be representatives of urban areas. In fact, nineteen of the forty-four persons elected were either functionaries or business men, a proportion that was certainly too high in terms of the populations represented.[41] Several of these persons were from Elbeuf, and

[40] *Cahier de Plaintes, Doléances et Remontrances Arrêté par les Commissaires Nommés le 1er de ce Mois par le Tiers Etat du Pont de l'Arche, pour être porté à l'Assemblée des Trois Ordres qui se Tiendra le 15 de ce Mois* (n. p., 1789). A copy may be found in the Bibliothèque Historique de la Ville de Paris under the call number 959554.

[41] LeParquier, "Les Assemblées Electorales"; Hippeau, *Gouvernement*, VI, 69–70.

one of them, the manufacturer Hayet, became a member of the commission of the Grand Bailliage that drew its *cahier*.[42]

II

It is not my intention to retrace here the entire political history of Elbeuf during the Revolutionary Period. I shall deal only with those events capable of throwing some light on the social structure of the city and on the changes it underwent at this time. The basic question to be answered is: How revolutionary was Elbeuf?

One thing is certain: the upper bourgeoisie, and particularly the manufacturers, had no intention of allowing whatever political changes that might intervene to loosen their hold on political power. They were quick to respond to any challenge. The first came, quite by accident, in the fall of 1788.

An Order in Council of September 30, 1788, ordered the municipality to call upon the forty most highly taxed inhabitants to aid it in picking eight persons who would, in turn, co-operate with the municipality in apportioning the capitation. This was done on October 23. Whether by accident or design, twenty-one of the forty, or almost exactly half, were manufacturers. The others included eleven merchants, two gardeners, one barber, two dyers, two rentiers, and one tool grinder. But the manufacturers were not happy about the results of the convocation, claiming that the date on which it was made (October 22) showed great haste on the part of the municipality, and moreover, that the date for which it was called (October 23) was the day of the fair of St. Romain, a day on which, it was known, many manufacturers would not be able to attend. The result was that of the eight persons chosen as tax commissioners, only one was a manufacturer. The others were four merchants, a dyer, a baker, and a tool grinder. Furthermore, said the manufacturers, they were represented by only two persons in the municipality (an assertion clearly contrary to fact) and so had not had an adequate voice in the apportionment of taxes. They wrote: " La communauté des fabricants à laquelle presque tous les autres habitants doivent leur existence, payant à peu près la moitié de la charge publique et renfermant probablement les quarante plus hauts cotisés, il était de toute justice qu'elle

[42] *Journal de Rouen* (April 25, 1789), pp. 137–38.

fournît au moins la moitié des huit adjoints à l'assiette de l'impôt."
They sent this protest to the *Bureau Intermédiaire* of the Department of the Andelys and Pont de l'Arche, asking that a new
assembly of forty be called, in which the election of at least four
manufacturers as tax commissioners would be assured. The Bureau,
completely at a loss as to how to reply, decided to ask the Elbeuf
municipality for its opinion on the matter. And here is the strange
thing: the municipality wrote back that it was in perfect agreement
with the manufacturers, that it had attempted to grant them
adequate representation in the first place, and that this was all a
frightful mistake. Upon receipt of this letter, the Bureau wrote to
the *Commission Intermédiaire* of the Provincial Assembly of
Rouen stating its advice in conformity with the above requests.
But by the time the Commission got around to answering, it had
only to reply that the whole thing was superfluous, as an Order in
Council of December 4 had decided that taxes would be assessed
in the old manner—by tax collectors appointed directly by the
municipality.[43]

I am inclined to feel that the whole thing was a tempest in a
teapot, a collossal misunderstanding. No one in Elbeuf bothered
to write to the *Bureau Intermédiaire* to oppose the manufacturers'
request, and, when one comes right down to it, everyone seems
to have been in agreement. Even if this were not so, the most
that can be said for this incident is that it was a petty quarrel
between two groups of upper bourgeois. The first interclass
incidents did not take place before 1789.

The principal actors in this episode were the municipality, the
bailli, two lawyers, Balleroy and Asse, and certain petits bourgeois.
If the last named were allied against the municipality, it was more
because politics makes strange bedfellows than because of common
interest.

In June, 1789, an incident occurred that was the first to create
bad feeling between the municipality and certain members of the
lower bourgeoisie. The tavernkeeper Leveneur accused the municipal officers of having conspired to rig the elections of deputies to
the assembly of Pont de l'Arche. They replied by stating that
Leveneur was out to destroy them, because he was dissatisfied
with the way in which taxes had been assessed. They defended

---

[43] *Arch. Mun.*, Délib., Vol. I (October 21 and 23, 1788); *Arch. Dép. de l'Eure*,
C 45 (October 28, November 12, and December 24, 1788).

themselves against the charge of having favored the manufacturers in this matter. Then they recounted their version of the elections: At the meeting of the primary assembly, they said, four persons besides those elected (a cardmaker, a retail merchant, a notary, and a retailer of salt and tobacco) had received some votes. Their partisans claimed that they should represent the city in place of three manufacturers and a lawyer who, said the municipality, had a majority of votes. After a stormy session that lasted twelve hours, the president of the primary assembly decided against the objectors. Nonetheless, they went to the Bailliage Assembly in an effort to make good their claim to represent the city. The president of the bailliage turned them down. The incident was closed —for the time being.[44]

On July 20, 1789, the municipality disbanded the bourgeois militia and substituted for it a corps of volunteer patriots. At the beginning, there were only thirty of them, but in August, because of disturbances due to the lack of grain, the corps was expanded until it included 181 persons divided into four companies. The corps had the right to elect, in conjunction with the municipality, its own officers. During the limited period of time anyone might join the corps, afterward the recommendation of two members and of the municipality would be necessary. The volunteers elected four officers to meet with two members of the municipality, in the presence of two to four other volunteers, to draw up a statute for the group, subject to the approval of the municipal committee as a whole. At the same time a public subscription was opened to buy arms.[45] In September the municipality assumed greater control of the volunteers by changing the system of election of officers to include two degrees of suffrage. Instead of direct election by all volunteers, the troops would now elect twelve of their number, three in each company, to join with the mayor and five *échevins* in choosing officers.[46]

On September 2, the municipality took on responsibility for " la police et sécurité de la ville " until orders were received from the king and National Assembly. It justified this action by saying that the *bailli*, whose job it had been to enforce police regulations, was often absent from Elbeuf, and that even when present he had refused to co-operate with the municipality in

[44] *Arch. Mun.*, BB⁸.   [45] *Arch. Mun.*, Series EE.   [46] *Arch. Nat.*, Dⁱᵛ 61.

forcing bakers to furnish bread.[47] It was easier to make this claim stand as the *bailli* and everyone else connected with the Haute Justice were naturally suspected of being tools of the aristocracy.

Still, the reaction came quickly. Leveneur, his anger intensified by his defeat on the question of delegates to the assembly of Pont de l'Arche, threatened to bring the matter up before the National Assembly. His complaint was, and he was no doubt correct, that the municipality was not representative of the community. " La municipalité [he wrote] vraie et tendre mère de famille doit renfermer en elle un grand désir d'établir un comité et une milice bourgeoise. Tout député de chaque corps doit former membre de ce comité; . . . alors la municipalité est la base et le fondement du vrai comité permanent." [48] But he knew full well that the manufacturers who controlled the municipality and who made of it a " cruelle marâtre pour le reste des citoyens " would never give in to his demands. It is likely that he was right in so thinking, although no evidence is found to substantiate his conclusions that the reason for this refusal was a fear of exposure of certain financial manipulations on their part. It is true that the city was deeply in debt at this time, but it is not correct to say that the manufacturers had created this debt for their own personal advantage. Very simply, they resisted the interference of other social strata because they wished to maintain power in their own hands.

Faced with this staunch refusal, Leveneur carried out his threat to bring the question to the attention of the National Assembly. In October, he wrote to the *Comité des Rapports*:

Ils [the manufacturers] ont formé un comité, n'ont pas voulu y admettre les deputés de la commune. Ces dits deputés sont obligés de présenter une requête à M. le juge dudit lieu avec copie d'un décret rendu le 7 de ce mois dans lequel ils annoncent être revêtus du pouvoir exécutif. Ils en ont donné des marques en la personne de Mr. Asse, faisant alors les fonctions de juge, et cela le 16 de ce mois pour avoir fait défenses à M. le maire de porter les décrets de cette nature vexatoire, et qui ont mis le trouble dans cette ville.[49]

Just what was this vexatious decree? First of all, it threatened with severe, military punishment all persons who refused to do

[47] *Arch. Mun.*, Délib., Vol. I (September 23, 1789).
[48] *Arch. Mun.*, BB[10].   [49] *Arch. Nat.*, D[xxix] 37.

guard duty. Second, it subjected to such duty all men between the ages of eighteen and seventy paying at least 12 livres in capitation. Persons who did not serve on the appointed day were fined three livres and made to stand guard the following day. The sick paid six livres a month in lieu of service. As Leveneur explains, a group of thirty persons had already obtained a show cause order from the *bailli* on the grounds that the corps in which the municipality was forcing people to serve was not a bourgeois militia, because it had not been constituted with the approval of a general assembly of the inhabitants. Moreover, to fix the age limit at seventy was illegal, since the National Assembly had exempted all persons over forty from service in similar bodies. Illegality never being limited to one aspect of a system, the municipality was constrained, said the petitioners, to use force in order to make people serve, and this too was illegal in the absence of a judicial order.[50] Leveneur himself went a step further than the persons who signed the petition. He asked the National Assembly to order the convocation of a general assembly of the city to rectify this situation and to form a real bourgeois militia. He added that this was absolutely necessary, because the volunteers were persecuting a famished population by protecting transports of grains out of the region.[51] Moreover, the commanders of the volunteers were Zins and Desilles, " deux presque gentilshommes, suffragant et conservateur du château du Prince de Lambesc." [52] This was a situation not to be tolerated. One can understand the attitude here expressed, when one knows that the two persons in question were indeed chevaliers of the Order of St. Louis, and that this accusation was written several months after the famous charge of the Tuileries of July 12 made by the Royal-Allemand Regiment with Lambesc at its head.

The *bailli* and the two lawyers of the Haute Justice reacted similarly to the pretentions of the municipality. To the complaints expressed above, they added still more. Hervieu de l'Homme, the *bailli*, accused the city of causing the current grain shortage by intimidating the cultivators of the region, and when he, the *bailli*, had attempted to prosecute a troublemaker, the city had sent its volunteers to release him, thus preventing justice from being done. The expedition was led by the aristocratic Zins in his capacity as

[50] *Arch. Mun.*, BB[10]   [51] See above, pp. 129.   [52] *Arch. Nat.*, D[xxix] 37.

commandant. Hervieu wrote: "J'ai été étonné qu'un officier décoré de la croix de St. Louis se soit prêté à un pareil acte de violence envers un officier de justice qui remplit son devoir, mais les expéditions militaires ont toujours attraits pour ceux qui ont sucé le lait meurtrier. . . ." [53] The municipality also threatened with military sanctions the *ancien avocat* Asse, who had replaced the *bailli* in his functions for a short time while the latter was on vacation, and had approved the petition of the thirty against the municipality.[54] For all these reasons, the *bailli* notified the municipality and the National Assembly that he had decided to end his judicial service until measures should be taken against the pretentions of the former body. His indictment of the municipal administration ran like this:

Elbeuf est une ville de fabrique, ce sont les fabriquants qui mettent eux-mêmes dans les charges municipales à l'exception du maire qui est nommé par le prince seigneur haut justicier. Ils ont [sic] parti de là pour se distribuer entr'eux les honneurs militaires et rien n'est capable de les arrêter dans leur marche. Les habitants réclament, soutiennent que la municipalité ne peut les assujetir à une contribution qu'ils n'ont pas consentie,[55] et lorsque je me dispose à leur faire rendre justice, je reçois une signification extra-judiciaire dans laquelle le corps de ville déclare être seul compétent et fait très *expresses défenses à toutes personnes* en quelque qualité qu'elles agissent de troubler le corps municipal à peine d'être poursuivi comme perturbateur du repos public.

J'espère, Monseigneur, qu'il vous sera facile de distinguer le contraste frappant et choquant des prétentions de la municipalité. Je serai dans mes fonctions regardé comme perturbateur du repos public et la municipalité qui n'a aucune espèce de jurisdiction pas même sur ses propres manufactures sera écoutée à se dire juge et partie dans tout ce qu'elle fera et décretera. Non, Monseigneur, à la tête des représentants de la nation occupés d'anéantir le despotisme, vous ne permettrez pas qu'il se réfugie et s'établisse impunément dans toutes les petites villes du royaume, vous ne souffrirez pas que pour défendre sa propriété, on attente à celle des autres, c'est cependant ce que l'on se permet ici, on envoye chez le laboureur ou le force la corde à la main d'apporter du bled qu'il apporterait librement si la propriété était respectée à la halle, mais le peu de bled que la crainte les fait apporter est à la discretion du peuple et le propriétaire perd 7 ou 8 francs par sac du prix qu'il le vendrait dans le marché voisin. Voilà, Monseigneur, la principale cause de la rareté des grains dans le marché de cette ville.[56]

---

[53] *Arch. Nat.*, D^{iv} 61; *Arch. Mun.*, BB^{10}.
[54] *Arch. Nat.*, D^{iv} 61.
[55] This is a reference to the tax in lieu of service in the volunteers.
[56] *Arch. Nat.*, D^{iv} 61.

It becomes more and more obvious as we read these documents that there is a power struggle between the municipality dominated by the upper bourgeois manufacturers and the judicial officers. The municipality had two objectives: to maintain calm in the city while retaining power in its own hands. To do so, it had to employ revolutionary measures. There can be no doubt that the creation of a permanent committee and of a corps of volunteers was extra-legal, but they were made necessary by the situation. So also was the assumption of police power. All of this annoyed the judiciary, accustomed to playing a leading role through the institution of the Haute Justice and threatened by these initiatives. The judicial officers protested and took advantage of a certain latent discontent among the lower bourgeois and, no doubt, the wage earners on questions of grain, representation, and taxation, in order to do so. It was only in that sense that a united front was possible between the judiciary and the other anti-municipal groups, for certainly the former would never allow itself to be a party to a seizure of power by the latter, as is clearly shown by Hervieu's attitude toward fixed prices on grain enforced by " le peuple." As Balleroy later wrote, it was dangerous to arm the textile workers, because " cette classe du peuple, la plus indigente, n'est pas incapable des meilleures intentions, mais elle peut aisément se tromper dans les moyens." [57]

The incident in which this conflict reached its high point was the arrest of Balleroy, a lawyer in the Haute Justice about whom a good deal more will be heard in the course of the Revolution. On October 13, he was convoked to do guard duty under the *ordonnance* of October 7. He refused, for reasons he later explained:

> Moi! Reconnaître l'existence du comité d'Elbeuf, formé par lui-même, ayant à sa tête le maire de ville, nommé par le Prince de Lambesc, dont le secrétaire est l'homme d'affaires de ce Prince! Prendre les armes sous le commandement d'officiers volontaires, dont le chef est M de Zins, essentiellement l'homme du Prince, dont un des officiers est M. Bosquier, partisan des chasses privilégieés . . . En vérité, ma conscience y répugnait invinciblement; cela ne se pouvait pas.

He claimed to be as patriotic as the next man but refused to recognize illegally constituted bodies. As a result, he was arrested on

---

[57] *Arch. Nat.*, AD XVI 76—Mémoire pour François-Pierre Balleroy, Avocat Plaidant à Elbeuf.

the evening of October 14 and made to stand guard until the following evening. During all this time he continued to protest and demanded an audience with the committee, but was refused. On October 16, he was sentenced by the municipality to be incapable of bearing arms, because of " propos impertinents et séditieux " and slanders against de Zins and Bosquier. He was then released and, as he said, moved to Paris, " le pays de la liberté." And all this because he had ventured to criticize the municipality's actions! Balleroy asked that the judgment against him be suspended, and that his case be referred to a competent tribunal before which he intended to accuse those responsible for his disgrace of scandalous conduct. The committee of the National Assembly to which this appeal was addressed decided to write to the Elbeuf municipality to have its comments on the matter.[58]

By December, when Balleroy wrote his pamphlet, the municipal officers had already had occasion to defend themselves. They protested that the steps taken by them to safeguard grain supplies were known to all the inhabitants, and that the thirty persons who had signed the anti-municipality petition were " presque tous sans propriétés, d'une classe facile à séduire, et dont plusieurs ont déjà déclaré que leur signature avait été surprise par un cabaretier établi dans cette ville depuis environ un an et demi, connu pour fraudeur et chef de cabale." [59] They added that their efforts to maintain order and calm would no doubt have been successful but for the intrigues of the *bailli* and the two lawyers, " tous trois citoyens étrangers et dévoués sans doute aux ennemis de l'état, puisque par des insinuations perverses, ils ont cherché à indisposer citoyens contre citoyens, et le peuple contre les officiers municipaux. . . ." [60] The *bailli* had consistently countered the intentions of the municipality in this domain by releasing its prisoners, including an " homme incendiaire " who had come from outside Elbeuf to incite the people to revolt, to burn the workshops and machines. On the other hand, the *bailli* had been opposed to the release of a prisoner who had done no more than insult the officers of the guard while under the influence of

[58] *Ibid.*

[59] *Arch. Nat.*, D^{vi} 61. The reference is to Leveneur.

[60] It is true that two of the three were " citoyens étrangers " in the sense that Hervieu was a lawyer at the Parlement de Rouen and was domiciled there, while Balleroy had come to Elbeuf from Pont de l'Arche the year before. Asse, however, had been on the capitation roll of Elbeuf for some years prior to the Revolution.

alcohol. What was true of the *bailli* was equally true of Asse, when he had temporarily assumed the former's functions. All that the municipality could do in December was to repeat the same system of defense.[61] At most, it would concede that it had been forced to resort to unusual methods: ". . . ceux auquels est confié le soin de contenir une multitude souvent excitée par les enemis du bien public ont une tache bien pénible à remplir, et pour y parvenir, ils sont souvent forcés d'employer dans ces temps désastreux les seuls moyens que commande une imperieuse necéssité." [62] In any case, their intentions were of the purest:

On nous taxe et on a voulu vous persuader, Messieurs, que le corps municipal de notre ville est imbu des principes de l'aristocratie.

Est-il possible de penser qu'une ville toute composée de négociants occupés sérieusement par des manufactures utiles et précieuses où il n'y a point de noblesse, où il n'y a pas une charge de judicature, qui a un intérêt majeur à l'abolition de toutes entraves féodales et fiscales ne soit pas disposée à recevoir avec reconnaissance tous les décrets de l'Assemblée Nationale, qui tous tendent au soulagement et au bonheur du peuple.[63]

At the same time, individuals, notably Bosquier, the *procureur syndic,* defended themselves against Balleroy's charges by absolutely denying accusations according to which they were clients of the Prince de Lambesc, and that Bosquier, in his capacity as a lawyer, had defended the Prince's hunting rights, that relic of the feudal regime. In reply Bosquier resorted to the argument of the sanctity of private property, attempting to show that the persons he had prosecuted had not merely invaded the Prince's eminent domain but that to which he had property rights exclusive of all feudal contracts.[64]

This campaign of mutual recrimination did have certain results, not always favorable to the municipality. First of all, the municipal officers were temporarily compelled to give up their police jurisdiction. There is a resolution in the deliberations of December 10, 1789, noting that the city was "sans police," and that, therefore, the municipality and the guard were unable to cope with the nightly disturbances of the peace. They ordered that all those arrested should be judged by the royal court at Pont de l'Arche. Shortly afterward, on February 18, 1790, Zins resigned his post as head of the guard, giving ill health as his reason.[65]

[61] *Arch. Nat.,* D^iv 61.
[62] *Arch. Nat.,* D^iv 61.
[63] *Arch. Nat.,* D^iv 61.
[64] *Arch. Nat.,* D^xxix 37.
[65] *Arch. Mun.,* Délib., Vol. I (December 10, 1789 and February 18, 1790).

In the interim, conflicts had not ceased. The elections of February, 1790, the first under the municipal law of December 14, 1789, resulted in the replacement of a great many upper bourgeois, particularly manufacturers, by lower bourgeois tradesmen and independent artisans. This change was accomplished only over the protests of the old municipality, which looked upon Balleroy as the cause of its troubles. After the election of a mayor, the primary assemblies met to choose municipal officers and notables. At 11 P. M. on the evening of February 10, Fouard, a chandler and commissioner of the section of St. Jean, brought the ballots to the municipality for verification. But the ballot box was presented " sans être ni fiscelée ny cachetée." The municipal officers still in power protested that this was highly irregular, and that it was clear that inadmissible means of ballot counting had been employed in the St. Jean section. Therefore, they said, the elections should be declared null and void. This action was all the more imperative as several of the citizens had voted without first having taken the oath of allegiance. It was finally decided, after much argumentation, to convoke the primary assemblies of both sections, and to pose to them the question of the regularity of the elections. On February 14, the sections voted to accept the results of the assemblies of the 10th.

The electoral dispute must be seen as another episode in the continuing struggle between the municipality on the one hand, and the judiciary supported by the lower bourgeois on the other. The old municipality wrote to the president of the National Assembly:

Les personnes bien intentionnées de notre ville gémissent sur l'esprit de cabale que le Sr. Balleroy, avocat, y a semé en répandant avec profusion la veille des élections un mémoire incendiaire tendant à exclure des places municipales nos citoyens les plus capables . . . [il emploie] divers moyens . . . pour obtenir les suffrages d'un peuple nombreux qu'il cherche à séduire par les plus belles promesses. . . .

To what extent Balleroy played a leading role in this affair we do not know, but we do know that his confrère and ally Asse, in his capacity as president of the section of St. Jean, staunchly defended the legitimacy of the electoral procedure.[66]

The result of this struggle was a defeat for the old municipality.

[66] *Arch. Nat.*, D[iv] 61; *Arch. Mun.*, BB[10].

Among those elected as new municipal officers were Balleroy and Asse, the latter becoming *procureur* of the commune. However, peace was not restored so easily; the old questions continued to arouse controversy. We can pass over Balleroy's attempt to deprive the mayor of a voice in the debates of the municipal council as being just a sign of personal rivalry,[67] but we cannot neglect the recurrence of the police question, which caused a split among members of the municipality. The law of March 20–23, 1790, granted the municipality "la police administrative et contentieuse" on a temporary basis. On May 4 the municipality voted to hold court sessions three times a week, and, on June 8, to defend its newly acquired prerogatives on the occasion of a suit brought by a worker against a manufacturer before the Haute Justice, as had been the tradition. Balleroy and four other municipal officers, all elected in February, 1790, protested, saying:

Nous n'avons pas cru que l'attribution que l'assemblée Nationale a faite provisoirement aux nouvelles municipalités s'étendît au delà de la partie administrative & du contentieux qui pouvait en résulter; le mot police a reçu dans notre esprit une distinction en police administrative et police privée, celle-ci (nous l'avons du moins pensé) est restée aux juges ordinaires. . . . La jugeomanie peut être un défaut des nouvelles municipalités. . . . Le bailli d'Elbeuf a l'exercice de la jurisdiction sur les manufactures par une attribution particulière. . . . Nous avons cru que pour le dépouiller de cette branche de sa jurisdiction il fallait au moins attendre qu'il le fût de la haute justice entièrement; un juge doit être respecté dans une ville: Réduisant [*sic*] peu a peu son autorité, c'est l'amener au point où étant encore besoin qu'elle soit interposée, elle peut n'avoir plus de force.[68]

The question was settled only by the suppression of the Haute Justice and its replacement by a justice of the peace in accordance with the law of August 16–24, 1790.

Was this a settlement? Hardly, for the dispute continued under a new form, with the aid of the vagueness of the law. The law setting up justices of the peace had given them jurisdiction without appeal in all cases involving sums up to 50 livres and with appeal up to 100 livres. On the other hand, they had no criminal jurisdiction, while the law of July 19–22, 1791, gave the police tribunals of the municipalities the right to impose fines of up to 500 livres and prison terms of up to eight days for infractions of municipal

[67] *Arch. Nat.*, D^{iv} 61; *Arch. Mun.*, Délib., Vol. I (March 4 and May 4, 1790).
[68] *Arch. Nat.*, D^{xxix} 37; see also *Arch. Mun.*, Délib., Vol. I (May 4 and June 8, 1790).

ordonnances. What was not clear was the extent to which jurisdiction over the manufacture fell within either competence. The
situation was made more explosive by the election of Balleroy
as justice of the peace in November, 1790, and his re-election in
December, 1792.[69] The manufacturers proposed an alternative
solution: the creation of special commercial courts. Of this
proposal Balleroy wrote:

> Les fabricants voudraient donc bien rétablir un tribunal spécial pour
> leur manufacture. Il serait composé de fabricants. . . . Ils s'imaginent
> qu'ils peuvent ôter aux ouvriers le droit de concourir à l'élection des juges.
> De plus, par cette haine que la Révolution a attirée à ses veritables
> zélateurs, il ne plaît pas à plusieurs d'entr'eux de comparaître devant moi—
> trois ont été nommés mes assesseurs et ils ont refusé l'honneur.
> Ce serait contre les principes de la liberté française, qui ont détruit les
> corporations jurandes et maîtrises, d'établir un tribunal de manufacture.
> Peut-être se fondent-ils sur la conservation que l'Assemblée Nationale a
> faite de la jurisdiction des patrons pêcheurs à Marseille. Eh bien, que
> par la raison de parité, l'élection des juges de manufacture se fasse et
> par les fabricants et par les ouvriers: Or les fabricants ne voudront pas
> de cela.
> Ils ont à dire que le juge de paix ne se connaît pas en manufacture,
> mais ses assesseurs s'y connaissent. Il y en a deux qui ont été contremaîtres
> de manufacture. Pourquoi les fabricants qui ont eu l'honneur d'être
> nommés ont-ils refusé? Au reste ce ne sera pas à cause de tel ou tel juge
> que les loix apporteront des modifications à la compétence des juges de
> la paix.[70]

On this last point Balleroy was no doubt correct. No special
tribunal was established in Elbeuf, and the municipality and the
justice of the peace were left free to continue their quarrels. But
the whole question was deprived of a good deal of its importance
by the law of September 27–October 16, 1791, which abolished
all supervision over manufactures. The conflict between municipality and judiciary now entered into a period of tranquillity not
to be disturbed until the year II.

In the meantime, there was no lack of problems to deal with in
Elbeuf. One of the first manifestations of exclusively popular
discontent took place on June 1, 1790, when a great number of
persons, including many textile workers, tried to gain admittance
to the primary assemblies. As they were not active citizens, they

---

[69] *Arch. Mun.,* Délib., Vol. II (November 23, 1790, August 25, 1791, and
December 18, 1792).

[70] *Arch. Nat.,* D^{iv} 61.

had no right to do so. They were successful in the parish of St. Jean, despite precautions taken by the municipality in issuing admission cards. The mayor dissolved and reopened the assembly several times in an effort to eliminate the " undesirable " elements, but he could do nothing to keep them out. Finally, he had to write to the *Comité de Constitution* of the National Assembly to ask what to do. We do not know what directions were given him, but we find no mention of similar incidents at a later date.[71]

The constitution and maintenance of a national guard created numerous problems as well, the first of which was simply obliging people to serve. By the time the municipality decided, in March, 1790, that in order to have adequate control over the volunteers there would have to be a bourgeois militia, the right to accomplish this transition had already been granted by the law on the municipalities of December 14, 1789. Based on this authorization, the municipality twice ordered " tous les bourgeois et citoyens " to do guard duty when called. The second time, on August 3, 1790, it threatened all who refused to serve with the loss of their rights as active citizens if they did not sign up before September 8. Workers were specifically freed of this obligation, and, at a later date, some workers who had signed up anyway were allowed to resign when they manifested a desire to do so. A fine of 2 livres was imposed on those who refused to serve, the proceeds to be used to pay the wages of replacements. Seizure of property was authorized in the event of a refusal to pay the fine.[72]

In general, however, and despite these vicissitudes, Elbeuf was more concerned with the state of its manufactures and its grain supply than with politics per se. Not until the autumn of 1793 did the city take up a new lease on political life, marked by the organization of a Société Populaire on 13 Brumaire II. This creation came after the establishment of similar groups in two of the smaller towns of the Canton of Elbeuf: Orival and Oissel. On 14 Brumaire, the Elbeuvians instructed their delegate in Paris to ask affiliation with the " Société Mère des Jacobins." [73] It cannot be said that they showed much initiative in so doing; rather, the Elbeuvians had waited to see which way the wind was blowing

[71] *Arch. Nat.*, D^{iv} 61.
[72] *Arch. Mun.*, Délib., Vol. I (February and March, 1790; July 7 and August 3, 1791) ; Délib., Vol. II (August 16, 1791, and March 16, 1792).
[73] *Arch. Nat.*, F^{1a} 548; *Arch. Dép.*, L 5620.

before committing themselves to full co-operation with the Revolutionary government.

TABLE 5–1

PRESIDENTS AND SECRETARIES OF THE SOCIÉTÉ POPULAIRE

Name	Profession	Rank	Date of Election
Pierre Henry Hayet	Manufacturer	President	14 Brumaire II
			30 Thermidor II
Modeste Fremont père	Dyer	President	30 Nivôse II
Denis Séjourné	Old Clothes Dealer	President	28 Pluviôse II
Moise Duruflé	Manufacturer	President	1 Germinal II
Boisrenoult	?	Secretary	30 Nivôse II
		President	28 Germinal II
Marin Duruflé	Manufacturer	President	28 Floréal II
Valdampierre	Notary	President	28 Prairial II
Denis Murizon	Manufacturer	President	28 Messidor II
Pierre Nicolas Bourdon	Manufacturer	President	28 Fructidor II
Charles Voranger	Cardmaker	President	28 Vendémiaire III
Garousse	?	President	1 Frimaire III
Alexandre Grandin	Manufacturer	President	1 Nivôse III
Joseph Flavigny	Manufacturer	President	2 Pluviôse III
Bachelet	?	Secretary	30 Nivôse II
Delaunay le jeune	Manufacturer	Secretary	1 Germinal II
Joseph Delacroix	Manufacturer	Secretary	1 Germinal II
Henry Delarue	Manufacturer	Secretary	28 Floréal II
Alexandre Adam	Manufacturer	Secretary	28 Floréal II
Mathieu Bourdon	Manufacturer	Secretary	28 Prairial II
Petitgrand fils	Manufacturer	Secretary	28 Prairial II
Mathieu Delarue	Manufacturer	Secretary	28 Messidor II
Jacques Grandin	Manufacturer	Secretary	28 Messidor II
Flavigny Gosset, le jeune	Manufacturer	Secretary	30 Thermidor II
Dosier	?	Secretary	30 Thermidor II
Amable Chefdru	Manufacturer	Secretary	28 Fructidor II
Bruno Anquetil	Manufacturer	Secretary	28 Vendémiaire III
Prosper Delarue	Manufacturer	Secretary	28 Vendémiaire III
J.-B. Tienterre	Merchant	Secretary	1 Frimaire III
Norbert Lefebvre	Manufacturer	Secretary	1 Nivôse III
Alexandre Bouic	Manufacturer	Secretary	2 Pluviôse III
Pierre Lecalier	Manufacturer	Secretary	2 Pluviôse III

Note: This list in incomplete.
Sources: *Arch. Dép.*, L 5618 and L 5620.

This prudence is perhaps explained by the composition of the Société. Unfortunately, we have found no list of members, but certain clues nonetheless exist. First of all, there was an initiation fee of 6 livres until 8 Thermidor II, when the figure was lowered to 2 livres.[74] When we consider that the first figure exceeded the tax payments necessary to be an active citizen, since it represented at least four days' and sometimes a week's wages, it becomes evident that it must have made it difficult for at least that one-third of the population excluded from voting rights by the Constitution of 1791 (and perhaps some others) to become members of the Société Populaire. The rule of the Elbeuf society was thus behind the times in relation to the Constitution of 1793, which had abolished the *cens*. At the same time, those who were financially unable to join were admitted to the galleries of the meeting hall and were sometimes consulted on important items of business, although usually after the society had voted its opinion. Secondly, if we look at Table 5–2, we find that of thirty-three posts of president and secretary of the society held by thirty-one persons, there were twenty-two manufacturers, one dyer, one notary, one card-maker, one merchant, an old clothes dealer, and four whose professions are unidentifiable. Add to this the fact that in the only session of purification held before the society as a whole, on 2 Messidor II, eighteen of the twenty-three persons permitted to continue as members of the society were manufacturers, along with two merchants, one notary, a locksmith, and a priest,[75] and the shadings begin to appear. The Société Populaire of Elbeuf was made up of bourgeois, no doubt of all levels, but was dominated to a large extent by the upper bourgeoisie, with the manufacturers at its head. This is a phenomenon that falls into the pattern of the municipality already described in Chapter 4: at the beginning of the Revolution and through 1792, there was a reaction against the upper bourgeois who had been associated with the old regime. The upper bourgeois began to regain their influence in 1793 and had already recovered it in large part by the year II.[76]

Protestations of revolutionary ardor and the acceptance of a revolutionary morality were not lacking in the Société Populaire of Elbeuf, even as the municipality, as we shall see, painted itself in the colors of the deepest radicalism in its public declarations. A good example of this is the choice of slogans made by the

[74] *Arch. Dép.*, L 5621; L 5618—8 Thermidor II.
[75] *Arch. Dép.*, L 5618—2 Messidor II.
[76] See Chapter 4 for a discussion of this point.

society on 8 Floréal II to be engraved on the walls of its meeting place:

> La Loi est la sauvegarde des citoyens.
> La Liberté est le droit de la nature.
> L'Egalité est la base républicaine.
> La Fraternité assure le régime des Républiques.
> La Mort est préférable à l'esclavage.
> Tout égoiste doit être exclus de la Société.
> La Probité et la vertu sont à l'ordre du jour.
> Le régime des Tyrans est passé.
> L'Humanité est un devoir sacré.
> Vivre libre ou mourir.
> Le fanatisme est abbatu.
> Le peuple français reconnaît l'être suprême et
>   l'immortalité de l'âme.
> La Liberté fera le tour du globe.
> La souveraineté réside dans le peuple.
> Vive la République, vive la Montagne.[77]

Another example is the constant effort of purification made by the society: On 3 Germinal II, candidates were asked if they had (1) signed the Constitution of 1793, (2) served personally in the guard, (3) signed any " arrêtés liberticides " or (4) signed a petition for the creation of another and rival Société Populaire. If the answers to these questions were satisfactory, the question of the civic qualities of the person was put to the society and the galleries. If they approved, the member was allowed to continue in the society. By Messidor, the list of questions had grown in length and rigorousness. Instead of four, they now numbered sixteen:

1. As-tu accepté la Constitution Républicaine?
2. As-tu pris des engagements envers la République, sont-ils remplis. S'ils ne le sont pas, justifie de la décharge?
3. N'as-tu signé ni rédigé aucuns adresses en faveur de la royauté?
4. Quelle parti as-tu pris à la mort de Capet?
5. As-tu rempli ta souscription à l'emprunt forcé et volontaire?
6. As-tu payé tes impositions de 92 et autres antérieures?
7. As-tu fait ton service en personne dans la garde nationale depuis que les lois l'exigent?
8. Ne t'es-tu point réjoui de nos ennemis?
9. As-tu des parents émigrés? Ne leur as-tu été d'aucuns secours depuis leur émigration, et n'as-tu point correspondu avec d'autres émigrés sans être leur parent?

[77] *Arch. Dép.*, L 5618—8 Floréal II.

10. N'as-tu signé aucune pétition tendant à former une autre société dans cette commune?
11. As-tu été noble, prêtre? Es-tu fils d'un ci-devant privilégié? N'as-tu point été attaché aux ci-devant fermes générales et aux ci-devant seigneurs?
12. As-tu toujours obéi à toutes les réquisitions qui t'ont été faites?
13. N'as-tu point fait de fausses dénonciations?
14. Ne t'es-tu point absenté de la Société sans aucunes causes legitimes durant quatre séances de suite?
15. T'es-tu conformé à la loi sur l'éducation publique?
16. Enfin qu'as-tu fait pour la République? [78]

Shortly after the drafting of this list of questions, a new procedure, suggested by Guimberteau, was adopted for the admission of members. A committee of six members was elected to examine the petitions for membership. All such petitions were in the future to be endorsed by six members of the society. The committee of six was to investigate and could in consequence accept, reject, or postpone the admission of an applicant. Only in the case of an outright rejection would it be necessary to make a report of the reasons to the society as a whole. When the applicant was presented for final acceptance by the majority of the society, one-half of his endorsers had to be present and, in the event of his rejection, they too were subject to sanctions. They could be definitively or temporarily ejected from the society or simply censured for their conduct.[79]

We do not mean to suggest by these remarks that the allegiance to the Revolution displayed in the above slogans, questions, and procedures was hypocritical—not at all. But the slogans chosen and the questions asked do have a character of their own. That is to say, they are exclusively political and exhibit little or no concern with social problems. We are not dealing here with the *sans-culottes* of the Parisian sections who mixed cries for bread and work into their denunciations of aristocratic conspiracies and foreign plots, but with a group of solid bourgeois generally satisfied with a social order that the Revolution had already changed to their advantage, and only occasionally dissatisfied with the workings and administration of the economy.

If the Société Populaire showed an occasional concern in the economy as regards manufactures and a constant one in ensuring

[78] *Arch. Dép.*, L 5618—3 Germinal and 6 Messidor II.
[79] *Arch. Dép.*, L 5621—21 Thermidor II; L 5618—18 Messidor II.

the grain supply of Elbeuf, its main functions lay elsewhere. First and foremost, it was a meeting place for the elite, who gathered there to hear the news and to discuss the problems of the day. This character had been conferred on it by its very creation; later, it took on other duties. On 9 Ventôse II, the municipality ordered that all persons requesting *certificats de civisme* would have to present themselves to the Société Populaire " pour y passer à la censure." [80] Until this time the municipality had jealously guarded its prerogatives in this matter, despite demands to the contrary on the part of the Société Populaire. Shortly afterward, the Société began, on the order of the Revolutionary government, to act as an electoral assembly for the nomination of municipal officers, subject to the approval of the representative of the people —not without some protests, let it be said. At one of the electoral sessions, several persons in the galleries demanded the right to vote, asking whether the society had become a primary assembly. One of them was denounced to the Comité de Surveillance for his pains " comme ayant troublé la Société dans ses délibera- tions." [81]

But political disturbances were, on the whole, rare during this period in Elbeuf. A list of political prisoners as of 1 Germinal II taken from the records of the Comité de Surveillance shows that there were eight, of whom six normally domiciled in Elbeuf. None of the offenses listed were unusually grave. First among the prisoners was Jean Baptiste Drouet des Fontaines, former noble and *conseiller aux requêtes* in the Parlement of Rouen, accused of having " montré de l'éloignement pour le gouverne- ment de la République "—nothing more specific than that. The other non-Elbeuvian was Racoir, postmaster at Pacy-sur-Eure, arrested as a result of the interception of a letter addressed to him showing that he was an escaped prisoner. Why he had originally been emprisoned is not known. His brother-in-law, Pascal Andrieu, manufacturer of Elbeuf, was also thrown into jail because he had given the criminal asylum. Two persons, Pierre Le Roux, who is listed as both a worker in linens and a thread merchant, and Jacques Delacroix, a comb and thread merchant, were jailed for engaging in commerce with an enemy power.

[80] *Arch. Mun.*, Délib., Vol. III (9 Ventôse II).
[81] *Arch. Dép.*, L 5618—17 Floréal II.

Isidore Petitgrand, a cardmaker who had recently turned manufacturer, was arrested for having used his position of commissioner
of the Société Populaire to procure meat for his own consumption.
A professor of Latin who had taken minor orders, Jacques Francois LeRoux, was in custody for having spoken against the juring
clergy in 1791 and for having retired from his post with the non-
jurors. He had already been declared suspect, thrown out of the
National Guard, and disarmed once before, in 1792. Finally, we
find Pierre Victorin Asse, now an " avoué au district de Rouen,"
imprisoned as a suspect. No other reason is given for his deten-
tion, and one wonders whether the manufacturers, who had
regained their influence in the municipality, were not trying to
settle old scores.[82]

The above-mentioned persons were joined in their prison cells
by Balleroy, whose arrest had been ordered by the Comité de
Sûreté Générale.[83] His arrest was the culmination of a long series
of disputes between himself and the municipality which had never
really ended, despite the comparative quietus of 1792. On June
27, 1793, the *procureur de la commune* denounced Balleroy for
the crime of *lèse-nation*, because he was reported to have said
that " la municipalité d'Elbeuf n'est composée que de canailles
élus par la lie du peuple." The municipality decided to refer
the matter to the Committee of Public Safety for investigation.
Apparently nothing came of this, for on 28 Brumaire II the
General Council voted unanimously to give Balleroy his civic
certificate.[84] But he pressed his luck a little too far. In July and
September, 1793, he had excited the wrath of the municipality
by claiming that he had a right to preside over primary assemblies
convoked to elect Elbeuf's military contingent and the *comité
de surveillance*. In the last instance, his attitude forced the disso-
lution of the assemblies before their work was finished. In Nivôse
and Pluviôse II, he circulated a petition in favor of the creation
of another Société Populaire, and he managed to obtain a considerable number of signatures. The General Council and the Société
Populaire reacted vigorously, the former by declaring, on 2 Pluviôse, that no one who had signed the petition would be granted
a civic certificate and calling for the prosecution of the ringleaders,

[82] St. Denis, *Histoire*, VII, 226–28.
[83] *Arch. Nat.*, F 4570.
[84] *Arch. Mun.*, Délib., Vol. III (June 27, 1793, and 28 Brumaire II).

the latter by excluding eighteen persons for periods ranging from one to three *décades*. Prominent among those excluded were the very people who had aided Balleroy in the quarrels of 1791: Tienterre, Rousselin, and Fouard.[85]

When finally brought before the Revolutionary Tribunal, Balleroy had a chance to explain his alleged counter-revolutionary actions. Not all of the things of which he was accused had to do with Elbeuf, but it is only those that did that we will consider here. First, he was asked whether he had in fact insulted the municipality. He replied:

Non: J'ai dit . . . qu'il fallait respecter les autorités constituées, mais que parmi les nombres des officiers municipaux il se glissait des brouillons nommés par une poignée de gens du peuple souvent à force d'eau de vie . . . [il] ajoute qu'il a parlé en mal de la faction d'Orléans parce qu'il a cru que deux officiers municipaux en étaient les partisans.

Had he declared against the Department of the Seine-Inférieure? "Never." Had he asked that Elbeuf be joined to the Department of the Eure? If so, what was his motive, "ce département étant soupçonné de vouloir se mettre en insurrection." He answered, ". . . qu'il a toujours dit qu'Elbeuf devait être du département de l'Eure à cause des subsistances; mais sans égard à l'insurrection, non pas du département, mais des administrateurs de ce département, insurrection contre laquelle il s'est récrié dans toutes les occasions."

Had he insulted the revolutionary assemblies by saying that "nos représentants ne sont que des enfants qui ne connaissent rien aux lois et ne savent ce qu'ils font"? Not at all, he answered: "Je dis: il échappe de ces fautes dans la rédaction des lois quelquefois les enfants ne feraient pas; non pas pour avilir nos législateurs mais pour marquer que l'esprit humain laissait échapper des omissions."

It would be easy to believe that a good deal of what Balleroy was supposed to have said was exaggerated in the reporting. Such things were bound to and did happen in many cases, as is practically inevitable in any revolutionary atmosphere. All the more so in this case, as there were people looking for any excuse they might seize upon to secure Balleroy's disgrace. Indeed, the Société

[85] *Arch. Dép.*, L 5621; L 5618—5 Pluviôse II; *Arch. Mun.*, Délib., Vol. III (2 Pluviôse II).

Populaire, the Comité de Surveillance, and the municipality were all bitterly against him, that latter writing that it " a toujours voulu le faire renfermer." On the other hand, Balleroy also had his partisans. A group of fifty-three of them sent a petition to the Revolutionary Tribunal in which they spoke against " Toutes les atrocités commises contre sa personne par une classe d'hommes que l'on connaît sous le nom de riches, de muscadins, et de leurs soudoyés." They added that almost all of the people who had declared against him were " aristocrates qui ont repugné à tout ce que dictait une révolution," and continued:

La République serait blessée dangereusement s'il arrivait qu'elle prononcât contre un de ses plus zélés défenseurs. . . . C'est à sa sagesse, c'est à son courage que la Révolution doit son maintien dans les contrées. C'est à ses lumières et à sa confiance que tout citoyen lui doit que la tranquilité et la soumission aux loix a été le partage de notre commune et de celles environnantes. Enfin depuis 5 ans [il est] en lutte contre les aristocrates déguisés sous le voile du patriotisme. . . .

What we have here is a continuation of the struggle of 1790–91 between the upper bourgeoisie, on the one hand, and the lower bourgeoisie, this time joined by the wage earners, on the other. Balleroy himself may have been nothing more than an adventurer; but he struck a responsive chord in public opinion with his declarations. He is not very trusting in regard to the capacities of the *menu peuple* in electoral questions, but that is fully explicable. One does not have to be a Michelet and share a blind faith in the " people " in order to consciously serve its interests. Members of revolutionary elites are often apprehensive of the ability of the very people they wish to aid to recognize their own interests. On the other hand, the pro-Balleroy petitioners spoke of their adversaries as " riches " and " muscadins," a claim which is reenforced by our knowledge of the composition of the municipality and the Société Populaire.

Balleroy was acquitted by the Revolutionary Tribunal on 18 Messidor II [86] despite a violent act of accusation drawn up by Fouquier Tinville, which went so far as to accuse him of being a partisan of the Vendée rebels who systematically had sought to debase the revolutionary authorities in the commune and the

[86] Balleroy's dossier may be found in the archives of the Revolutionary Tribunal, *Arch. Nat.*, W 401, dossier 928.

department.[87]   It is understandable that Balleroy, on his return
to Elbeuf, should have been out for revenge. The pamphlet he
wrote on this occasion is a virtual history of Elbeuf during the
Revolution, and it is, on that account, worth citing at length:

> La République [he began] doit triompher sur tous les points de la
> France et le peuple doit éprouver partout les bienfaits.
>
> Cependant, en la commune d'Elbeuf, il y a eu une longue conspiration
> contre le peuple dans tout le cours de la Révolution. Elle a usé toutes les
> formes et, au temps de l'influence des Hébert et des Delacroix, elle a
> pris leurs exemples et leurs conseils. Voici les faits:
>
> [Before the Revolution] les fabriquants en général et surtout les plus
> fortunés d'entre eux faisaient cause commune avec les officiers et les
> valets de Lambesc au préjudice de la liberté du commerce et des ouvriers
> qu'ils employaient. [The means to this end were two-fold: a conspiracy
> not to admit anyone but masters' sons to membership in the manufacture,
> and the preservation of a discriminatory tax system (*tarif*), by which]
> les denrées de première nécessité payaient trois quarts de plus que les
> matières de fabrication.
>
> Les contestations qui s'élevaient entre les fabriquants et les ouvriers
> étaient jugées dans un bureau de quatre fabriquants, présidé par le bailly
> de la haute justice [Blin] qui était leur homme. De là, il résultait les
> plus cruelles vexations sur la classe la plus laborieuse.
>
> Cette coalition d'officiers de Lambesc et de fabriquants se condensait
> pour ainsi dire plus fortement tous les jours par les mariages entre les
> uns et les autres.
>
> Dans cette [*sic*] état, la commune d'Elbeuf offrait un contraste frappant.
> Les fabriquants avaient tous le ton et les airs de la noblesse et tous, en
> effet, tendaient à devenir propriétaires de fiefs et à acheter des charges
> d'anoblissement qui, dans l'ancien régime, étaient flétries de ridicule par
> l'epithète de ' savonnettes à villains.'
>
> Dans cet état encore, il est évident que la Révolution français de 89 ne
> fut pas reçue à Elbeuf de leur part avec satisfaction; elle renversait leurs
> privilèges exclusifs et choquait cruellement leur amour propre. Elle ne
> le fut, en effet, qu'avec colère et délire. L'action infâme de leur patron
> qui sabra vieillards aux Tuileries le 14 juillet [*sic*] ne fit que renforcer
> de son exemple, leur aversion naturelle contre ce grand événement politique
> qui donnera le bonheur au monde par la liberté et l'égalité.

Here he proceeded to relate the old charges about the organization
of the permanent committee and the National Guard. Although
he conceded that they had sometimes served the commonweal, he

---

[87] Balleroy's attacks on the departmental administrators had earned the Société
Populaire of Elbeuf a reprimand from its Rouen affiliate which denounced it to
the District, because of the " peu de patriotisme ou pour mieux dire de l'aristocratie
et du fanatisme existant dans la commune d'Elbeuf." See Felix Clérembray, *La
Terreur à Rouen* (Rouen and Paris, 1901), p. 311.

contended that the organizers' aims had been to take up arms against the Revolution. When he, Balleroy, had tried to serve the Revolution, he was subjected to constant abuse on the part of the conspirators. They tried to prevent his election as justice of the peace, even registering priests in the National Guard so as to have their votes. In the elections of 1792, those of them who were elected had systematically refused to serve, so that in order for the elections to be completed, the District of Rouen had to send commissioners to Elbeuf.

Since August 10, these counter-revolutionaries had tried to " se montrer les plus ardents révolutionnaires." Although they had prevented the formation of a Société Populaire ever since 1791, they were now quick to form one that would be under their control. When Balleroy had challenged them in this design, they denounced him to the Revolutionary Tribunal, their object being to

rétablir les abus de l'ancien régime sous les formes républicaines à l'égard de la fabrication des draps. Ils ne virent qu'avec colère l'établissement d'une foule de nouveaux concurrents que leur a suscités la liberté du commerce et qu'ils apellent dédaigneusement ' les fabricants de la Révolution.' . . . Un autre juge de paix, qu'ils auraient fait nommer à leur dévotion, bien partial, sans vergogne, bien dans leur système, aurait lors des contestations fréquentes qui s'élèvent entre les fabriquants et leurs ouvriers, appris à ceux-ci à ne pas demander souvent justice avec espoir de l'obtenir. Ainsi, les formes seules auraient été changées, et le fond des abus êut été conservé.

Balleroy's acquittal had foiled the plot against liberty in Elbeuf. But while he was gone, " l'épouvante et la consternation ont été mis à l'ordre du jour contre le peuple," he said. A *sans-culotte* shoemaker who accused Henry Delarue *fils*, one of Balleroy's accusers, of lying was thrown into jail by order of the temporary justice of the peace. The Comité de Surveillance had held up the transmission of the pro-Balleroy petition for two days and had threatened certain *sans-culottes* with imprisonment when they went to visit Balleroy in Paris, although they had permission from the public prosecutor to do so. Even children who had sung rhymes in favor of Balleroy (Vive la loi! Vive la République! Vive Balleroy!) had been threatened with punishment if they kept on. And the harassment was not over: " Tous les jours, ce sont des pièges et Balleroy en est à sentir qu'il était plus heureux dans sa prison."

Balleroy did not hesitate to name the members of the cabal he denounced. There were fifteen of them: ten manufacturers, two dyers, a landowner, a lawyer, and Desilles, the Chevalier de St. Louis who had been in Lambesc's employ. Balleroy wanted it understood that

en parlant des fabriquants de l'ancien régime en général, on n'entend pas parler de tous individuellement mais seulement de l'esprit de la masse, qui a de mauvais effets. Il en est qui ont reçu la sagesse de secouer ce vieil esprit comme il est quelques nouveaux fabricants qui, étourdis de la grosse fortune qu'ils ont faite, ont eu la folie de s'en imprégner.

On the other hand, those who were responsible for seditious acts were the vilest sort of individuals, as for instance Vedic, who was known as a " libertin, mauvais mari, mauvais fils. Accablé de dettes et maintenant sauvé d'Elbeuf pour éviter les poursuites." [88]

Balleroy's class conception of the conflict is, I think, correct. But it is more difficult to check up on the specific charges he leveled at the bourgeois. For instance, can we speak of an alliance between the bourgeois and the ducal officers?

The officers of the duchy who were responsible for overseeing the Prince de Lambesc's interests included *gens de loi* of the Haute Justice, tax farmers, and others whose functions were largely honorary. The bourgeois who controlled the pre-revolutionary municipalities seem to have got along very well with them, as witness the absence of any significant quarrel and the election of two of the Prince's men to head the volunteer patriots in 1789. Furthermore, the municipality reacted not at all to the charge of Lambesc at the Tuileries on July 12, 1789; they did not denounce him for it, as they surely would have done had there been any bad feeling between them.

Certain bourgeois families held ducal offices. In 1763 we find a Grandin as lieutenant, a Godet as verderer, a Maille as a lawyer in the Haute Justice. By 1772 this same Jean-Louis Maille had succeeded to the post of *ancien avocat* and replaced the *bailli* whenever the latter was unable to serve. The same year saw Nicolas Bourdon as lieutenant of forests. Later, Jean-Baptiste Grandin occupied the honorary functions of *garde-marteau*.[89] There was also some intermarriage between the two groups.

[88] The above is cited from St. Denis, *Histoire*, VII, 316–39. I have been unable to find the original manuscript.
[89] St. Denis, *Histoire*, V, 458.

On the other hand, it cannot be said that the bourgeois pursued nobility through venal offices or other means. As we have seen, there was only one case of ennoblement through purchase of an office, that of a *secrétaire du roi*, and one refusal by the crown of an Elbeuvian who had wanted to be granted noble status under the scheme for honoring commercial men. Nor does it appear that the upper bourgeoisie of Elbeuf bought an inordinate amount of noble land, although some among them were large landed proprietors. Our somewhat fragmentary researches on this point have uncovered only one such instance: the purchase of the fief of Busset at St. Martin de Cléon by Jean Baptiste Pierre Grandin in 1783.[90]

On his arrival back in Elbeuf, Balleroy tried to assert his authority over the Société Populaire, which was then undergoing one of its periodic purges. He tried to gain control of the committee of six appointed to " purify " the membership, claiming that he should have a place therein because he had been declared trustworthy by the Revolutionary Tribunal. The elections of 25–26 Messidor gave him a seat on the committee, but he was dissatisfied with the rest of the results. Certain of those elected were guilty, he said, of participating in a " conjuration contre le people," and he demanded new elections. In this endeavor he had support from the poorer sections of the population, those who could not afford to be members of the Société Populaire but occupied the galleries instead. So enthusiastic was their welcome for Balleroy that they several times kept the Société from continuing its sessions, on account of " le trouble et le bruit qui s'était [*sic*] fait entendre." [91]

The municipality, as might be expected, reacted adversely. It wrote to the Comité de Sûreté Générale to request the presence of the representative of the people in Elbeuf. The municipal officers defended themselves against Balleroy's accusations and in turn accused him of having cultivated a great resentment in regard to them because of the incidents of 1789. They wrote:

De là, ces haines, ces animosités particulières qui aveuglent souvent au point de confondre l'intérêt général avec l'intérêt privé. . . . [Balleroy] annonce dans la Société Populaire qu'il a dénoncé plusieurs citoyens aux comités de salut publique, de sûreté générale, et à l'accusateur public du Tribunal révolutionnaire. Le bruit se répand que la dénonciation est

---

[90] *Arch. Dép.*, C 2895.   [91] *Arch. Dép.*, L 5618—18–26 Messidor II.

nombreuse. Chacun, malgré le temoignage de sa bonne conscience, craint pour soi; il redoute de se voir enlever du sein de sa famile. L'inquiétude devient générale et la fermentation se [manifeste]. . . . [For these reasons the General Council wishes the representative to come] pour prendre connaissance des faits & interposer sa médiation pour mettre fin à ses dissensions.[92]

Guimberteau arrived on 7 Thermidor and made a speech calling for unity in the commune. His appeal apparently went unheeded. On 9 Thermidor, Balleroy resigned his post as justice of the peace, claiming that he was surrounded by enemies on all sides. On the 16th, he wrote a letter to the Comité de Salut Public to justify his conduct. The fall of Robespierre had given the opposing faction new arms against him, for he was suspected of having been the Incorruptible's friend and henchman. In his letter he proclaimed his innocence and assumed the style of the day in writing of the " execrable Robespierre." Precious little good it did him, for on 17 Thermidor the Comité de Sûreté Générale ordered his arrest. On the 20th Guimberteau declared in a speech to the Société Populaire that he was entirely satisfied with the explanations given by the persons accused of misdeeds by Balleroy. The " germs of division " had been definitively crushed in Elbeuf. The Société Populaire was never to mention the name of Balleroy again.[93]

Presumably this interdict was lifted long enough for the Société to hold a symbolic session of self-purification on 28 Thermidor. The *rapporteur* was Henri Delarue the younger, one of the manufacturers who were Balleroy's *bêtes noires*. There is no point in going through the matter in its entirety once again. The tone of this funeral oration is, however, interesting. Balleroy is here a conspirator, a creature of Robespierre " altère du sang des patriotes." Like Robespierre, he owed his influence to threats of terror, " menaçait les patriotes de l'échafaud, proclamait l'arrêt de mort de ceux qu'il calomniait." His partisans were " sansculottes égarés et séduits, mais fanatisés au point de crier: Vive Balleroy! Vive Robespierre!," in which they were joined by " une douzaine de personnes, beaucoup d'enfants, et quelques filles de

[92] *Arch. Mun.*, Délib., Vol. IV (7 Thermidor II).
[93] *Arch. Dép.*, L 5618—7 and 20 Thermidor II; *Arch. Nat.*, D III 270–16 Thermidor II; *Arch. Mun.*, Délib., Vol. IV (10 Thermidor II).

moyenne vertu." [94] In brief, a few more days would have been sufficient for Balleroy to make another hundred victims of Robespierrism. Even when he was arrested, Balleroy had had the gall to say that " Elbeuf ne serait jamais tranquille à moins qu'on lui coupe les doigts et la langue." And at this very moment

Il intrigue encore du fond de sa prison; on colporte des pétitions pour le réclamer. Le fameux président [Cofinhal of the Revolutionary Tribunal, accused of having defended Balleroy at his first trial] sorcier et fanatique est dans ce moment à Paris, muni d'une pétition signée d'un petit nombre de femmes, d'enfants et de quelques filles de mauvaise vie. Avant de s'acheminer pour Paris, il a été trouver le devin, il a fait tirer les cartes, et l'oracle, qui avait été consulté la première fois, et qui avait annoncé qu'il serait mis en liberté, a répondu qu'il sortirait encore triomphant, mais avec plus de difficulté. Cet espoir est consolant, et la troupe fanatisée en est ravie.[95]

Despite the fears expressed here, Balleroy, released on 20 Prairial III,[96] never returned to Elbeuf. From this time on, the city was extraordinarily calm until the end of the Empire. There can be no doubt that Balleroy's fall was due to 9 Thermidor and the ensuing reaction, which armed his enemies against him. He could no longer count on his super-republicanism and sansculottism to win him sympathies at the higher levels of government against the plans of his local adversaries. Nor should we be astonished at the speed of his discomfiture, considering the extraordinarily close liaisons established by the committees of government between Paris and the provinces both before and after Thermidor. Deprived of a vigorous leader, the *sans-culottes* of Elbeuf (was this not true in most of France?) ceased to be an effective political force. The disturbances of 1789–94 gave way to the generalized apathy of the bourgeois republic.

The apathy manifested itself in the failure and/or refusal of the citizens to do guard duty. This was true of the officers as well as of the rank and file. On 8 Floréal III, the general Council called upon the District to reorganize the Guard " considérant que depuis l'affreuse pauvreté de subsistances, les citoyens de cette commune et particulièrement les ouvriers obligés de parcourir les

---

[94] Note the curious, if common, attempt made by Balleroy earlier and now by his enemies to associate sexual virtue with political morality.
[95] [Henri Delarue fils] *Discours Prononcé à la Société Populaire de la Commune d'Elbeuf. Bibliothèque Nationale*, Lb⁴⁰ 2685.
[96] *Arch. Nat.*, F 4570.

campagnes pour se procurer des vivres se dispensent de satisfaire au commandement qui leur est fait pour le service et donne pour excuses des motifs puissants." [97] On 21 Floréal, not a single person showed up for guard duty, and on the same day the municipality shortened the period of service required from twenty-four hours to the hours between dusk and 2 A. M. The municipality was constantly obliged to use sanctions to enforce the obligation of service, going so far as to punish those who failed to show up at the required time with two days of imprisonment.[98] On 7 Floréal IV, the replacement tax was set at the equivalent of two days' wages (25 livres in assignats or 2 livres in coin). The next day the Guard was reorganized in accordance with the law of 28 Prairial, which dispensed the " gens malaisés " from service. Despite the reorganization, the situation did not get any better. On 1 Fructidor IV, we find the notation that " le service de la garde nationale est négligé au point de compromettre la sûreté publique." In the months just before and after, several of the elected officers refused to take up their commissions.[99]

What was to be done? On 22 Nivôse V, the departmental administrators wrote to the city administrators urging them to " stimulate the zeal " of the Guard, and, on 12 Pluviôse, the police commissioner was given the power to require its aid in emergency cases, without waiting for an order from the justice of the peace or the *commissaire du pouvoir executif*. On 7 Fructidor, the municipality ordered all persons " qui voudront jouir de leurs droits d'activité " to join the Guard; those who did not join would not only lose their rights as active citizens but would also be taxed three francs every time they would normally have done service.[100] All these measures seem to have been without effect, for we find continuing complaints of the inefficiency of the National Guard. In Frimaire and Nivôse VI, there were complaints that there was no control exercised over " les crimes qui se commettent journellement dans les environs," to which the municipality replied by saying that the Guard's activities were nil due to the lack of money to buy supplies.[101]

[97] *Arch. Mun.*, Délib., Vol. IV (8 Floréal III).
[98] *Arch. Mun.*, Délib., Vol. IV (21 Floréal III) and Vol. V (19 Vendémiaire IV).
[99] *Arch. Mun.*, Délib., Vol. V (7–8 Floréal, 27 Messidor, 4 Thermidor, 1 and 24 Fructidor IV).
[100] *Arch. Mun.*, Délib., Vol. V (22 Nivôse, 12 Pluviôse, and 7 Fructidor V).
[101] *Arch. Mun.*, Délib., Vol. VI (2 Frimaire, 23 and 29 Nivôse VI).

We doubt that this was the only reason. Again and again the municipal records show refusals to serve. In Brumaire VII, the municipality ordered everyone convoked to respond, whether they claimed exemption or not, until a re-examination of the law was made. All temporary exemptions were revoked. On 22 Frimaire, the commandant declared that the guard post was almost always lacking part of its contingent of troops, and so it was decided to create a pool of replacements on which to draw in case of need.[102] The same problems continued in the year IX, when the Guard was confided to " quelques remplaçants qui ne sortent pour ainsi dire point du corps de garde, sinon le jour, qu'ils vaquent à leurs affaires comme s'ils n'étaient point de service." Happily, disturbances requiring Guard action were rare at this time, and the establishment of a brigade of gendarmerie was sufficient to ensure public order. At the end of the year IX, actual service was no longer required of the guardsmen, although they remained subject to call, particularly for night patrols on " les anciens jours de dimanches et fêtes." [103]

A parallel apathy was seen in the municipality. The elections of the year IV lasted nine months. In Brumaire, efforts were made several times to convoke the primary assemblies, but few people bothered to come. Such elections as were held resulted in the victory of persons who had received as few as fourteen votes, and those elected often refused to take up their posts. The General Council was convinced that no one wanted to administer a city where famine was raging; and on 24 Prairial, the Minister of the Interior was obliged to fill the vacancies still existing by decree. Even then, certain of those nominated declined. The municipality that was finally installed on 29 Messidor was none too zealous. Several months later the records show a denunciation of officers who did not attend meetings and neglected their work by the commissaire du directoire exécutif.[104]

The only incident to break up this uneventful apathy took place in the year VII. In Vendémiaire, an anonymous denunciation of Louis Lemercier, wood merchant, municipal officer, and president of the cantonal administration, was sent off to the depart-

---

[102] Arch. Mun., Délib., Vol. VI (7 Brumaire and 22 Frimaire VII).
[103] Arch. Mun., Délib., Vol. A (9 Vendémiaire and 2e jour complémentaire IX).
[104] Arch. Dép., L 231; Arch. Mun., Délib., Vol. V (Brumaire–Frimaire IV, and 2 Nivôse V).

mental Directory. Lemercier, who had bought the chateau of Elbeuf, Bizy, and La Londe, was accused of having headed a party of "hommes terrés" at the elections of the year VI. Not satisfied with the results of the elections, he and a group of his supporters had seceded from the primary assembly. There resulted a total disorganization of that assembly which left him master of the situation, and so he was able to obtain the above offices. Armed with these newly acquired powers, he announced his intention to "republicanize" the city—that is, according to his adversaries, terrorize it. Because he was in disagreement with the commandant of the National Guard, he attempted to get the municipality to ask for the posting of a contingent of two hundred regular troops in Elbeuf. His maneuver failed, but he asked the department to send troops anyway to protect him against physical violence. The department refused. From that time on, his despotic acts increased enormously. He threatened with prison all persons who he felt were less than zealous during the *fêtes républicaines*; he refused export certificates to manufacturers. In general, this *nouveau riche* conducted himself like the lord of the manor.

That was one side of the story. The investigation ordered by the Ministry of the Interior and carried out by Delaistre, *commissaire du directoire près l'administration centrale du département*, had quite different results. On 8 Frimaire VII, Delaistre expressed the opinion that as far as the authors of the denunciation were concerned, Lemercier's greatest crime had been the purchase of national lands that had belonged to certain " ci-devant grands personnages émigrés." He said the electoral schism had been warranted, and that it had resulted in no trouble or disorder. Finally, he justified Lemercier's zealous conduct toward persons who were negligent in performing their republican duties, saying that ". . . la commune d'Elbeuf n'est pas celle de tout notre département qui mérite de jouir de la plus belle réputation du côté du patriotisme, plusieurs des principaux fabricants qui l'habitent ne sont point les chauds amis de notre gouvernement républicain." [105]

Lemercier was thus saved—for the moment. A year later, however, he was suspended from his functions as a municipal officer by the departmental administration on charges of having falsified

---

[105] *Arch. Nat.*, F II Seine-Inférieure 13.

tax rolls in his favor. The charges were brought by the municipality, which was at that time dominated by the manufacturers.[106]
We have no way of knowing whether they were just or not, but
we are tempted to see this affair as an episode in the struggle for
power between the bourgeois manufacturers and those who were
rash enough to challenge their authority.

Elbeuf's relations to the central government—any central government—were rarely, if ever, strained. There were occasional
disputes, but not on political matters. Rather, it was economic
and especially fiscal questions that gave rise to complaints on the
part of the city.

Complaints about taxes did not, of course, start with the Revolution. All our evidence, starting with the *cahiers* and running
through the Prefect's reports under the Empire, seems to show
that the Generality of Rouen and, subsequently, the Department
of the Seine-Inférieure were overtaxed in proportion to other
sections of the country.[107] As soon as the opportunity presented
itself, the Elbeuvians were quick to call attention to their plight.

In 1788 the municipality wrote that the 65,472 livres it paid
in taxes each year was a great burden, particularly unjust because
Louviers paid only 37,218 livres a year, although the wealth and
population of the two cities were about equal. The government
could not continue to oppress both workers and manufacturers
at this time, when to do so was to harm one of the most important
French industries.

The root of the trouble lay in the 10 sols per livre added to
the *tarif* without, the Elbeuvians maintained, legal justification.
It had to be done away with, but the *tarif* itself was to remain.
To throw the baby out with the bath would cause " l'arbitraire
dans l'assiette des impositions, l'arbitraire destructeur de l'industrie, traînant à sa suite la haine, la vengeance, les dissensions
intestines " to reappear.[108]

So spoke the municipality dominated by upper bourgeois manufacturers. Its lower bourgeois opponents like Leveneur, along with
Balleroy and du Homme, did not agree. They favored outright

---

[106] *Arch. Dép.*, L 231; *Arch. Nat.*, F[1b] Seine-Inférieure 13.

[107] See, for instance, *Arch. Nat.*, 40 AP 3—Mémoire présenté au ministre des
finances par le préfet sur la situation du département de la Seine-Inférieure relative
aux contributions (an X), folio 251 verso–253 verso.

[108] *Arch. Mun.*, BB[8]— August, 1788.

abolition of the *tarif* (" cet odieux impôt "), because it was a
burden on the lower bourgeois retailers and on the wage earners,
whose food bill it raised considerably.[109] The appeal of the municipality went unheeded in 1788, and the 10 sols per livre surtax
was abolished only with the *tarif* in 1790. By that time fraud
in the evasion of indirect taxes had become a common practice
in Elbeuf.[110]

Good year, bad year, old regime, new, Elbeuvians did not cease
to protest what they considered to be exclusively high taxes. In
November, 1791 and April, 1792, complaints were voiced against,
in the first case, the *contribution foncière*, in the second, the
contribution mobilière.[111] The claim was that the city could meet
its quota of the land tax only " en payant la troisième partie et
plus de ses revenus fonciers," whereas the maximum had been
set at one-sixth of the net average revenue by the National Assembly. The *contribution mobilière* was simply said to be "une
surcharge effrayante." In both cases, reductions were accorded.[112]
Despite this, difficulties of collection continued, and it was only
after the department had authorized payment in assignats at face
value that final payments were made.[113]

In so far as concerns the *contribution mobilière*, Elbeuf seems
indeed to have paid more than its legitimate part in comparison
with Rouen. An estimate of the year V puts Rouen's population
at 13.8 times that of Elbeuf (80,000 to 5,785), but it paid a
contribution mobilière only nine times as high in 1791 and 1792.
This was not the case for the *contribution foncière*, where the
proportion was more just at 16–17 to 1. Of course, these calculations consider only proportions between population and taxation
and ignore the question of comparative wealth. Elbeuf, as an
exclusively manufacturing town, may very well have had proportionately more non-real property than Rouen. Be that as it may,
starting in 1793 Elbeuf's taxation, although still subject to great
variations, greatly decreased in proportion to that of Rouen, which

[109] *Arch. Nat.*, D^{vi} 50.
[110] *Arch. Nat.*, AD XVI 76, Décret portant défenses de troubler la perception
des droits du tarif, etc., September 3, 1789; D^{vi} 50 and 51.
[111] *Arch. Mun.*, Series G.
[112] *Arch. Mun.*, Délib., Vol. II (November 5, 1791, and April 2, 1792); see
also Series G—November 17, 1791.
[113] *Arch. Mun.*, Délib., Vol. V (17 and 26 Vendémiaire V).

fact no doubt explains the absence of complaints for several years thereafter.[114]

Unhappily, this time did not persist, and, under the Empire, the complaints began coming once again thick and fast. Particularly unpopular were the *patentes* and the *portes et fenêtres*. As Beugnot wrote in the year X:

> La contribution des portes et fenêtres devient insupportable dans beaucoup de localités. On trouve telle partie du département, par exemple, le canton d'Yvetot et celui d'Elbeuf, dont les bâtiments exclusivement destinés à des fabriques ne présentent à tous les aspects que de longues files de fenêtres, élevées les unes au-dessus des autres, en 2, 3 et jusqu'à 4 étages. Ces fenêtres ne sont dans la réalité que des instruments de fabrique et sembleraient, à ce titre, exemptées d'une contribution qui doit frapper l'opulence acquise et non pas l'industrie laborieuse; mais le contraire est décidé et cet impôt des portes et fenêtres devient une surcharge accablante pour certaines localités.[115]

The final subject of fiscal discontent was the *octroi*. This tax, so reminiscent of the old regime, had been re-established in certain cities under the Directory. At the end of the year XIII, 2,283 communes had established an *octroi*, and by 1811, 11 per cent of the receipts were going to the central government, which was tempted by this fact to extend the system to as many cities as possible. Already in the year IX, the municipality of Elbeuf had voted to avoid the establishment of an *octroi* by ordering the collection of a surtax of 20 per cent on all *contributions mobilières* of over 15 francs, and even on those under 15 francs, if the taxpayer was judged to be in sufficiently easy circumstances. In all events, care was to be taken to avoid taxing " tous les citoyens composant la classe ouvrière." [116] The curious thing is that the municipality was composed at this time of members of the class that had staunchly upheld the *tarif* in 1789. Why this difference in attitude? Simply because under the old regime the *tarif* replaced an even more onerous tax, the *taille*, while the *octroi* was meant not to replace, but to be an additional burden.

All the maneuvers to avoid the establishment of an *octroi* failed. If anything, the *octroi* established in 1812 was more favorable to the manufacturers than the old *tarif* and disastrous for

---

[114] *Arch. Dép.*, L 538; *Arch. Mun.*, Series G.

[115] *Arch. Nat.*, 40 AP 3—Mémoire already cited, 253 verso–254 recto.

[116] Godechot, *Institutions*, p. 550; *Arch. Mun.*, Délib., VIII (25 Prairial and 1 Messidor IX).

the wage earners. Not only was it in no way progressive but it taxed only food items, leaving aside the raw materials of the manufacture.[117] For a time, it even went so far as to tax the wine that workers brought into Elbeuf in their lunch baskets.

Quarrels with the central government over fiscal arrangements do not necessarily indicate hostility to the Revolution—far from it. They were rather the continuation of an old tradition and, all things considered, were no more, and perhaps less, violent than under the old regime. There are other questions that may better measure Elbeuf's loyalty to the Revolution: religion and emigration.

Elbeuf's attitude toward religion, as in most other matters, was moderate. Certainly there was no deviation to the left. If there were any atheists in the commune, their influence was not felt. On doctrinal matters the local authorities were in total agreement, not with dechristianization but with the establishment of revolutionary worship. On 13 Messidor II, the General Council wrote to the Convention:

Vous avez consacré par votre décret du 18 Floréal dernier une grande et sublime vérité en reconnaissant l'existence de l'être suprême et l'immortalité de l'âme. Le peuple français avance à grands pas vers sa glorieuse destinée. Déjà le féroce anglais s'applaudissaient [sic] des semences d'athéisme que ses agents avaient jetté parmi nous pour anéantir la liberté. Déjà dans le même dessin, les apôtres d'une nouvelle doctrine à laquelle ils ne croyaient pas eux-mêmes, avaient élevé leurs ridicules autels. Insensés! Pouvaient-ils donc ignorer que vous étiez là pour punir de semblables forfaits. Vous l'avez fait et vous avez dignement rempli notre attente. Vous l'avez remplie en proclamant les principes inoubliables si consolant pour la vertu, si désolant pour le crime. Ces Principes d'une justice éternelle qui protège notre liberté naissante et qui veille sans cesse sur les jours de nos représentants en détournant les poignards dirigés contr'eux par la tyrannie. Avec tous les français, nous l'avons honoré le 20 Prairial. Cet être suprême, ce père de la nature, nous lui avons adressé nos voeux pour qu'il continue à vous couvrir de son égide invisible. Ce jour vit par la pompe et l'allégresse générale dans notre commune la plus belle de toutes les fêtes. Il fut comme l'avant coureur de l'existence heureuse que nous préparent les précieux germes dont vous venez d'ensemencer le territoire français. Législateurs, achevez votre ouvrage, continuez à tenir d'une main ferme les rênes que le peuple vous a confié et restez à votre poste, jusqu'à la fin de vos glorieux travaux.[118]

---

[117] *Arch. Mun.*, Délib., Vol. VIII (February 15, 1812 and February 4, 1815); Délib., Vol. B (November 13, 1812).

[118] *Arch. Mun.*, Délib., Vol. IV (13 Messidor II).

Thus Elbeuf took up Robespierre's line against the more radical one of the Paris Commune, but only after having flirted with the cult of reason and having opened a temple of reason in the former church of the parish of St. Jean, converted from Catholicism for the occasion. The experiment was short-lived, of about three months duration, having begun on 10 Ventôse II. But it was not until a year later (26 Ventôse III) that the temple was completely disaffected, having served in the meantime for the worship of the Supreme Being.[119]

There was no gratuitous persecution of the Catholic church in Elbeuf. All measures taken were meant to further the announced aims of secularization and the abolition of superstition. Indeed, if we leave aside the single incident of the deportation of non-juring priests, persecution is hardly the correct term.

On 29 Brumaire II, the General Council wrote:

que tout ce qui peut entretenir la superstition, relever le despotisme du clergé et perpetuer l'ignorance du peuple par des pratiques minutieuses [devrait être aboli], qu'il ne peut exister de liberté ni de gouvernement républicain partout où les ministres du culte ont des moyens de subordonner les actes civils à des cérémonies religieuses, que bientôt ils parviennent à se créer au milieu de l'état un idole . . . dont ils ne tardent pas à faire un despote ou un tyran pour en être ensuite protégé . . . que le règne de la raison et de la morale universelle approche et que c'est aux magistrats du peuple à en affermir les bases en concurant à détruire les frivoles inductions de la crédulité et du mensonge. . . .

For these reasons, the General Council now prohibited the exhibition of religious statues outside of houses, the wearing of religious habits, and street processions. No baptism or marriage registers might be kept by priests. No sales of relics or religious objects were to be tolerated and, if discovered, the sellers were to be fined and considered " charlatans suspects." The ringing of bells for church services was forbidden as was the use of Latin in cemeteries. A tricolor cloth was to be substituted for the pall at funerals. The silver plate of the churches was to be collected and turned over to the government. Finally and by far most important, Sunday was to be abolished as the day of rest in favor of *décadi*.[120]

Although certain of its forms were altered, the content of

[119] *Arch. Mun.*, Délib., Vol. III (10 Ventôse II); Délib., Vol. IV (26 Ventôse III).

[120] *Arch. Mun.*, Délib., Vol. III (29 Brumaire and 21 Ventôse II).

Catholicism was left intact. Formal freedom of worship remained, even under the Revolutionary government and the Directory. On the other hand, there can be no doubt that the government did encourage the break with Catholicism by requisitioning the Church of St. Jean for the *culte de la raison*, for instance. Priests were also encouraged to follow the example of Gobel, constitutional bishop of Paris, by renouncing their posts. Seven priests, all those remaining in the city, did so in Ventôse and Germinal II.[121]

Such right-wing resistance as manifested itself in Elbeuf was of no great importance, although there can be no doubt that a large part of the population remained profoundly attached to Catholicism. At worst, there was a recurring need for the municipality to enforce the prohibition of business on *décadi*. When a rumor circulated after the fall of Robespierre that the observance of Sunday would soon be re-established, the General Council of the city made short work of it by announcing that all persons who worked on *décadi* would be regarded as " more than suspect." In the year VI, all priests had to be invited to celebrate mass on *décadi* and in the year VII there is additional evidence to show that the problem was still current. At the same time, the " réunions décadaires" were being regularly celebrated, "mais pas encore avec toute la pompe et la décence dignes de son objet."[122] Those who insisted on holding to Sunday worship finally won out on 7 Thermidor VIII, when the obligation to respect *décadi* was abolished.

It is true that any serious opposition that might have been forthcoming was seriously weakened by the departure of the non-juring priests in September, 1792, in conformity with the law of August 26 of the same year, which ordered the deportation to Guiana of those who had not left the country within fifteen days. There was yet another reason, the weakening of religious ties of the educated bourgeois as they came to accept certain deistic principles. It cannot be said that free-masonry exercised any direct influence in Elbeuf, since there was no lodge established there before 1810. But there can be no doubt that a commercial and

---

[121] *Arch. Mun.*, Délib., Vol. III (Ventôse–Germinal II) ; see also Emile Sevaistre, *Le Personnel de l'Eglise Constitutionnelle en Normandie* (1791–1795) (Paris, 1925), I, 239–40.

[122] *Arch. Mun.*, Délib., Vol. IV (21 Fructidor II) ; Délib. Vol. VI (12 Nivôse VI and 9 Brumaire VII) ; *Arch. Dép.*, L 231.

manufacturing bourgeoisie with its wide contacts outside of Elbeuf
was influenced by the new ideas of the philosophes, perhaps
through the intermediary of the Académie de Rouen or the masonic
lodge established there in 1750.[123]

Given a decimated clergy and an upper bourgeoisie largely
indifferent to the question, only the wage earners and petit bourgeois would protest against the religious policy of the Revolution.
On 30 Pluviôse IV, Marin Duruflé, himself a manufacturer and
commissaire du directoire in the Elbeuf municipality, analyzed
the situation in the following terms:

Ou peut affirmer que la basse classe des citoyens en général désirait
la réintégration des ministres du culte catholique et la liberté de l'exercer.
Tous ses partisans se sont portés avec zèle pour la réparation de ces édifices,
et ils continuent de les fréquenter avec assiduité les fêtes et *dimanches*;
ils paraissent fort attachés à leurs principes . . . mais personne ne les trouble
dans leur exercice; il pourrait bien y avoir les $\frac{3}{4}$ des citoyens de cette
opinion.

Le nombre de ceux qui ne suivent aucun culte peut être de $\frac{3}{16}$e des
habitants, mais on peut assurer qu'ils ne seront jamais dangereux.

Quant à ceux qui tenaient aux réfractaires, il pourrait y avoir à peu
près $\frac{1}{16}$, mais depuis la retraite de leurs ministres, ils font probablement
leur exercice à petit bruit et sans éclat, car on ne s'en aperçoit en aucune
façon, rien ne donne à penser que la malveillance dirige les opinions
d'aucun de ces individus, c'est bien plutôt une suite de leur bonne foi ou
pieuse inquiétude qui les fait penser ainsi avec sévérité.

Il n'y a en ce moment de temples que les deux églises fréquentés par
les catholiques suivant les ministres soumis aux lois.

Depuis longtemps il n'existe extérieurement dans cette commune aucun
signe religieux.

On peut aussi affirmer que l'esprit et les principes des ministres de ce
culte sont bons et qu'ils se font un devoir de se conformer à la loi; ils
ne font que des prônes et point de discours ou de prédications.[124]

To reach this stage of tolerance had taken some time. Between
Ventôse II and Ventôse III there had been no Catholic worship
in Elbeuf, not because it was forbidden, but because all the priests

---

[123] Michel Join-Lambert, "La Pratique Religieuse dans le Diocèse de Rouen de
1707 à 1789," *Annales de la Normandie*, V (1955), 35–49; de Loucelles, *Histoire
Générale de la Franc-Maçonnerie en Normandie, 1739–1875* (Dieppe, yr. 5875
[1875]), pp. 4, 131–32. L'Union lodge of Elbeuf, founded in 1810, was given
its constitution in 1812. There were seventeen members in 1813, but the lodge
"tomba en som . . ." in the same year. Reconstituted in 1822, it had thirty-three
members in 1828. The Revolution of 1830 "amena une perturbation qui causa
la mise en sommeil de l'Union" from which it had not yet recovered in 1875.

[124] *Arch. Dép.*, L 231.

had resigned. On 3 Ventôse III, the Convention voted a decree guaranteeing freedom of worship, but forbidding the use of churches, which were, of course, the property of the state. This prohibition was repealed by a decree of 11 Prairial that allowed the use of churches that had not yet been sold, provided they were shared by all sects in the commune. The reason given for this decree was that it was difficult to exercise proper surveillance over worship in private homes, but, in fact, it was a surrender to public pressure. At Elbeuf in the months between the two decrees, direct action had been taken, particularly by women. On 5 Germinal III, an " immense concourse " of citizens came to the city hall with a petition signed by eighty-eight women demanding the opening of the churches. The General Council invoked the law of 3 Ventôse, saying it was powerless to comply with this request, but offered to bring the matter to the attention of the District Administration and asked the petitioners to name two delegates to accompany its own commissioners. The crowd refused to accept this offer and instead persisted in asking for the keys to the churches, for which they were willing to pay a rent. In describing what happened next, the municipality wrote:

> Un grand nombre de citoyennes ont escaladé la barre du conseil, en nous demandant à grands cris de leur remettre [les clés] en ajoutant qu'ils ne nous laisseraient pas tranquilles, qu'elles ne nous quitteraient pas, et nous ont fermé tout passage. Toute voie de représentations étant devenue inutile, le tumulte et les cris croissant, nous nous sommes trouvés contraints apres six heures d'une séance orageuse, pour éviter des suites plus fâcheuses, de leur remettre provisoirement les clefs.

This action avoided more serious trouble such as occurred at neighboring Oissel, where the crowd ripped down the tricolor from the city hall, cut down the tree of liberty and replaced it with a calvary.[125] On 9 Germinal the Elbeuf demonstrators complied with a decision of the District ordering them to return the keys, nonetheless maintaining that they saw no reason to be so deprived, since churches had already been reopened in the neighboring District of Louviers. Taking up this argument, the General Council authorized the opening of the Church of St. Etienne on 14 Germinal. The District of Rouen followed suit on 5 Floréal by

[125] *Arch. Nat.*, D § I 20—5 Germinal III; *Arch. Mun.*, Délib., Vol. IV (5 Germinal III).

allowing the return of *lettres de prêtrise* to priests who asked for them. By 15 Prairial, four of the seven who had given up their functions in the year II and one new priest had announced their intention of resuming their posts. Henceforth, Catholic worship was restored in Elbeuf, and its free exercise was protected by the municipality, so long as it conformed to the law.[126]

Emigration and religion were closely related problems. In Elbeuf, eleven of the eighteen priests were either deported or left voluntarily in 1792. Theirs was the largest contingent among the *émigrés*. In fact, there were only seven lay *émigrés*, and none of those who were true residents of Elbeuf left for political reasons. Lambesc, the first to leave, cannot be counted as a resident of the city. The same is true of his bodyguard, Delarue de la Mare Hybert. André Lucas de Tourville was the son of a *conseiller* of the Parlement de Rouen, and there is no information on the de Mouilles sisters, cited by Bouloiseau as being domiciled in Elbeuf. None of the last three names appears on the tax rolls of the pre-Revolutionary period. The most, then, that can be said is that, if they actually did live in the city, they were recent arrivals. The dyer Constant le Bourg and the manufacturer Waast Robert Constant Dupont, both residents of long standing, emigrated to escape their creditors after they had gone into bankruptcy, in 1789 and 1791 respectively.[127] This is just one more sign of the essential conformity and/or indifference prevalent in the city, except among the clergy. Even the clerical emigration failed to arouse any counter-revolutionary sympathies, if we may be permitted to reason from a lack of evidence. None of the non-juring clergy returned to Elbeuf before the signature of the Concordat on 8 Thermidor IX. In fact, it was only a year later that the presence of three of them was noted.[128]

The apathy exhibited in almost all circumstances by the citizens and administrators of Elbeuf was the sign of a basically non-revolutionary nature. Non-revolutionary, not counter-revolutionary, be it understood. This attitude dictated a certain conformity, in

---

[126] *Arch. Mun.*, Délib., Vol. IV (9 and 14 Germinal, 5 Floréal and 15 Prairial III); *Délib.*, Vol. A (28 Frimaire XI).

[127] *Arch. Mun.*, Délib., Vol. IV (2 Messidor III).

[128] *Arch. Nat.*, F⁷ 3689¹; *Arch. Mun.*, Délib., Vol. A (17 Fructidor and 2 Messidor X); Bouloiseau, *Liste des Emigrés, passim*; Sevaistre *et al., La Déportation du Clergé Orthodoxe*, pp. 85, 112.

order to be sure that the city would be left to itself, that higher authority would not interfere. Now, there are two ways of conforming: the first is simply to obey orders, the second is to go one step beyond the order, so as to impress higher authority with your loyalty. There are examples of both approaches in Elbeuf.

It was, of course, expected that Elbeuf should give its consent to, and rejoice in, the great victories of the Revolution. This it did, the municipality ordering ceremonies to celebrate the principal events. In 1790, the Federation of the National Guard was feted by the singing of a mass and the taking of the civic oath by the municipal officers, clergy, and National Guard. The news of the arrest of the royal family on its flight to Varennes in 1791 was the occasion of a *Te Deum* and a display of fireworks. The National Guard was called out to give a certain éclat to the day, and the population was compelled to light up their houses as a sign of joy, subject to a fine of 50 livres for failure to comply.[129]   In September, 1791, and August, 1792, the same measures were taken, when the news of the king's acceptance of the Constitution and of the suspension of the executive power arrived. On both these occasions, however, there were no religious ceremonies, the situation vis-à-vis the church having evolved in the meantime.[130] The tradition thus established was maintained throughout the Revolution in the form of fêtes of both the political and non-political varieties. They were most ardent under the Revolutionary government of the year II, while they reached their lowest level of public enthusiasm under the Directory, only to take up a new lease on life under the Consulate and Empire.

Great care was taken (and rewarded by public participation) in the preparation of the fêtes of the year II. The celebration of the first anniversary of May 31 on 12 Prairial II was intended to have the participants "jurer de nouveau haine implacable au fédéralisme, monstre hideux qui voulait renverser la République et nous replonger dans les fers de l'esclavage." It was carried out with the best of results. A local musician even composed several songs for the occasion, remarkable less for their poetry than for their typical sentiments, as witness one of them, *La Prière à l'Eternel*:

---

[129] *Arch. Mun.*, Délib., Vol. II (July 14, 1790 and June 24, 1791).
[130] *Arch. Mun.*, Délib., Vol. II (September 17, 1791 and August 16, 1792).

La Liberté fut ton ouvrage;
Son feu dévore notre coeur.
Par elle, fier de Ta grandeur,
L'homme est devenu Ton image.
Tu vois de stupides brigands
Vouloir nous détruire pour elle.
Combats pour nous; c'est Ta querelle
Dieu bon, tonne sur les tyrans.

Women's Chorus:

Détruis les tyrans, et la guerre
N'affligera plus les mortels.
Paix bienfaisante, Tes autels
Seront relevés sur la terre.
A nos chastes embrassements
Rends nos époux couverts de gloire
Rends par une prompte victoire
Le tendre père à ses enfants.

Liberty, the defeat of tyrants, a profound desire for peace, a certain revolutionary puritanism—in short, all were a thorough reflection of the aspirations of the moment.[131]

Even a simple *fête décadaire* of this period showed all the signs of a heightened revolutionary consciousness. One finds a contemporary counterpart in Cuba, with which more than one comparison might be made. Take, for example, the fête of 20 Nivôse II. Because of what I feel to be its intrinsic interest, I am taking the liberty of reprinting the description in full:

La fête était composée de 4 hommes à cheval suivis d'un piquet de gardes nationaux portant une banière avec cette devise: *Vivre libre ou mourir,* des jeunes gens composant la première réquisition ayant la plupart le sac sur le dos avec une dont la devise était *Nous sommes tout prêts à combattre nos ennemis, que la patrie nous emploie.* Des enfants au-dessous de l'âge de dix huit ans en très grand nombre, respirant la gaîeté vive et charmante de l'innocence exempte de peine et de soucis portant pour devise *L'Espoir de la patrie.* D'un groupe de vieillards dont un laboureur âgé de 96 ans et marchant avec facilité, ce groupe portait pour bannière cette devise: *Nous n'avons plus que de vous à vous offrir.* La statue de la victoire dans tout son éclat etait portée à hauteur d'hommes et frappait non moins la mémoire que les yeux [pour commemorer] les victoires récentes remportées sur nos ennemis par la reprise de l'infâme Toulon, la levée du siège de Landeau & la destruction si ardemment desirée des fanatiques rebelles de la Vendée.
Un groupe compris de citoyennes de tout âge où brillait [*sic*] tout à

[131] *Arch. Mun.,* Délib., Vol. III (11 Prairial II); St. Denis, *Histoire,* VII, 264–65.

la fois la vénération des mères, la dignité des épouses et les grâces des filles. Leur bannière était *Nous décernerons la récompense aux vainqueurs*. La beauté semblait s'être jointe à la décence et à la joie vive et pure. La Société populaire venait ensuite portant pour bannière *Nous sommes l'effroi des Tyrans*. Au milieu d'elle était élevée la statue de la liberté ayant son bonnet à la main. Un groupe de musiciens jouaient tous les airs patriotiques et révolutionnaires. On voyait ensuite les bustes de Pelletier [de Saint-Fargeau] et de Marat avec la déclaration des droits de l'homme et un faisceau de piques puis la statue de la raison devant laquelle deux jeunes citoyennes portaient une vase d'où sautaient des flammes. Enfin, les autorités constituées, savoir le comité de surveillance ayant pour bannière *Les conspirateurs sont surveillés*, la justice de la paix, *La Loi et la paix* et le conseil général de la commune, *Le But de la société est le bonheur commun*.

Un piquet de gardes nationaux avec trois cavaliers fermait la marche ayant à sa tête un tableau de la reprise de Toulon avec ces paroles: *Aux braves républicains qui ont repris Toulon*. Cette marche est partie de la maison commune . . . a pris la rue de la réunion au bout de laquelle . . . elle a placé au lieu du christ le faisceau de piques, symbole de l'union surmonté d'un bonnet de la liberté. Ce faisceau fait le plus bel effet sous un beau dôme soutenu par quatre pilliers d'une belle architecture.

Elle est revenue à la Révolution devant la maison commune où une montagne en gazon etait disposée et elle y a planté un beau chêne. Le vieillard de 96 ans a eu l'honneur de la plantation avec deux belles citoyennes et les chefs des autorités constituées et le président de la Société populaire. Le vieillard a été embrassé par tous et on a vu la joie percer encore sur son auguste visage malgré ses rides. Le génie de la liberté semble avoir procuré un de ses événements propre à tuer le fanatisme, la superstition et accroître la confiance de la Révolution. L'épouse d'un des deux commandants de la garde nationale etait accouchée le matin d'une fille. Les père et mère ont desiré que la naissance fût constatée par l'officier publique sur la montagne lors de la plantation de l'arbre de la liberté. Cet acte important et dégagé de toutes idées superstitieuses a été dressé à cet effet au désir des pères et mères et de tout le peuple qui dans un concours immense y a donné ses plus vifs applaudissements. Cette fille de la liberté a été nommé Cornélie en mémoire de la mère des illustres grecs [sic] qui périrent victime de l'aristocratie en haine de leur amour pour le peuple. Un feu de joie a été allumé, l'on a dansé. Tout s'est confondu dans les épanchements de la gaiété et des danses nombreuses. Les jeunes gens avaient préparé un banquet civique, où le peuple a pris part dans tout l'essor de la joie.[132]

Here we have the true revolutionary spirit that bound together the living—men and women, young and old, rich and poor—and the dead, the ancients who had fought against aristocracy and

---

[132] *Arch. Dép.*, L 5618—20 Nivôse II.

tyranny. Under the circumstances, it is perhaps pedantic to note that the person who drew up the report, in his haste to find a good classical analogy, attributed Greek nationality to the Roman Gracchi.

If the fêtes of the year II were capable of stimulating a new burst of *joie de vivre* in the old men of the commune, ardent revolutionary feeling ceased to be in good taste under the Directory. The new order of march for the fêtes included only public authorities and the National Guard most of the time. Rarely is mention made of public participation. For the first time complaints as to lack of money necessary to conduct the fêtes are heard— this on the occasion of the *Fête de la Reconnaissance* of the year V. The municipal commissioner of public works was nonetheless charged " de s'occuper d'un mode de fête nationale qui présente sans frais toute la dignité qu'elle exige." But whatever preparations he may have made proved useless, for neither the National Guard nor any other citizens showed up to take part. The same experience was repeated several times during the following months, even as concerns fêtes of some importance, for instance those of July 14, 9 Thermidor, and August 10.[133] The old spirit was again in evidence, albeit to a much lesser degree than formerly, in the year VI at the fête of the anniversary of the execution of Louis XIV and of the sovereignty of the people. Still, it appears that the non-political celebrations attracted the greatest numbers of citizens, whereas the report of that of July 14 makes no mention of popular participation. Moreover, the municipality was much excited over the attitude of the National Guard, some of whose members " se sont conduits avec indécence et se sont rendus au piquet en habits indécents et sous les vêtements qu'ils ont coutume d'apporter dans leurs ateliers de fabrique les jours de travail." Shortly afterward, the president of the municipal administration called upon " tous les citoyens à terminer la fête [du 9–10 Thermidor] par des amusements, des danses et des jeux." If he felt called upon to do so, it is evidently because the population had not exhibited much enthusiasm and had thus exceeded the indifference even of the administrators, who were no doubt interested in keeping up appearances. In the future, precautions were to be

---

[133] *Arch. Mun.*, Délib., Vol. V (29 Nivôse, 4 and 10 Prairial, 10 and 26 Messidor, 9 and 23 Thermidor V).

taken well in advance. For the very significant first anniversary of the coup d'état of 18 Fructidor, it was ordered that national guardsmen wear decent clothes and not *sans-culottes*, those who did not conform being threatened with disciplinary action and a replacement tax.[134] The results obtained do not appear to indicate that this was the means to arouse public enthusiasm, which did not reappear until the abolition of all but two of the republican fêtes on 3 Nivôse VIII.[135] Even their replacement by the *Fête de St. Napoleon* (August 15) did not arouse any excitement, in the short run. It was observed without either pomp or circumstance until the second year of its existence (1806).[136]

In addition to the fête, all the changes of regime, whether constitutional or simply *de facto* and whether submitted for public approval or not, gave rise to protestations of loyalty on the part of the city of Elbeuf. In 1793, the General Council approved the new Constitution "qui vient de paraître comme l'aurore d'un beau jour qui luit sur tous les français," even before the vote of the primary assemblies. This action was ratified unanimously by the active citizens, although it must be added that only 195 persons out of 1,095 eligible bothered to vote. There was nothing unusual in the event, this sort of unanimity being common in the area, as witness the following figures:

Name	Pro	Con	Active Citizens in 1791
Rouen (25 of 26 sections)	3,445	25 (and 21 abstentions)	
Darnetal	124	0	?
Grand Couronne	39	3	183
Caudebec & Val sur la Londe	145	–	304
Sotteville-sous-le-Valle and Trouville-la-Rivière	80	4	221
St. Etienne de Rouvray	101	5	172

In other words, as is so often true in yes-no plebiscites, only the yea-sayers expressed themselves, and it is probable that even some of them abstained.[137]

[134] *Arch. Mun.*, Délib., Vol. VI (2 Pluviôse, 30 Nivôse, 10 Floréal, 10 and 26 Messidor, 9, 10 and 23 Thermidor, 10 and 13 Fructidor VI).

[135] *Arch. Mun.*, Délib., Vol. VII (9 Thermidor VII). The two fêtes not abolished were those of July 14 and 1 Vendémiaire (New Year).

[136] *Arch. Mun.*, Délib., Vol. B (27 Thermidor XIII and August 15, 1806).

[137] *Arch. Mun.*, Délib., Vol. III (July 8, 1793); *Arch. Nat.*, B II 28, Nos. 368, 966; D^{iv} *bis* 52.

Just one year later, Robespierre fell. So did Elbeuf—into temptation. No more than thirty-six hours after the Incorruptible's capture, all the public authorities of the city adopted resolutions congratulating the Convention on having discovered and put an end to the "complots liberticides" of the tyrant and his accomplices.[138] From this time forward it appears to have been a simple matter to get anyone to agree to anything—or almost. Here, for instance, is the vote on the Constitution of the year III:

Name	Pro	Con
Elbeuf	163	10
Rouen	5,428	30
Darnetal	77	5
Caudebec	Unanimous	(no figures available)
Grand Couronne	24	15
Franqueville	55	0

Curiously enough, of the above-mentioned cities, only Elbeuf, by a vote of eighty-five to twenty-five, rejected the co-optation decrees of 5 and 13 Fructidor III prescribing that two-fifths of the new assemblies be made up of members of the Convention. The two sections of the city used almost identical words in announcing their decision: "Cette article [paraît] contraire aux droits du peuple et tendre évidemment à compromettre sa souveraineté.[139] The assertion was correct, but why the citizens should have allowed this issue among all others to shake them out of their torpor, even for a moment, is a mystery. It was, in any case, the city's political paroxysm. Never again did Elbeuf wander from the path blazed by the national government. The examples are many; one will suffice.

Hayet, the *commissaire du directoire* in Elbeuf, caught the spirit of Brumaire perfectly, when he wrote:

Certes elles feront époque dans les annales de la République, ces journées mémorables dont les heureux résultats arrêtant tout d'un coup les mouvements désordonnées et convulsifs du corps politique, présages de sa ruine, préparent l'établissement de la liberté sur des bases immuables. C'est assurément dans ces circonstances où le gouvernement actuel veut sincèrement le bien et qu'il est investi de grands pouvoirs pour l'opérer, que nous devons l'aider de tous nos efforts pour le maintien de la tran-

---

[138] *Arch. Mun.*, Délib., Vol. IV (11–12 Thermidor II); *Arch. Nat.*, C 311 (dossier 1231).
[139] *Arch. Nat.*, B II 61.

quillité publique. Le canton qui est resté si calme et si patient au milieu de la détresse générale ne manquera pas de se montrer le même lorsque le moment est enfin venu de croire à un ordre de choses réparateur des maux passés. L'allégresse qui s'est manifesté ici lors de la nouvelle des grands changements survenus annonce que l'espoir est le sentiment qui y domine et que le bon ordre n'y sera encore que mieux affermi.[140]

In writing this, he no doubt took care to properly impress his correspondent, but we have found no evidence to indicate that he colored his account unduly.

Republic, Empire, Restoration—Elbeuf manifested a perfect *jem'enfoutisme* by changing with the wind, and sometimes when there was only a slight breeze. Four hundred fifty-four citizens said yes to the heredity of the throne in the year XII, again a unanimous vote. In the whole of the *arrondissement* of Rouen there were only three negative votes to 19,613 affirmative ones on this issue, none of which kept the municipality from solemnly giving its approval to the decrees of April 2–3, 1814, proclaiming the fall of Napoleon. It called for the restoration of the Bourbons, comparing the demagoguery and tyranny of Bonaparte to the " autorité tutélaire et paternelle de ses rois sous lesquels la France avait acquis tant de splendeur & de puissance." Of course, they also took care to demand a constitution " qui va rendre indissolubles les doux liens qui, désormais, uniront le monarque à la France, nous fera enfin retrouver notre patrie." This insistence compensated somewhat for their utter abnegation before the allies. On September 19, 1814, the municipal officers took the oath of allegiance to the new regime. And on March 14, 1815, after Napoleon had landed in France, they sent Louis XVIII the following letter:

Déjà nous commencions à goûter le bonheur que nous avait promis le retour du meilleur des rois et la [promesse?] d'une paix profonde préparait l'entière restauration du bon empire . . . [mais] l'impitoyable ennemi machinait les plus sinistres projets: Qu'ôse-t-il espérer de son affreux délire? Croit-il que la France peut oublier et ses serments et vos bienfaits? Non, Sire, nous ne serons point de vils parjures et nous ne perdrons point de vue que la charte et le roi sont la seule garantie de nos propriétés et de notre liberté. C'est donc autour du trône que nous nous empressons de nous rallier en vous offrant et nos coeurs et nos bras.[141]

---

[140] *Arch. Dép.*, L 231.
[141] *Arch. Nat.*, B II 831ᵃ; *Arch. Mun.*, Délib., Vol. VIII (April 9, 1814 and March 14, 1815); Délib., Vol. B (April 14, 1814).

This protestation of loyalty did not stop the same people, two weeks later, from writing to Napoleon:

Des événements extra-ordinaires vous avaient éloigné de nous. Mais le bonheur de la France, toujours présent à votre souvenir, était dans votre exil l'unique objet de vos méditations. Par son retour miraculeux, Votre Majesté vient consommer ce [sic] grand oeuvre. Les moyens, sire, vous en sont connus. Un pacte constitutionnel basé sur trois pouvoirs sagement balances qui garantissent son inviolabilité, à la nation sa liberté, à chacun sa propriété, aux tribunaux leur indépendance, à l'Europe sa tranquillité. Nous osons le dire, sans l'adoption de ces principes, point de bonheur pour le peuple, point de gloire ni de stabilité pour le trône. Mais, sire, nous n'en pouvons douter, pénétré de ces grandes vérités, votre génie en saura faire la juste application, car vous l'avez dit vous-même *les rois sont faits pour les peuples, et non les peuples pour les rois.* C'est ainsi qu'en assurant la félicité publique, vous mériterez le juste titre de grand, c'est ansi que vous rendrez le trône inébranlable et Napoléon immortel.

On April 20, they took the oath of loyalty to Napoleon. Shortly thereafter 103 voters unanimously approved the *Acte Additionel aux Constitutions de l'Empire* which granted the guarantees asked for in the above letter.[142]

This political hurdle jumping shows that the desire for peace and economic disturbances had indeed rendered the Empire unpopular by 1814, but that Elbeuvians would have been willing, as always, to accept any government had it promised certain reforms.

Throughout the Revolution, the municipality showed a disposition to go one step beyond the conformity demanded of it. Most of its actions were purely symbolic. It planted a tree of liberty in June, 1792, and added the word " revolutionary " to its name, when it was fashionable to do so in the year II. In the latter year, it changed certain street names to conform to revolutionary images, so that we find streets called equality, liberty, fraternity, union, reunion, and the mountain. On the other hand, the decline of the enthusiasm of the year II caused it to change the names of the sections from liberty and equality to simply north and south—and this not more than six weeks after the beginning of the Thermidorean Reaction. The street of the Mountain soon disappeared as well, and in the year X the streets all got back their original names, with the exception of the Rue Bonaparte.[143]

[142] *Arch. Mun.*, Délib., Vol. VIII (April 1 and 20, 1815); *Arch. Nat.*, B 11 941ª.
[143] *Arch. Mun.*, Délib., Vol. II (June 29, 1792); Délib., Vol. III (11 Pluviôse

Other gestures of this sort were also made, as when the Société Populaire congratulated the Convention on its decree abolishing slavery, and the municipality celebrated Napoleon's victory that put Malta under French control. In the first instance, the wool manufacturers, unlike their colleagues in the cotton industry, had nothing to lose, for they did sell their cloth in the colonies to clothe the slaves. Their merchandise was much too good for that purpose. In the second case, there was a good reason for rejoicing. As the municipal officers themselves wrote: "L'isle de Malte contient une population de 150 mille âmes; elle est tres fortifiée et ouvre à la République le commerce du levant qu'elle interdira à ses ennemis." [144]

It should not be thought, however, that only economic matters aroused interest in Elbeuf. On the contrary, the Société Populaire, unaware of the imminent danger it was in, took care to congratulate the Convention on the closing of the Jacobin club, "which had a tendency to compete with it [the Convention]." [145] Elbeuvians were thus careful to protect their reputation against accusations of counter-revolutionary activity. In the case where they found some basis for a complaint, they sought to remove it. In 1792, the municipality of Pont de l'Arche wrote that Elbeuf was a center of seditious propaganda in whose mail packet royalist newspapers were often found. Their Elbeuf colleagues investigated and did find thirteen copies of Beche's *Chronique Nationale et Etrangère*, which they ordered burned on the spot. This incident seems to have been exceptional, for only one person was arrested in Elbeuf for sedition after the year II. On one other occasion, during the First Restoration, several worker blacksmiths were arrested, because they had "disturbed the peace with repeated cries of: Long Live the Emperor! adding words most injurious to the person of the King." [146]

For the rest, the municipality staunchly denied that any of its citizens might be dangerous politically, whether as Robespierrists,

---

and 19 Nivôse II); Délib., Vol. IV (3 Vendémiaire III); Délib., Vol. VI (27 Floréal VI); Délib., Vol. VIII (4 Thermidor X).

[144] *Procès-verbal de la Convention Nationale, Imprimé par Son Ordre* (Paris, Year II), XXXI, 234; *Arch. Mun.*, Délib., Vol. VI (16 Messidor VI); *Arch. Dép.*, L 5620.

[145] *Arch. Dép.*, L 5620.

[146] *Arch. Mun.*, Délib., Vol. II (September 15 and 16, 1792); *Arch. Nat.*, F⁷ 3689²; St. Denis, *Histoire*, VIII, 346.

defenders of the non-juring clergy, or Bonapartists, according to the fashion. When Leneuf Tourneville, commandant of the National Guard of Fécamp, wrote to them from Paris that "il a aperçu au faubourg Antoine des citoyens [d'Elbeuf], grands partisans de Balleroy et en cette qualité terroristes lesquels ont échappés à la vigilance [de la municipalité]," they replied that they knew of no one fitting the description. In the year VI, they reported that domiciliary visits had yielded no non-juring priests, *émigrés*, or suspect foreigners. Twice in the course of the year VII, the *commissaire du directoire* swore up and down that there was nothing to be feared from Elbeuf. In answer to a ministerial inquiry, he wrote: "Quoique les habitants de ce canton n'aient pas en général toute l'énergie désirable pour le triomphe & l'affermissement des principes & que même il y en ait parmi eux plusieurs qui passent pour n'être pas amis du nouvel ordre des choses, je n'en connais aucun qui soit dans le cas d'être désigné dans le sens indiqué par le ministre. . . ." And once again, at the beginning of the Second Restoration:

[Les habitants] sont tous pénétrés du bonheur [du retour de Louis XVIII] et d'attachement à sa personne. Il faut sans doute en excepter quelques mauvais esprits, que le manque d'éducation et de malheureuses dispositions rendent récalcitrants à toute autorité. Il s'en trouve dans tous les pays et surtout dans ceux de fabrique comme le nôtre, où abonde une quantité d'ouvriers étrangers, souvent débauchés et perturbateurs, surtout depuis l'établissement des mécaniques.[147]

But the higher authorities were not much impressed by these protestations of loyalty. If it is true that Elbeuf was rarely the object of their wrath and that they even were confident of its loyalty, writing that there were "point de malveillants ni d'agitateurs" and that "l'esprit de cette commune est très bon," they never praised the city for its revolutionary exuberance.[148] It seems, however, that this was the case for the entire department of the Seine-Inférieure, if we can believe Beugnot, the very conscientious and capable prefect who wrote in the year VIII:

Les habitans sont éloignés de l'ardente énergie qui abat les trônes, mais ils possèdent les vertus fortes et paisibles qui consolident les gouverne-

---

[147] *Arch. Mun.*, Délib., Vol. IV (13 Prairial III) ; *Délib.*, Vol. VI (4 Thermidor VI) ; *Arch. Dép.*, L 231 ; St. Denis, *Histoire*, VIII, 387–88.
[148] *Arch. Nat.*, D § I 17.

ments. Fidèles aux deux grandes divinités qui enrichissent la terre, au travail et à l'economie, l'esprit de conservation est leur esprit dominant. Le seule loi révolutionnaire dont ils aient conservé un souvenir profond est la loi du maximum. Le surplus ne les a que médiocrement émus. S'ils s'occupent de la politique c'est dans les rapports qu'elle a avec leurs intérêts. Au reste, ils aiment beaucoup l'autorité qui protège, et le gouvernement existant est, par cela même qu'il existe, celui qu'ils préfèrent.[149]

What more perfect description of good bourgeois living in a society where their existence and that of their class is in no way seriously threatened?

The images of the Seine-Inférieure as seen by Beugnot and of Elbeuf as seen by the *commissaire du directoire près du département* two years earlier coincide. The latter seems to us to sum up the attitude of Elbeuvians all through the Revolution. He said:

La petite ville d'Elbeuf entièrement livrée à des operations manufacturières et mercantiles n'a jamais eu de part a la Révolution.

On peut assimiler cette commune à l'âne de la fable qui, déterminé a porter le bât, s'inquiète fort peu de l'avenir et paît tranquillement en attendant l'impulsion qu'on voudra lui donner.

L'on n'y remarque qu'un seul principe d'action politique qui lui a été donné par le fanatisme et la superstition.

L'on peut donc dire que les administrateurs et les administrés ne tiennent à la République qu'autant qu'elle n'exigéra pas d'eux la sacrifice de leurs jouissances et leur paisible apathie.

Les exceptions à ce caractere général sont infiniment rares et le peu de bons citoyens que récèle cette commune n'ose accepter les fonctions publiques pour ne pas se mettre en but [sic] aux haines et aux tracasseries.

This letter was written on 11 Ventôse VI apropos of the removal of three municipal officers accused of sheltering non-juring priests. It was no doubt more exact than the figurative language employed in an anonymous denunciation written at the same time, which spoke of the manufacturers as being " tous aristocrates, quoique la majeure partie doive leur fortune à la Révolution et que la dépreciation du papier monnaie leur ait procuré la faculté de se réhabiliter et acquiter leurs bilans avec rien." [150] It is clear that an aristocrat was, for this writer, anyone who was less than devoted to the Revolution.

The proof is now abundant. The bourgeois of Elbeuf, whose

---

[149] *Arch. Nat.*, F[20] 256.

[150] Two copies of this statement exist: *Arch. Nat.*, F[1b] II Seine-Inférieure 13; *Arch. Dép.*, L 231.

opinion it is that is expressed by the municipality and other public authorities, were so many vicars of Bray. They, too, found that loyalty no harm meant—any kind of loyalty, and within limits. In short, they made their peace with the Revolution by adjusting each time to its successive stages. Their adaptability was rewarded, for, even when their motives were recognized, no attempt was made to dislodge them from control of municipal affairs.

This is not to say that the bourgeois did not have certain preferences. They did, and we have seen them amply expressed—in the *cahier*, appeals to the king and to the assemblies, municipal ordinances, and, last but not least, in the demand for a constitution during both the First Restoration and the Hundred Days. Their aims were two-fold: the creation of a Revolution that would preserve their power at the local level and enhance it on the national level; and the protection of their gains against popular revolutionism of the *sans-culottes* and, later, the counter revolution of the restored Bourbon monarchy. There are many ways to skin a cat, and the bourgeoisie, within the limits set by its objectives, used everyone of them.

It is difficult to imagine the Elbeuf bourgeoisie taking the initiative in the revolutionary agitation of the spring of 1788. It became revolutionary, because it was caught up in the wave of Revolution that came from outside the city. Despite the rhetoric they employed, the bourgeois of Elbeuf were, like their colleagues in the large cities of Normany, never more than constitutional monarchists of a very mild variety. Their essential conservatism made them suspect in the eyes of the *sans-culottes*, who successfully challenged their rule at a very early date. But in the long run the lower bourgeois and the wage earners were too preoccupied in making a living, too much a part of the eighteenth-century status system, too lacking in class consciousness to form a movement that might effectively challenge the domination of the bourgeoisie. By 1793 the latter had regained much of its influence and power. After Thermidor, the bourgeois found themselves very much at home in the various political arrangements that followed, throughout the Directory, Consulate, and Empire. Their rule was, in fact, consolidated during this period. Elbeuf was and remained a city of notables.

APPENDIX

Because of a lack of tax rolls for the period of the Empire, it is impossible to make a detailed social structure analysis for the post-revolutionary, as has been done for the pre-revolutionary, period in Elbeuf. It is nonetheless possible, thanks to the lists of one hundred most highly taxed individuals in each commune drawn up in 1812,[1] to investigate changes that occurred within the upper bourgeoisie.

The first phenomenon worthy of note is that by which manufacturers and rentiers now had even greater representation among the one hundred than before the Revolution. There were now sixty-two manufacturers (sixty in 1785), fifteen rentiers (four in 1785), and twelve merchants (ten in 1785). For the rest, there was little, if any, change. There were now five grocers, two surgeons, a notary, a baker and two carpenters on the list.

There were now sixty-seven families on the list, as compared with a high of sixty (in 1780) in any single year before the Revolution. Twenty-two of these families had plural representation, a figure that marked no change from the pre-revolutionary average. But was it the same families that had plural representation at both times?

Of the twenty-two families having plural representation in 1812, thirteen occupied a similar position at some time before the Revolution, four had had only single representation, and five had been unheard of at that time. Of forty-five families now singly represented, twenty-eight had not been on the list before the Revolution, eleven had been in a similar position, and six had had plural membership. Of eighty-five families there were to be found on the list of one hundred most highly taxed individuals at some

[1] *Arch. Nat.*, F[1c] III Seine-Inférieure 2. In the year XI, there had been seven Elbeuvians among the 550 most highly taxed individuals in the department. They were all manufacturers: Adrien Bataille, Pierre Nicolas Bourdon, Louis and Prosper Delarue, Pierre Henri Hayet, Grandin and Lemercier.

TABLE A–1

THE 100 MOST HIGHLY TAXED INDIVIDUALS IN ELBEUF IN 1812

(in Francs & Centimes)

Name	Profession	Income	Tax Paid
Haylet, Henri (mayor)	Manufacturer	15,000	1,256.17
Quesné, Matthieu	Manufacturer	15,000	1,154.06
Bourdon, Nicolas	Manufacturer	10,000	926.54
Duruflé, Constant	Manufacturer	12,000	807.03
Grandin, Alexandre	Manufacturer	12,000	805.61
Lefort, Jean-Pierre	Manufacturer	10,000	792.56
Lecalier, Jacques	Manufacturer	6,000	779.12
Delarue père, Louis	Manufacturer	3,000	749.60
Godet, Constant	Manufacturer	15,000	722.74
Flavigny, Robert	Manufacturer	15,000	721.31
Louvet, Charles	Manufacturer	4,000	687.69
Sevaistre père, Mathieu	Manufacturer	10,000	661.51
Delacroix, père, Henri	Manufacturer	10,000	637.53
Saint-Amand, Jacques	Carpenter	4,000	631.69
Hayet, Jean-Pierre	Wine Merchant	4,000	629.47
Patallier, Pierre	Manufacturer	8,000	603.38
Delaunay, Amable	Manufacturer	3,000	614.84
Glin, Jean-Baptiste	Manufacturer	10,000	600.92
Frontin, Mathieu	Rentier	10,000	597.97
Menage, David	Manufacturer	8,000	592.52
Bourdon, Robert	Manufacturer	5,000	570.49
Patallier l'âiné, Laurent	Manufacturer	6,000	569.79
Delaunay, Jean-Baptiste	Manufacturer	5,000	567.59
Bourdon, Victor	Manufacturer	6,000	553.02
Bourdon, Mathieu	Manufacturer	3,000	546.75
Sevaistre fils, Mathieu	Manufacturer	6,000	535.61
Henry, Augustin	Manufacturer	8,000	528.03
Delarue père, Henri	Rentier	4,000	521.69
Tassel fils, Alexandre	Manufacturer	3,000	509.98
Lefevre père, Félix	Manufacturer	5,000	505.30
Devé, Augustin	Manufacturer	5,000	501.02
Belec, Jean	Manufacturer	3,000	495.41
Delaleau, Jacques	Rentier	8,000	491.70
Lambert père, Jouin	Rentier	12,000	480.18
Adam père, Alexandre	Manufacturer	6,000	480.18
Leroy, Denis	Grocer	6,000	461.79
Vidcoq, Thomas	Manufacturer	6,000	458.09
Sevaistre, Louis	Rentier	4,000	456.09
Grandin, Louis-Jacques	Manufacturer	6,000	447.12
Corblin, Amable	Manufacturer	3,000	444.91
Heraut, François	Cloth Merchant	2,000	437.25
Louvet, Nicolas	Manufacturer	3,000	430.87
Grandin, Jean-Baptiste-Pierre	Rentier	10,000	424.74
Turgis, Pierre	Manufacturer	6,000	407.79
Loizelet, Louis	Baker	3,000	400.89
Patallier, Nicolas	Rentier	8,000	397.79
Cartier, Victor	Merchant	4,000	387.38
Chefdrue, Benjamin	Rentier	1,500	376.77
Quesné, Louis-Jacques	Manufacturer	3,000	393.69
Huaut, Jean-Baptiste Servant	Rentier	5,000	374.66

TABLE A–1 (Continued)

THE 100 MOST HIGHLY TAXED INDIVIDUALS IN ELBEUF IN 1812

(in Francs & Centimes)

Name	Profession	Income	Tax Paid
Capplet père, Charles	Rentier	2,000	373.19
Maille, Parfait	Merchant	10,000	369.05
Vinet, Constant	Merchant	3,000	367.63
Lecalier, Pierre	Manufacturer	2,000	352.55
Maille-Louvet	Manufacturer	6,000	348.85
Eloy, Nicolas-André	Wine Merchant	3,000	342.55
Godet, Albert	Manufacturer	8,000	337.47
Rouvin, Jean-Baptiste	Manufacturer	3,000	335.15
Lenoble, Amable	Manufacturer	2,000	331.45
Grandin, Louis	Rentier	2,000	329.31
Capplet, Amédée	Manufacturer	4,000	315.46
Boutry, André	Manufacturer	2,000	304.03
Lalman, Honoré	Manufacturer	4,000	291.18
Lefort, Alexandre	Manufacturer	3,000	290.30
Bachelet, Auguste	Manufacturer	3,000	275.93
Desfresches	Manufacturer	4,000	275.56
Deshayes, Louis	Manufacturer	2,000	269.50
Lason père, Pierre-Louis	Grocer	2,000	256.77
Dantan, Jacques	Merchant	2,000	251.69
Lejeune fils, Pierre	Manufacturer	1,200	242.38
Desgenetez, Gabriel	Manufacturer	2,000	244.09
Lingois, Pierre	(ex-) Notary	2,000	239.36
Dantan, Jean-Baptiste	Manufacturer	2,000	238.36
Lesieux, Jacques	Grocer	2,000	234.68
Tassel père, Alexandre	Manufacturer	8,000	229.82
Tienterre, Jean-Baptiste	Manufacturer	2,000	240.32
Gerdret, Hyppolite	Manufacturer	4,000	224.21
Delacroix père, Jacques	Rentier	1,500	222.10
Leroy, le jeune, Mathieu	Manufacturer	1,500	216.83
Lefevre, François	Manufacturer	1,500	215.87
Lambert, Hyppolite	Manufacturer	5,000	206.28
Quesné, Louis Joseph	Rentier	2,000	197.20
Gauthier, Antoine	Surgeon	3,000	191.16
Lebourg, Prosper	Merchant	1,200	188.06
Voranger, Louis-Jacques	Manufacturer	1,000	182.90
Langlois, Michel	Rentier	6,000	182.90
Lasnon fils âiné,	Grocer	1,500	181.45
Hayet, Charles-Prosper	Grocer	1,000	181.45
Lemercier, Paschal	Merchant	1,200	181.46
Peuffier, Auguste	Surgeon	2,000	180.76
Delarue fils, Louis	Manufacturer	2,000	170.11
Mors, François	Joiner	4,000	178.62
Huet, Hyppolite	Merchant	2,000	177.72
Duruflé, Marin	Rentier	2,000	177.52
Lalman, Constant	Manufacturer	4,000	171.17
Barbe fils, Jean-Baptiste	Merchant	3,000	169.26
Poteau, Roch	Rentier	1,200	167.
Valentin, Henri	Merchant	1,000	158.34
Sevaistre, Eugène	Manufacturer	2,000	158.11

" Old " families that had plural representation both before and after the Revolution:

Bourdon	Louvet
Grandin	Godet
Sevaistre	Delacroix
Quesné	Lefebvre
Delarue	Leroy
Patallier	Maille
Hayet	Maille-Louvet

" Old " families that had plural representation after, single representation before, the Revolution:

Dantan	Tassel
Capplet	Lambert

" Old " families that had single representation both before and after the Revolution:

Adam	Henry
Chefdrue	Gauthier
Deshayes	Lebourg
Desgenetez	Lenoble
Delaleau	Huaut
Glin	

" Old " families that had single representation after, plural representation before, the Revolution:

Duruflé	Flavigny
Frontin	Lejeune

" New " families that were unknown before, but have plural representation after, the Revolution:

Delaunay	Lalman
Lefort	Lasnon
Lecalier	

" New " families that were unknown before, but have single representation after, the Revolution:

Bachelet	Barbe
Belec	Boutry
Cartier	Corblin
Desfreches	Devé
Eloy	Gerdret
Huet	Heraut
Langlois	Lemercier
Lesiex	Lingois
Loizelet	Menage
Mors	Peuffier
Poteau	Rouvin
Saint-Amand	Tienterre
Turgis	Valentin
Vidcoq	Vinet
Voranger	

Source: *Arch. Nat.*, F^{1c} III Seine-Inférieure 2.

time before the Revolution, only thirty-four—the hard core—
continued to find a place in 1812. The conclusion is that there
was certain amount—even a great deal—of mobility between
the middle and the upper bourgeoisies. We have already seen
that this pattern did not extend much further downward in the
social scale, i. e., wage earners and all but a few lower bourgeois
did not make the jump into the upper bourgeoisie. Moreover,
falling back into the middle bourgeoisie did not necessarily deprive
the ex-upper bourgeois of his political influence in the commune,
as seen in Chapter 5.

The average income of this group of one hundred was 4,803
francs, and the median income was 4,000 francs. Four persons
had an income of 15,000, three of 12,000, eight of 10,000, seven
of 8,000, eleven of 6,000, six of 5,000, twelve of 4,000, sixteen
of 3,000, twenty of 2,000, five of 1,500, four of 1,200, and four
of 1,000 francs per year. These figures show that there was no
significant difference between Elbeuf and the rest of the department as to the definition of what could be considered comfortable
income. The lists of candidates for municipal office drawn up
under the Empire and consisting of solid bourgeois citizens show
that throughout the department of the Seine-Inférieure, 4,000 to
7,000 francs was a nice, round annual income.[2]

[2] Etienne Dejean, "Une Statistique de la Seine-Inférieure au Début du Siècle
Dernier sous l'Administration de Beugnot," *La Révolution Française*, LI (1906), 43.

BIBLIOGRAPHY

PRIMARY MANUSCRIPT SOURCES

ARCHIVES NATIONALES, PARIS

AD XVI 75, 76—Printed Material on Local History.
AF III 262, 302—Political and Economic Affairs under the Directory.
40 AP 3, 15—Papers of Beugnot, Prefect of the Seine-Inférieure, 1801–1806.
B II 28, 61, 831^a, 941^a—Popular Votes on Constitutions and Referendums of the Revolutionary Period.
B III 168—*Cahier des Doléances* of the Third Estate of Elbeuf.
C 138, 180, 311—Minutes of the Revolutionary Assemblies and Related Documents.
D § I 17, 20—Papers of the Representatives on Mission Concerning Political Affairs in Elbeuf, an III.
D III 270—*Comité de Législation (Convention)*.
D IV 61—*Comité de Constitution (Constituante)*.
D IV *bis* 17, 38, 46, 52—*Comité de Division (Législative et Convention)*.
D VI 50, 51—*Comité des Finances (Constituante et Législative)*.
D XXIX 37—*Comité des Rapports (Constituante)*.
F^{1a} 435—General Administration of France.
F^{1b} II Seine-Inférieure 13—Administrative Personnel.
F^{1c} III Seine-Inférieure 1, 2, 3, 7—Public Opinion and Elections.
F^{1c} V Seine-Inférieure 1, 2—*Conseils Généraux*.
F^7 3639, 3689$^{1-2}$—*Police Générale* of Revolutionary Period.
F^7 4570—*Comité de Sûreté Générale*.
F^{12*} 30, 31, 156, 157—Commerce and Industry.
F^{12} 204, 205, 206, 560, 652, 678, 749^b, 751, 760, 871^a, 926, 1344, 1348, 1363, 1364, 1365, 1366, 1367, 1389–90, 1391, 1557, 1559, 1568, 1585, 2007, 2412, 2517—Commerce and Industry.
F^{20} 25, 125, 256, 311, 382, 399—Population Statistics.
H^1 1420, 1666—Local Administrations to 1790.
W 401—Papers of the *Tribunal Révolutionnaire*, The Balleroy Affair.

ARCHIVES DEPARTEMENTALES DE LA SEINE–MARITIME, ROUEN.

Series C—Pre-Revolutionary Administration:
C 129—Correspondence concerning the Manufacture of Elbeuf.
C 185, 193, 256, 261, 274, 390, 560, 586, 2193—Tax Rolls and Fiscal Documents.
C 202, 211—Municipal Administration of Elbeuf.
C 2210, 2211, 2212—Mendicity in Elbeuf and Environs.
C 2745—Maps of Elections of the Généralité de Rouen.

SERIES L—Administration in the Revolutionary Period:
    L 204, 205, 209, 211, 214—Elections in Elbeuf.
    L 231—General Administration of Elbeuf, years IV–VIII.
    L 404, 405, 407, 411, 427—Grain Prices.
    L 536, 528, 806—Taxes in Elbeuf.
    L 2331—General Administration of Elbeuf, 1791–92.
    L 2336—List of Active Citizens of Elbeuf.
    L 2349, 2361, 2371—Revolutionary Disturbances.
    L 2350—List of Nobles and Foreigners Domiciled in Elbeuf.
    L 2401, 2405—Commerce and Industry in Elbeuf.
    L 2495—*Caisse Patriotique d'Elbeuf.*
    L 5618, 5619, 5620, 5621—Records of the *Société Populaire* of Elbeuf.
    L 5808—Justice of the Peace of Elbeuf.
    L 6396—Municipal Elections in Elbeuf, 1790–93.
SERIES M (unclassified)—Statistics on Commerce and Industry.
SERIES Q (unclassified)—Bankruptcies, 1785–1807, 26 boxes and packages.
SERIES Q (unclassified)—National Lands, 1791—year VII, 34 sales registers, indexed.
SERIES Q (unclassified)—*Mutations après décès*, 1792–1806, 6 registers.
VITAL STATISTICS (*Etat-Civil*)—Parish Registers, 1793 (year II).

ARCHIVES MUNICIPALES DE LA COMMUNE D'ELBEUF

    AA (unclassified)—Municipal Administration before the Revolution.
    BB[2, 3, 4, 8, 9, 10, 11]—Elections and Municipal Administration before the Revolution.
    CC (unclassified)—Pre-Revolutionary Tax Rolls and Fiscal Documents.
    D—Deliberations of the Municipal Government, 1780–1816, 10 registers, as follows:
        I—1780–1790
        II—1790–February, 1793
        III—February 5, 1793–19 Prairial II
        IV—19 Prairial II–3e jour complémentaire, year III
        V—1 Vendémiaire IV–2 Vendemaire VI
        VI—12 Vendémiaire VI–30 Pluviôse VII
        VII—1 Ventôse VII–7 Pluviôse VIII
        A—7 Pluviôse an VIII–29 Fructidor XII
        B—6 Vendémiaire XIII–May 12, 1816
        VIII—1 Nivôse an IX–September 25, 1817
    F[1]—Population Statistics.
    F[4]—Grain Prices and Documents Concerning Shortages.
    G (unclassified)—Taxes of Revolutionary Period.
    HH—Records of the *Manufacture Royale.*
    II—*Contribution Patriotique* of 1789.
VITAL STATISTICS (Etat Civil)—Marriage registers, 1800, 1805, 1810, 1815.

ARCHIVES DEPARTEMENTALES DE L'EURE, EVREUX

    C 41, 42, 43, 44, 45—Papers of the *Assemblée Départementale des Andelys et de Pont-de-l'Arche*, 1788–1789.

BIBLIOTHÈQUE DE LA VILLE DE ROUEN

DELARUE, PROSPER. "Notice sur la Ville et sur les Fabriques d'Elbeuf en Brumaire, an XIII (Octobre–Novembre, 1804)," dated October 24, 1804. Unpublished manuscript. Call number, MS. g. 1 (suppt. 709).
HAYET, PIERRE HENRY. "Notice Historique sur la Ville d'Elbeuf, 30 Mai 1822." Unpublished manuscript. Call number, MS. g. 1.

BIBLIOTHÈQUE DE LA VILLE D'ELBEUF

DUPONT, FRANCIS. "Notes Manuscrites sur Elbeuf," dated 1782.
ROUSSEL AVOCAT. "Chapitres Contenant l'Histoire de la Ville d'Elbeuf sur Seine et Environs." Unpublished manuscript, date 1830.

PRIMARY PRINTED SOURCES

ANONYMOUS WORKS

Addresse de Remerciment Présentée au Roi par les Officiers Municipaux de la Ville de Rouen, en Assemblée Générale. Rouen, 1789.
Arrêté du Parlement de Normandie du Mercredi, 25 Juin 1788. Rouen, 1788.
Cahier d'Instructions, Délibérations et Protestations de l'Ordre des Avocats au Parlement de Normandie. Rouen, 1789.
Cahier des Plaintes, Déléances et Remontrances Arrêté par les Commissaires Nommés le 1er de ce Mois par le Tiers-Etat du Bailliage du Pont-de-l'Arche pour être porté à l'Assemblée des Trois Ordres qui se Tiendra à Rouen le 15 de ce Mois. N. p., 1789.
Considérations du Tiers-Etat de la Province de Normandie sur la Forme des Futurs Etats-Généraux. N. p., 1788.
Discours à Prononcer dans l'Assemblée Générale de Tous les Bailliages de la Province de Normandie, pour la Rédaction des Cahiers et pour l'Election de Leurs Députés aux Etats-Généraux. Rouen, 1789.
Edit du Roi Contenant Règlement pour l'Administration des Villes & Principaux Bourgs du Royaume Donné à Compiègne au Mois d'Août, 1764. Paris, 1764.
Exposition Publique des Produits de l'Industrie Française, an X, Procès-verbal des Opérations du Judy. Paris, an XI.
Intrépidité des Onze Volontaires Patriotes de la Ville d'Elbeuf Qui . . . Ont Attaqué Quatre Mille Furieux Qui Pillaient un Bateau de Bled Destiné pour l'Approvissionnement de la Capitale. N. p., 1789.
Journal de Normandie. Rouen, 1785–1791.
Liste des Electeurs du Département de la Seine-Inférieure Nommés en Exécution de la Loi du 29 Mars 1791. Rouen, 1791.
Mémoire présentée au Roi par les Avocats au Parlement de Normandie sur les Etats-Généraux. Rouen, 1788.
Observations de la Chambre de Commerce de Normandie sur le Traité de Commerce entre la France et l'Angleterre. Rouen, 1788.
Procès-verbal de l'Assemblée Nationale Imprimé par son Ordre, Troisième Livraison, Vol. VII. Paris, 1790.
Procès-verbal de la Convention Nationale Imprimé par son Ordre, XXXI. Paris, year II.
Procès-verbal des Séances de l'Assemblée Administrative de la Seine-Inférieure aux Mois de Novembre et Décembre, 1791, Seconde Session. Rouen, 1791.

Rapport des Travaux du Département de la Seine-Inférieure depuis le 15 Décembre 1791 jusqu'au Renouvellement en Novembre, 1792. Rouen, n. d.

Rapport des Travaux du Département de la Seine-Inférieure depuis le Mois de Novembre, 1792, jusqu'au Renouvellement au 1er Brumaire, an IV. Rouen, year V.

Compte-Rendu de l'Administration Centrale du Département de la Seine-Inférieure depuis le 1er Brumaire an IV jusqu'a l'Organisation du Nouveau Système Administratif, Établi par la Loi du 28 Pluviôse an VIII. Rouen, year VIII.

Seconde Exposition des Produits de l'Industrie Française, an IX, Procès-verbal des Opérations du Jury. Paris, year X.

OTHER WORKS

BERNIER, ABBÉ P. (ed.). "Voyage de Antoine-Nicholas Duchesne au Havre et en Haute Normandie en 1762," in Société de l'Histoire de Normandie, *Melanges,* IV, 187–275. Rouen, 1898.

BEUGNOT, J. C. *Exposé Sommaire de son Administration Présenté par le Préfet du Départment de la Seine-Inférieure au Conseil-Général à l'Ouverture de la Session de l'an X.* Rouen, year X.

DE BOILEAU, M. L. J. *Recueil de Règlements et Recherches Concernant les Municipalités.* 4 vols. Paris, 1784–85.

DELARUE FILS, HENRI. *Discours Prononcé à la Société Populaire de la Commune d'Elbeuf.* N. p., year II.

DEMANDOLX, J. F. *Discours sur les Moyens . . . de Faire Cesser la Mendicité dans la Province de Normandie.* Avignon, 1780.

DUHAMEL. *Etat de la Magistrature en France pour l'année 1789.* Paris, 1789.

DUPLESSIS, MICHEL TOUSSAINT CHRÉTIEN. *Description Géographique et Historique de la Haute Normandie.* 2 vols. Paris, 1740.

DUPONT DE NEMOURS, P. S. *Lettre à la Chambre de Commerce de Normandie: Sur le Mémoire qu'Elle a Publié Relativement au Traité de Commerce avec l'Angleterre.* Rouen, 1788.

EXPILLY, L'ABBÉ. *Dictionnaire Géographique, Historique et Politique des Gaules et de la France.* 4 vols. Amsterdam, 1763–64.

GERBAUX, FERNAND, and SCHMIDT, CHARLES. *Procès-verbaux des Comités d'Agriculture et de Commerce de la Constituante, de la Législative & de la Convention.* 4 vols. Paris, 1906–10.

GUILBERT. *Voyage Fait par le Premier Consul en l'an XI de la République dans les Départements de l'Eure et de la Seine-Inférieure.* Rouen, n. d.

HIPPEAU, CAMILLE. *Le Gouvernement de Normandie ou XVIIe et au XVIIIe Siècles—Documents Tirés des Archives du Château d'Harcourt.* 9 vols. Caen, 1864.

HOUARD, DAVID. *Dictionnaire du Droit Normand.* 4 vols. Rouen, 1780–82.

JOURDAN, ISAMBERT and DECRUSY. *Recueil Général des Anciennes Lois Françaises depuis l'an 420 jusqu'à la Révolution de 1789.* 28 vols. and index. Paris, 1821–33.

DE LA ROCHEFOUCAULD, FRANÇOIS, *Voyage en France, 1781–1783,* ed. JEAN MARCHAND. Paris, 1933.

LEBÈGUE, ERNEST. *Procès-verbal de la Commission Intermédiaire de l'Assemblée Provinciale de Haute Normandie, 1787–1789.* Paris, 1910.

LE PECQ DE LA CLOTURE. *Collection d'Observations sur les Maladies et Constitutions Epidémiques.* Rouen, 1778.

LOISEL DE BOISMARE. *Dictionnaire du Droit des Tailles.* 2 vols. Caen, 1787.

MESSANCE. *Nouvelles Recherches sur la Population de la France*. Lyon, 1788.
————. *Recherches sur la Population des Généralités d'Auvergne, de Lyon, de Rouen, etc*. Paris, 1766.
MOREAU DE BEAUMONT. *Mémoires Concernant les Impositions et Droits en Europe*. 4 vols. Paris, 1768–69.
NECKER, JACQUES. *De l'Administration des Finances de la France*. Paris, 1784.
NOEL, S. B. J. *Second Essai Sur le Département de la Seine-Inférieure*. Rouen, 1795.
PEUCHAT, J., and CHANLAIRE, P. G. *Description Topographique et Statistique de la France*. Vol. VIII. Paris, 1811.
ROLAND DE LA PLATIÈRE. *Encyclopédie Méthodique—Manufactures, Arts et Métiers*. 3 vols. Paris, 1785.
SAUGRAIN, C. M. *Dictionnaire Universel*. 3 vols. Paris, 1726.
SAVARY DES BRUSLONS, JACQUES. *Dictionnaire Universel de Commerce*, ed. PHILEMON-LOUIS SAVARY. Nouvelle édition, 3 vols. Paris, 1748.
THOURET, J. G. *Avis des Bons Normands à Leurs Frères Tous les Bons Français de Toutes les Provinces et de Tous les Ordres sur l'Envoi de Lettres de Convocation aux Etats-Généraux*. Rouen, 1789.
————. *Suite de l'Avis des Bons Normands*. Rouen, 1789.
VITALIS, J. B. *Annuaire Statistique du Département de la Seine-Inférieure pour l'an XII de l'Ere Française*. Rouen, year XII.

SECONDARY SOURCES

BIBLIOGRAPHY AND WORKS ON METHOD

BEAUREPAIRE, CHARLES DE ROBILLARD DE. *Inventaire Sommaire des Archives Communales* [de Rouen] *Antérieures à 1790*. Rouen, 1890.
BOISSONADE, PROSPER. *Les Etudes Relatives à l'Histoire Economique de la Révolution Française* (1789–1804). Paris, 1906.
DAUMARD, ADELINE, and FURET, FRANÇOIS. "Les Archives Notariales et la Mécanographie," *Annales-Economies-Société-Civilisations*, XIV (1959), 676–93.
FRÈRE, EDOUARD B. *Manuel du Bibliographie Normand*. 2 vols. Rouen, 1858–60.
GONNET, PAUL. "Archives Fiscales et Histoire Sociale," *Revue d'Histoire Economique et Sociale*, XXXVI (1958), 432–43.
GOUBERT, P. "Des Registres Paroissiaux à l'Histoire, Indications Pratiques et Orientation de Recherches," in Comité des Travaux Historiques et Scientifiques, *Bulletin d'Histoire Moderne et Contemporaine*, I (1956), 5–22.
HATIN, EUGÈNE. *Bibliographie Historique de la Presse Française*. Paris, 1866.
HYSLOP, BEATRICE F. *Répertoire Critique des Cahiers de Doléances pour les Etats-Généraux de 1789*. Paris, 1952.
————. *Supplément au Répertoire Critique des Cahiers de Doléances pour les Etats-Généraux de 1789*. Paris, 1952.
LEFEBVRE, GEORGES. "Un Colloque pour l'Etude des Structures Sociales," *Annales Historiques de la Révolution Française*, No. 147 (April–June, 1957), pp. 99–106.
————. "Recherches sur les Structures Sociales aux XVIIIe et XIXe Siècles," Comité des Travaux Historiques et Scientifiques, *Bulletin d'Histoire Moderne et Contemporaine*, I (1956), 53–61.
MARTIN, ANDRÉ, and WALTER, GÉRARD. *Catalogue de l'Histoire de La Révolution Française*. 5 vols. Paris, 1936–43.

PERROT, J. C. " Sources et Difficultés de l'Histoire des Villes au XVIIIᵉ Siècle: l'Exemple de la Basse Normandie," *Annales de Normandie*, VIII (December, 1958), Supplément, 25–29.

REINHARD, MARCEL. " La Population des Villes, sa Mesure sous la Révolution et l'Empire," *Population*, IX (1954), 279–88.

SANSON, V. *Répertoire Bibliographique du Département de la Seine-Inférieure pendant la Période dite Révolutionnaire (1781–1901).* 5 vols. Paris, 1911–12.

SAINT-JACOB, P. DE. " Une Source de l'Histoire Sociale au XVIIIᵉ Siècle; La Table des Contrats de Mariage dans les Fonds du Contrôle des Actes," *Actes du 84ᵉ Congrès Nationale des Sociétés Savantes, Dijon, 1959—Section d'Histoire Moderne et Contemporaine.* Paris, 1960, pp. 415–18.

SAINT-LEGER, A. DE. " Les Mémoires Statistiques des Départements pendant le Directoire, le Consulat, et l'Empire," *Le Bibliographe Moderne*, XIX (1919), 1–45.

SEVESTRE, ABBÉ EMILE. *Essai sur les Archives Municipales et les Archives Judiciaires des Chefs-lieux de Département et de District en Normandie pendant l'Epoque Révolutionnaire.* (1787–1801). Paris, 1912.

TUDESQ, A. J. " L'Etudes des Notables, Inventaire des Sources et Projets d'Enquêtes," in Comité des Travaux Historiques et Scientifiques, *Bulletin d'Histoire Moderne et Contemporaine*, I (1956), 25–52.

VERNIER, J. *Répertoire Numérique des Archives Départementales—Seine-Inférieure—Période Révolutionnaire—Série L.* Rouen, 1914.

WORKS ON NORMANDY

BALLIN, G. " Notice sur la Ville d'Elbeuf," *Revue de Rouen* (1834).

BARBE, LUCIEN. " Histoire de l'Industrie du Drap à Louviers," *Bulletin de la Société d'Etudes Diverses de l'Arrondissement de Louviers*, II (1894), 24–136.

BARTHELEMY, CHARLES. *Histoire de la Normandie Ancienne et Moderne.* Tours, 1858.

BAUDOT, M. " La Structure Sociale à Louviers en 1760," *Nouvelle Revue Historique du Droit Français et Etranger*, 4th Series, XXXVI (1958), 627–28.

BAUDRILLART, M. *Les Populations Agricoles de la France, I—La Normandie.* Paris, 1880.

BEAUREPAIRE, CHARLES DE ROBILLARD DE. *Recherches sur la Population de la Généralité et du Diocèse de Rouen avant 1789.* Evreux, 1872.

———. *Renseignements Statistiques sur l'Etat de l'Agriculture vers 1789.* Rouen, 1889.

BERNIER, PAUL D. *Essai sur le Tiers-Etat Rural ou les Paysans de la Basse Normandie au XVIIIᵉ Siècle.* Rouen, 1893.

BESNIER, ROBERT. *La Coutume de Normandie, Histoire Externe.* Paris, 1935.

BOULOISEAU, MARC. *Liste des Emigrés Déportés et Condamnés pour Cause Révolutionnaire dans le District de Rouen.* Paris, 1937.

———. *Le Séquestre et la Vente des Biens des Emigrés dans le District de Rouen.* Paris, 1937.

BOURDE, A. J. " L'Agriculture à l'Anglaise en Normandie au XVIIIᵉ Siècle " *Annales de Normandie*, VIII (1958), 215–33.

BOURDON, MATHIEU. *Etude sur l'Importance Commerciale et Manufacturière de la Ville et du Canton d'Elbeuf.* Caen, 1863.

BRISSON, CHARLES. *Elbeuf, Ma Ville.* Rouen, 1951.

———. " Origines et Développement de l'Industrie Drapière à Elbeuf et à Louviers," *Etudes Normandes*, livraison 5, numéro 13 (1952), pp. 209–24.

CLÉREMBRAY, FELIX. *La Terreur à Rouen.* Rouen, 1901.

COEURET, GEORGES. *L'Assemblée Provinciale de Haute Normandie (1787–1789)*. Paris, 1927.

DARDEL, PIERRE. "Crises et Faillites à Rouen et dans la Haute Normandie de 1740 à l'an V," *Revue d'Histoire Economique et Sociale*, XXVII (1948), 53–71.

————. *Histoire de Bolbec des Origines à la Révolution*. 2 vols. Rouen, 1947.

————. "Importateurs et Exportateurs Rouennais au XVIIIᵉ Siècle, Antoine Guymonneau et ses Opérations Commerciales," *Bulletin de la Société Libre d'Emulation du Commerce et de l'Industrie de la Seine-Inférieure* (1949–52), pp. 83–147.

DARSEL, J. "Les Privilèges d'Elbeuf en Matière de Taille et de Capitation," *Annales de Normandie*, IX (1959), 117–20.

DAVIES, ALUN. "The New Agriculture in Lower Normandy, 1750–89," in Royal Historical Society, *Transactions*, 5th Series, VIII (1958), 129–46.

DEJEAN, ETIENNE. *Un Préfet du Consulat, Jacques-Claude Beugnot*. Paris, 1907.

————. "Une Statistique de la Seine-Inférieure au Début du Siècle Dernier sous l'Administration de Beugnot," *Révolution Française*, L (1906), 512–37, and LI (1906), 30–52.

DELARUE, PROSPER. "Histoire Appliquée à l'Industrie Normande," *Revue de Rouen* (1835).

DESMAREST, CHARLES. *Le Commerce des Grains dans la Généralité de Rouen à la Fin de l'Ancien Régime*. Paris, 1926.

DUBOIS, GEORGES. "La Normandie Economique à la Fin du XVIIᵉ Siècle d'après les Mémoires des Intendants," *Revue d'Histoire Economique et Sociale*, XXI (1933–34), 337–88.

————. "Les Subsistances dans la Seine-Inférieure de 1793 à 1795," *Bulletin de la Société Libre d'Emulation du Commerce et de l'Industrie de la Seine-Inférieure* (1935), pp. 199–264.

DUCHEMIN, LOUIS. "L'Impôt sur le Revenu en Normandie (Dixième et Vingtième) avant la Révolution," *Recueil des Travaux de la Société Libre d'Agriculture, Sciences, Arts et Belles-Lettres de l'Eure*, 5th series, V (1898), 31–97.

D'ESTAINTOT, ROBERT. *Recherches sur les Hautes Justices Féodales Existant en 1789 dans les Limites du Département de la Seine-Inférieure*. Rouen, 1892.

EVRARD, F. "Les Ouvriers du Textile dans la Région Rouennaise 1789–1802," *Annales Historiques de la Révolution Française*, No. 108 (1947).

————. "Les Subsistances en Céréales dans le Département de l'Eure de 1788 à l'an V," in Commission de Recherche et de Publication des Documents Relatifs à la Vie Economique de la Révolution, *Bulletin Trimestriel* (1909), pp. 1–96.

GAILLARDON, CHARLES. "L'Industrie et les Industriels de Normandie au Moment de la Convocation des Etats-Généraux de 1789," *Revue d'Etudes Normandes*, III (1908–9), 22–33, 133–53, 258–69.

GENESTAL, R. "L'Histoire du Droit Public Normand," in Société des Antiquaires de Normandie, *Bulletin*, XXXVII (1926–27), 76–149.

GUILMETH, A. A. *Histoire de la Ville d'Elbeuf*. Rouen, 1842.

JOIN-LAMBERT, M. "La Pratique Religieuse dans le Diocèse de Rouen de 1707 à 1789," *Annales de Normandie*, III (1953), 247–74, and V (1955), 37–49.

LEBRETON, THEODORE ELOI. *Biographie Normande*. 3 vols. Rouen, 1857–61.

LECARPENTIER, GEORGES. "La Propriété Foncière et la Vente des Biens Nationaux d'Origine Ecclésiastique dans la Seine-Inférieure, et Spécialement dans le District de Caudebec," *Revue Historique*, LXXVII (1901), 70–82.

LE COCQ DE VILLERAY, PIERRE FRANÇOIS. *Abrégé de l'Histoire Ecclésiastique, Civile et Politique de la Ville de Rouen.* Rouen, 1759.

LEGRELLE, ARMAND. *La Normandie sous la Monarchie Absolue.* Rouen, 1903.

LÉONARD, EMILE C. *Histoire de la Normandie.* Paris, 1944.

LE PARQUIER, E. "Les Assemblées Electorales de 1789 dans les Baillages Secondaires de la Haute Normandie," *La Normandie,* XIII (1906), 1–12, 32–42.

———. "Une Enquête sur le Paupérisme et la Crise Industrielle dans la Région Rouennaise en 1789," *Bulletin de la Société Libre d'Emulation du Commerce et de l'Industrie de la Seine-Inférieure* (1935), pp. 127–97.

———. *Ouvriers et Patrons dans la Seconde Moitié du XVIIIᵉ Siècle.* Rouen, 1933.

———. "Le Rôle et l'Influence de Rouen en Normandie dans la Période de la Préparation des Etats-Généraux en Normandie en Novembre et Décembre, 1788," *Bulletin des Etudes Locales dans l'Enseignement Public, Groupe de la Seine-Inférieure* (Mai, 1930–Mai, 1931), pp. xix–xxxvi.

LEROY, CHARLES. "Measures de Capacité en Usage en Haute Normandie aux XVIIᵉ et XVIIIᵉ Siècles," *Bulletin de la Société Libre d'Emulation du Commerce et de l'Industrie de la Seine Inférieure* (1936), pp. 49–96, and (1937), pp. 155–218.

———. *Paysans Normands au XVIIIᵉ Siècle.* 3 vols. Rouen, 1929.

LOTH, ABBÉ. *Les Conventionnels de la Seine-Inférieure.* Rouen, 1883.

DE LOUCELLES. *Histoire Générale de la Franc-Maçonnerie en Normandie, 1739 à 1875.* Dieppe, 1875.

McCLOY, SHELBY T. "Government Aid to Large Families in Normandy, 1764–1786," *Social Forces,* XVIII (1940), 418–24.

MAILLE, PARFAIT. *Histoire de la Ville et de la Fabrique d'Elbeuf.* 3 vols. Elbeuf, 1859–1863.

MOURLOT, F. "La Comparution Individuelle des Citoyens du Tiers-Etat aux Assemblées Electorales des Paroisses pour les Etats-Généraux de 1789," in Comité des Travaux Historiques et Scientifiques, *Bulletin des Sciences Economiques et Sociales* (1906), pp. 172–87.

———. *La Question de la Mendicité en Normandie à la Fin de l'Ancien Regime.* Paris, 1903.

OLPHE-GALLIARD, G. *Les Industries Rurales à Domicile dans la Normandie Orientale.* Paris, 1913. (111ᵉ Fascicule de la Bibliothèque de la Science Sociale).

OUIN-LACROIX, CHARLES. *Histoire des Anciennes Corporations d'Arts et Métiers et des Confreries Religieuses de la Capitale de la Normandie.* Rouen, 1850.

PERROT, J. C. "Pêche, Commerce et Gens de Mer en Normandie sous l'Ancien Régime," *Annales de Normandie,* VII (1958), 388–92.

PETIT, L. *Histoire de la Ville d'Elbeuf.* Rouen, 1856.

PRENTOUT, H. "L'Histoire de Normandie," *Bulletin de la Société des Antiquaires de Normandie,* XXXVII (1926–27), 1–52.

———. "La Normandie," *Revue de Synthèse Historique,* XIX (1909), 52–71, 203–22, and XX (1910), 37–72, 188–220, 306–21.

ST. DENIS, HENRI. *Histoire d'Elbeuf.* 12 vols. Elbeuf, 1894–1905.

———, and DUCHEMIN, P. *Notices Historiques sur les Communes des Environs d'Elbeuf.* 8 vols. Elbeuf, 1885–90.

SÉE, HENRI. "The Normandy Chamber of Commerce and the Commercial Treaty of 1786," *Economic History Review,* II (1930), 308–13.

SERVIN, A. N. *Histoire de la Ville de Rouen . . . depuis sa Fondation jusqu'en l'Année 1744.* Rouen, 1775.

SEVESTRE, EMILE, EUDE, XAVIER, and LE CORBEILLER, EDOUARD. *La Déportation du Clergé Ordinaire pendant la Révolution.* Paris, 1913.

SEVESTRE, EMILE. *Le Personnel de l'Eglise Constitutionelle en Normandie (1791–1795), I-Liste Critique des Insermentés et Assermentés (Janvier–Mars, 1791).* Paris, 1925.

SION, JULES. *Les Paysans de la Normandie Orientale.* Paris, 1909.

VIDALENC, JEAN. "La Bourgeoisie à Evreux en 1789," in Commission de Recherche et de Publication des Documents Relatifs à la Vie Economique de la Révolution, *Compte-Rendu de l'Assemblée Générale de 1939, I—La Bourgeoisie Française de la Fin de l'Ancien Régime à la Restauration.* Besançon, 1942.

————. "Quelques Remarques sur le Rôle des Anglais dans la Révolution Industrielle en France, Particulièrement en Normandie, de 1750 à 1850," *Annales de Normandie,* VIII (1958), 273–90.

WADDINGTON, FRANCIS. *Histoire du Protestantisme en Normandie de 1685 à 1797.* Paris, 1862.

WALLON, HENRI. *La Chambre de Commerce de la Province de Normandie, 1703–91.* Rouen, 1903.

GENERAL WORKS

AFANASSIEV, GEORGES. *Le Commerce des Céréales en France à la Fin du XVIIIe Siècle.* Paris, 1894.

ANCHEL, ROBERT. "Une Enquête du Comité de Salut Public sur les Draperies en l'an III," in Commission de Recherche et de Publication des Documents Relatifs à la Vie Economique de la Révolution, *Bulletin Trimestriel d'Histoire Economique de la Révolution* (1913), pp. 371–89.

AUBERT DE LA CHESNAYE DESBOIS, FRANCOIS ALEXANDRE. *Dictionnaire de la Noblesse.* 12 vols. Paris, 1770–78.

AYNARD, JOSEPH. *La Bourgeoisie Française, Essai de Psychologie.* Paris, 1934.

BABEAU, HENRI. *Les Assemblées Générales des Communautés d'Habitants en France du XIIIe Siècle à la Révolution.* Paris, 1893.

BALLOT, CHARLES. *L'Introduction du Machinisme dans l'Industrie Française.* Lille and Paris, 1923.

BARBER, ELINOR G. *The Bourgeoisie in 18th Century France.* Princeton, 1955.

Biographie Universelle Ancienne et Moderne. Supplément, Vol. LXX. Paris, 1842.

BLACKER, J. G. C. "Social Ambitions of the Bourgeoisie in 18th Century France," *Population Studies,* XI (1957), 46–63.

CAHEN, LÉON. "Une Novuelle Interprétation du Traité Franco-Anglais de 1786–1787," *Revue Historique,* CLXXV (1939), 257–85.

CANARD, M. "Essai de Semantique: le Mot 'Bourgeois,'" *Revue de Philologie Française et de Littérature,* XXVII (1913), 32–47.

CARON, PIERRE. "Une Enquête sur les Prix après la Suppression du Maximum," Commission de Recherche et de Publication des Documents Relatifs à la Vie Economique de la Révolution, *Bulletin Trimestriel* (1910), pp. 1–134.

CHABAUD, ALFRED. "Essai sur les Classes Bourgeoises Dirigeantes à Marseille en 1789," Commission de Recherche et de Publication des Documents Relatifs à la Vie Economique de la Revolution, *Compte Rendu de l'Assemblée Générale de 1939, I—La Bourgeoisie Française de la Fin de l'Ancien Régime à la Restauration.* Besançon, 1942.

CHOULGUINE, ALEXANDRE. "L'Organisation Capitaliste de l'Industrie Existait-

Elle en France à la Veille de la Révolution," *Revue d'Histoire Economique et Sociale*, X (1922), 184–218.

Cobban, Alfred. *The Myth of the French Révolution.* London, 1955.

X Congresso Internazionale di Scienze Storiche. *Atti.* Rome, 1957.

————. *Riassunti.* Rome, 1957.

Danière, A. "Feudal Income and Demand Elasticity for Bread in Late 18th Century France," *Journal of Economic History*, XVIII (1958), 317–31.

Delavenne, M. A. *Recueil Généalogique de la Bourgeoisie Ancienne.* 2 vols. Paris, 1954–55.

Esmonin, Edmond. "L'Abbé Expilly et Ses Travaux de Statistique," *Revue d'Histoire Moderne et Contemporaine*, IV (1957), 241–80.

Foster, Charles G. "Honoring Commerce and Industry in 18th Century France." Unpublished Ph. D. Dissertation, Harvard University, 1950.

Godechot, Jacques. *Les Institutions de la France sous la Révolution et l'Empire.* Paris, 1951.

Haag, Emile and Eugène. *La France Protestante.* 10 vols. Paris, 1846–59.

Hayem, Julien. "La Répression des Grèves au XVIIIᵉ Siècle," in his *Mémoires et Documents pour Servir à l'Histoire du Commerce et de l'Industrie en France.* Paris, 1911, I, 116–77.

Kolabinska, Marie. *La Circulation des Elites en France, Etude Historique depuis La Fin du XIᵉ Siècle jusqu'à la Grande Révolution.* Lausanne, 1912.

Labrousse, Ernest. *La Crise de l'Economie Française à la Fin de l'Ancien Régime et au Début de la Révolution.* Paris, 1943.

————. *Esquisse du Mouvement des Prix et des Revenus en France au XVIIIᵉ Siècle.* 2 vols. Paris, 1933.

————. "Voies Nouvelles vers une Histoire de la Bourgeoisie Occidentale aux XVIIIᵉ et XIXᵉ Siècles," in *Relazioni del X Congresso Internazionale di Scienze Storiche.* Florence, 1955, IV, 365–96.

Landes, David S. "The Statistical Study of French Crises," *Journal of Economic History*, X (1950), 195–211.

Lardé, Georges. *La Capitation dans les Pays de Taille Personnelle.* Paris, 1906.

Lefebvre, Georges. *La Révolution Française.* 3rd ed. Paris, 1957.

Léonard, Emile G. "La Bourgeoisie Protestante et sa Position Politique et Religieuse du XVIIIᵉ Siècle à la Restauration," in Commission de Recherche et de Publication des Documents Relatifs à la Vie Economique de la Revolution, *Compte-Rendu de l'Assemblée Générale de 1939, I—La Bourgeoisie Française de la Fin de l'Ancien Régime à la Restauration.* Besançon, 1942.

————. "Les Protestants Français au XVIIIᵉ Siècle," *Annales d'Histoire Sociale*, II (1940), 5–20.

Leuilliot, Paul. "Réflexions sur l'Histoire Economique et Sociale à propos de la Bourgeoisie en 1789," *Revue d'Histoire Moderne et Contemporaine*, I (1954), 131–44.

Lévy-Bruhl, H. "La Noblesse de France et le Commerce à la Fin de l'Ancien Régime," *Revue d'Histoire Moderne*, Nouvelle Série, No. 8 (May-July, 1933), 209–35.

Marion, Marcel. *Dictionnaire des Institutions de la France aux XVIIᵉ et XVIIIᵉ Siècles.* Paris, 1923.

Matthews, George T. *The Royal General Farms in 18th Century France.* New York, 1958.

Méhée de la Touche. *Histoire de la Prétendue Réovlution de Pologne.* Paris, 1792.

Mirot, Albert. *Manuel de Géographie Historique de la France.* 2nd ed., 2 vols. Paris, 1950.

MORAZÉ, CHARLES. *La France Bourgeoise, XVIIIᵉ-XXᵉ Siècles.* Paris, 1946.

MURET, PIERRE. *La Prépondérance Anglaise.* Paris, 1949.

NORMAND, CHARLES. *La Bourgeoisie Française au XVIIᵉ Siècle.* Paris, 1908.

PAGÈS, GEORGES. "La Vénalité des Offices dans l'Ancienne France," *Revue Historique,* CLXIX (1932), 477–95.

PARRAIN, CHARLES. "Une Vieille Tradition Démocratique: les Assemblées de Communauté," *La Pensée,* I, No. 4 (1945), 43–48.

PETIT-DUTAILLIS, CHARLES. *Les Communes Françaises, Caractères et Evolution des Origines au XVIIIᵉ Siècle.* Paris, 1947.

REINHARD, MARCEL. "Elite et Noblesse dans la Seconde Moitié du XVIIIᵉ Siècle," *Revue d'Histoire Moderne et Contemporaine,* III (1956), 5–37.

SCHMIDT, CHARLES. "La Crise Industrielle de 1788 en France," *Revue Historique,* XCVII (1908), 78–94.

SCHNERB, ROBERT. "La Dépression Economique sous le Directoire après la Disparition du Papier Monnaie," *Annales Historiques de la Révolution Française,* No. 61 (1934).

SCOVILLE, WARREN C. "The Huguenots in the French Economy, 1650-1750," *Quarterly Journal of Economics,* LXVII (1953), 423–44.

SÉE, HENRI. *La France Economique et Sociale au XVIIIᵉ Siècle.* Paris, 1933.

———. *Histoire Economique de la France.* 2 vols. Paris, 1939–42.

———. "Le Rôle de la Bourgeoisie Bretonne à la Veille de la Révolution," *Annales de Bretagne,* XXIV (1919–20), 405–33.

SOBOUL, ALBERT. "La Communauté Rurale (XVIIIᵉ–XIXᵉ Siècles). Problèmes de Base," *Revue de Synthèse,* 3ᵉ Série, VII (1957), 283–315.

SZEFTEL, M. "La Règle de Vie Exemplaire des Nobles et l'Evolution Sociale de la France de l'Ancien Regime," *Revue de l'Institut de Sociologie Solvay,* XVI (1936), 603–40.

TARLÉ, E. V. *L'Industrie dans les Campagnes en France à la Fin de l'Ancien Régime.* Paris, 1910.

THORE, PIERRE-HENRI. "Essai de Classification des Catégories Sociales à l'Intérieur du Tiers-Etat de Toulouse," *Actes du 78ᵉ Congres National des Sociétés Savantes, Toulouse, 1953.* Paris, 1954. pp. 149–65.

VOLVELLE, MICHEL. "Structure et Répartition de la Fortune Foncière et de la Fortune Mobilière d'un Ensemble Urbain: Chartres de la fin de l'Ancien Régime à la Restauration," *Revue d'Histoire Economique et Sociale,* XXXVI (1958), 385–98.

WARNOTTE, D. "Les Vertus Bourgeoises, Leur Origine, Leur Signification," *Revue de l'Institut de Sociologie Solvay,* XIX (1939), 1–14.

WILLIAMS, PRESTON B. "The French Bourgeoisie on the Eve of the Révolution." Unpublished Ph.D. Dissertation, University of Texas, 1950.

YOUNG, ARTHUR. *Travels in France and Italy During the Years 1787, 1788 and 1789.* Everyman Edition. New York, n.d.

———. *Voyage en France en 1787, 1788 et 1789.* Ed. and trans. Henri Sée. 3 vols. Paris, 1931.

INDEX

THE JOHNS HOPKINS UNIVERSITY
STUDIES IN
HISTORICAL AND POLITICAL SCIENCE

✦ ✦ ✦

✦ ✦ ✦

THE JOHNS HOPKINS PRESS

BALTIMORE

THE JOHNS HOPKINS UNIVERSITY STUDIES IN HISTORICAL AND POLITICAL SCIENCE

A subscription for the regular annual series is $8.00. Single numbers may be purchased at special prices. A complete list of the series follows. All paperbound unless otherwise indicated.

ii

SEVENTY-EIGHTH SERIES (1960)

1. The Nobility of Toulouse—An Economic Study of Aristocracy in the Eighteenth Century. By Robert Forster.
   Cloth 5.00
2. The Union Pacific Railroad—A Case in Premature Enterprise. By Robert William Fogel. . . . . Paper 3.00; Cloth 3.50

SEVENTY-NINTH SERIES (1961)

1. Enterprise and Anthracite: Economics and Democracy in Schuylkill County, 1820-1875. By Clifton K. Yearley, Jr.
   Paper 4.00; Cloth 5.00
2. Birth Rates of the White Population in the United States, 1800-1860: An Economic Study. By Yasukichi Yasuba.
   Paper 5.00

EIGHTIETH SERIES (1962)

1. The Road to Normalcy: The Presidential Campaign and Election of 1920. By Wesley M. Bagby
   Paper 4.00; Cloth 4.50
2. The Decline of Venetian Nobility as a Ruling Class. By James C. Davis.
   Paper 3.50; Cloth 4.00

EIGHTY-FIRST SERIES (1963)

1. The First Ottoman Constitutional Period: A Study of the Midhat Constitution and Parliament. By Robert Devereux. Cloth 6.00
2. Elbeuf During the Revolutionary Period: History and Social Structure. By Jeffry Kaplow. . . . . Cloth 6.50